THE CHRISTIAN WOMAN'S GUIDE TO CHILDBIRTH

Also by Debra Evans

The Complete Book on Childbirth

The Mystery of Womanhood

Heart & Home

Fragrant Offerings

Beauty for Ashes

Without Moral Limits

Blessed Events

Preparing for Childbirth

The Woman's Complete Guide to Personal Health Care

Beauty and the Best

Christian Parenting Answers (General Editor)

Women of Character

Kindred Hearts

Ready or Not, You're a Grandparent

The Christian Woman's Guide to Sexuality

The Christian Woman's Guide to Personal Health Care

Women of Courage

The CHRISTIAN WOMAN'S GUIDE TO CHILDBIRTH

Debra Evans

CROSSWAY BOOKS • WHEATON, ILLINOIS
A DIVISION OF GOOD NEWS PUBLISHERS

The Christian Woman's Guide to Childbirth

Published by Crossway Books
a division of Good News Publishers
1300 Crescent Street
Wheaton, Illinois 60187

Cover design: Design Point Inc.

Cover photo: CORBIS /Australian Picture Library

First printing 1999

Printed in the United States of America

A substantial portion of the material in this book was previously published in *The Complete Book on Childbirth*, copyright © 1986 by Debra Evans and published by Tyndale House Publishers, Inc. This new edition has been revised and thoroughly updated.

This book was current to the best of the author's knowledge at the time of its publication, but before following any advice contained within it, you should, of course, verify information with an appropriate health-care provider or agency. All medical decisions should be made with the guidance and advice of the reader's own health-care provider. The information presented in this book is based on an in-depth review of recent medical literature. It is intended only as an informative resource guide and is not intended to replace the advice of anyone's own health-care agency or provider, with whom one should always confer before starting any medical treatment, herbal therapy, diet, or exercise program.

Library of Congress Cataloging-in-Publication Data

Evans, Debra.
The Christian woman's guide to childbirth / Debra Evans.
p. cm.
Includes bibliographical references and index.
ISBN 1-58134-104-0 (alk. paper)
1. Pregnancy—Religious aspects—Christianity. 2. Childbirth—Religious aspects—Christianity. 3. Christian life. I. Title.
RG526.E86 1999
618.2—dc21 99-25846
CIP

15 14 13 12 11 10 09 08 07 06 05 04 03 02 01 00 99
15 14 13 12 11 10 9 8 7 6 5 4 3 2 1

DEDICATION

to Phyl Kenney, RN—

for welcoming the Parents Preparing in Christ class

to St. Elizabeth Community Health Center

with your warm smile and a great big hug

CONTENTS

ACKNOWLEDGMENTS

Though I cannot thank them individually, I am indebted to the many expectant parents I have worked with since 1973. Martha Hutchens and Cathy Newhouse were instrumental in making the original Parents Preparing in Christ program in East Lansing, Michigan, a reality in 1978. Phyl Kenney, R.N., was especially supportive at St. Elizabeth's Community Health Center in Lincoln, Nebraska. Deb Klopping, Trina Sollars, and Cinda Childers provided typing skills, transforming notes and handwritten scribbles into a legible manuscript. My friend and pastor, Dave Argue, gave insightful assistance concerning Scripture. Rogene Argue's prayers were an invaluable aid. Dr. Sam Fuenning, Director of Athletic Medicine at the University of Nebraska, conveyed the affirming power of Christ's love through his example and encouragement. Dr. Roger Bruce read and critiqued the manuscript. Meg Bruce, R.P.T., provided additional help as she reviewed many chapters along with her husband. Carol Newsom provided vital prayer support. Members of my small group—Janet and Fred Smith, Rich and Susie Newcomer, Mick and Cheryl Martin, Scott and Di Keller, and Tom Eggert—supported me through many weeks of Wednesday night updates. Sally Herman, Barb Pett, Barb Woodhead, and Lori Marcuson provided timely expressions of friendship. My parents, John and Nancy Munger; my sisters, Kerry Olson and Nancy Shallow; and my husband's family, Betty and Stan Gorman, Sue Beckwith, and Diane Vincent, cheered me on from Mexico, Michigan, and Arizona.

The revision of this book was made possible through the collaborative effort of Crossway Books' excellent staff—Lila Bishop, Jill Carter, and Joe Rosewell. I greatly respect and appreciate your long hours of work on The Christian Woman's Guides. And warm thanks to Crossway's management team as well: Lane Dennis, Brian Ondracek, Fred Rudy, Randy Jahns, Geoff Dennis, and Marvin Padgett.

My deepest gratitude goes to the five people who shared the cost of creating this book—my daughters, Joanna and Katherine; my sons, David and Jonathan; and my husband, Dave. I love you very much.

FOREWORD

In this book Debra Evans, educator and mother of four, has worked diligently to consolidate in a clear and personal manner what she has learned about childbirth. I feel that she has created a balance between the biblical perspectives on childbearing and the scientific techniques. Her aim is to help pregnant women, as well as those close to them, to experience childbirth with joy and dignity.

She exposes the reader to choices that must be made, not only in the who, where, and how of delivery, but also in the adjustments that must be made by new parents and friends of the newborn. She explains the "babymoon," when rest and patience are essential, and she elaborates on the pros and cons of breastfeeding and bottle-feeding as well as on the importance of nurturing. Not only does Evans help the reader through the stages of a "normal" birth, but she also thoroughly describes cesarean birth, a technique too frequently used and therefore not to be ignored. She deals professionally with what to expect during a cesarean birth and covers other possible complications to birth and the remedial steps.

Debra Evans has succeeded both from a practical perspective and a deeply Christian point of view to give a preparation for childbirth that is comforting and realistic. May her book, through its clear presentation, help many to know that bringing new life into the world can be one of the most rewarding experiences of our lives.

Ingrid Trobisch

INTRODUCTION

He tends his flock like a shepherd: He gathers the lambs in his arms and carries them close to his heart; he gently leads those that have young.

ISAIAH 40:11

This beautiful word picture was painted by God to reassure us of his never-ending love, to describe how he personally cares for those who draw near to him for help. During the childbearing process, you will be faced with many decisions, questions, challenges, and issues. It's easy to feel anxious or fearful concerning the outcome of your pregnancy—to wonder about the health of your baby, how the labor will go, and what impact an infant will have on your lives.

The birth of a child is a major event in the life of a family. Becoming a parent is an experience unlike any other. It's an exhilarating event, challenging crisis, and amazing achievement all at once—a fork in the road that brings many different changes that are impossible to ignore. "There were two, and now there's a third human being, a new spirit, finished and complete, unlike the handiwork of man; a new thought and a new love," the Russian author Fyodor Dostoevsky wrote about this momentous life passage. "It's positively frightening. . . . And there's nothing grander in the world."

The transition from being a couple to becoming parents is both exciting and demanding, perhaps more so than any other change you will face together. It's natural to think that your parenting experience will start with your baby's arrival. But a closer look confirms what recent research and the Bible tell us: The shaping of your child's life began long before birth, even before conception took place. A number of factors are already influencing who your baby is—and is still becoming. As a psalm of David tells us, "All the days ordained for me were written in your book before one of them came to be" (Ps. 139:16).

Your remaining months of pregnancy will benefit from your willingness to learn about birthing and breastfeeding prior to greeting your little one for the first time. *The Christian Woman's Guide to Childbirth* is specifically designed to help you and your husband meet this need, whether you're in the early weeks of pregnancy or right in the midst of preparing yourself to give birth in just a few weeks. I offer you a feast of support, encouragement, and useful tips to sample as you await your baby's arrival. The options described here are designed to be savored slowly as you take what you need, when you need it, and leave the rest for later—or abandon an idea entirely. I don't guarantee that you'll like everything I say. Women's birthing and mothering preferences vary tremendously, as do parents' lifestyles and their beliefs about raising children. I know you'll use your best judgment to decide which ideas and suggestions will be helpful to you.

If you're feeling some anxiety about all of this, that's perfectly understandable. According to the renowned pediatrician Dr. T. Berry Brazelton, "The feelings of being overwhelmed, of feeling anxious, of not knowing what is best, of caring too much, of being inexperienced and inadequate are universal ones for all parents. In fact, the amount of anxiety that a new parent experiences may parallel just how much he or she cares about doing well by that baby" (*On Becoming a Family: The Growth of Attachment*, Delacorte Press, 1981).

Over time, these feelings will subside as you grow in wisdom and ability as a mom. Giving birth for the second or third time will be substantially different from giving birth the first time around. Nothing can substitute for the experience real life brings on your parenting journey. But the companionship of friends helps to make the going easier.

The Christian Woman's Guide to Childbirth will encourage you to deepen your dependence on God and his Word, increasing your confidence in his ability to gently protect and guide you. It offers a biblical perspective of childbirth in addition to practical advice for dealing with the physical and emotional changes of childbearing. As you become more familiar with the process of childbearing, it will become easier for you to understand the unique spiritual, emotional, and physical changes associated with pregnancy and childbirth. As you read through these pages, I hope you will marvel at God's good design for the new life that he has created within your body.

Thank you for inviting me to join you on your grand adventure. And welcome, baby, to your new family.

> *Praise be to the God and Father of our Lord Jesus Christ, the Father of compassion and the God of all comfort, who comforts us in all our troubles, so that we can comfort those in any trouble with the comfort we ourselves have received from God.*
>
> 2 CORINTHIANS 1:3-4

ONE

GETTING READY FOR CHILDBIRTH

They will not toil in vain or bear children doomed to misfortune;
for they will be a people blessed by the Lord.

ISAIAH 65:23

Deep within your body, securely nestled in your womb, your child is growing. From the moment of conception, your baby's life has begun to unfold according to God's perfect plan.

Our Creator's design for fetal growth and development is incredibly intricate, woven together in a beautiful way through many minute details. The physiological aspects of pregnancy are nothing less than astounding. Did you know, for example, that as an embryo, your baby started secreting a substance to prepare your breasts for lactation *before* implantation took place? Or that your entire immune system was initially suppressed to avoid mounting a biological assault on your little one?

While many of the processes linked to your pregnancy escape notice, other changes in your body eventually become unmistakable: the increase in your respiratory rate, which supplies extra oxygen to your uterus and the baby; a slowing down of digestive processes, often resulting in heartburn and constipation; hormone shifts resulting in skin softness, breast fullness, and complexion changes. As you've experienced these physical changes, you may have noticed your emotions changing as well.

As you prepare for your baby's entry into the outside world, you may feel weak, tired, frustrated, or frightened at times. That's okay. It isn't unusual to feel pulled in many different directions by friends, family, and society. Being a Christian doesn't automatically confer some sort of "super-humanity" on believers that exempts us from experiencing a wide range of emotions. Instead, it means that our emotional strength rests upon our reliance on God's unfailing love and acceptance. Learning to come to God with your arms wide open will help you embrace his love for you anew each day.

Being human, we tend to hug our fears and concerns close to ourselves rather than trust God with our wayward hearts. It takes real effort to depend on our heavenly

Father to meet our needs. We must *choose* to walk with him day by day as we get to know the Lord better and talk with him often. This pregnancy, your upcoming birth experience, and mothering this little one will provide you with almost unlimited opportunities for spiritual growth, enabling you to become increasingly aware that God's Word is *true*. Know that the Lord's grace will always be sufficient for you as you draw near to him with a sincere heart, even when things happen that you weren't planning on. In all circumstances, the comfort of the Holy Spirit will be present to sustain you.

Although your due date may seem a long way off, the coming months will give you time to prepare for your baby's arrival in much the same way that your engagement gave you a chance to get ready for your wedding. This period of waiting can be both fruitful and fulfilling as you move closer in time to that incredible moment when you hold this precious child in your arms. Between now and then, take advantage of this opportunity to get ready for mothering.

There are a number of things you'll want to consider as you plan to make this birth as safe and as special as possible: Where will the event take place? Who will serve as your birth attendant and support team? What things are important to you and your husband in terms of promoting your values and beliefs during birth and the immediate recovery period? Numerous books, classes, maternal-child health advocates, and childbirth organizations offer information for your consideration and education. Take advantage of these resources!

Protect your pregnancy by eating well, getting plenty of rest, exercising sensibly, and avoiding exposure to harmful substances such as cigarette smoke and alcohol, in any amounts. Your pregnancy is not a disease or an illness but a physiological state that is wonderfully normal. In spite of how complicated this entire process seems to us, God's design for labor and birth is not geared for frequent complications. Your body is capable of accomplishing amazing tasks during pregnancy and childbirth, especially if you take care of yourself wisely. Also, encourage your husband to assume a greater degree of responsibility for the birth by including him in your prenatal care and education.

Most of all, enjoy these months of intimate sharing with your developing baby. Dream! Go for long walks! Sing lullabies! Marvel as your belly shifts and sways while your baby somersaults! Pregnancy isn't just a time of waiting and hoping. It's a time for participating in the exuberant joy of creation. These will be remarkable, memorable months worth enjoying and experiencing to the fullest.

It is essential to practice the walk of the feet in the light of the vision.

OSWALD CHAMBERS

LOOKING AHEAD TO THE WORK OF LABOR

Conceiving a child is a most intimate act. The birth of that child is no less intimate. A woman's total being becomes completely absorbed in the process of giving birth.

Labor is not just something that happens to you. It is the fundamental effort required to bring new life into the world. When this experience is shared, childbirth allows a couple to come to terms with the fruition of their sexuality and becomes a landmark event in the history of their family.

As I recently spent an hour watching the highlights from a triathlon event on television, I could hardly believe my eyes. Nearly 1,000 men and women traveled all the way to Hawaii to compete in a race that required them to swim two and one-half miles in the Pacific Ocean (that's 200 lengths in an Olympic-sized pool), then run out of the water to change and cycle 112 miles on a bike, only to return back to the starting point, change again, and run a 26-mile marathon.

What a testimony to the strength and endurance of the human body. Yet today many women worry about their bodies giving birth to a baby—*a normal physiological function for which we were specifically designed*—even without our participation in any type of voluntary advance training for labor. Both the triathlon and giving birth involve intense physical effort and a certain degree of pain once the event begins. But when we give birth, what a reward awaits us!

THE FIRST STAGE OF LABOR

A quick overview of normal labor and birth at this point may be helpful to you. Later chapters will present detailed information concerning a wide variety of options for you to consider as your baby's arrival approaches.

Though it still isn't known exactly what triggers the childbirth process to begin, labor starts when shifting hormone levels in the bloodstream and substances secreted by the baby and the placenta cause the muscles of the uterus to contract and retract. Across the top of the womb lie three thick layers of muscle, called the *fundus*, which begin to press down upon the baby intermittently. The contractions of these muscles gradually move the baby down against the opening of the uterus, called the *cervix.*

During pregnancy the cervix typically remains firm and closed to prevent a premature birth. When the time nears for your baby to be born, the cervical area will soften and become more elastic. As a result, when the muscles in the upper part of the uterus press down, the part of the baby lying closest to the cervix stretches it open. About 96 percent of the time it is the baby's head that presses down on the cervix (called a *vertex presentation*). About 3 percent of the time the baby's buttocks lie at the opening to the uterus (called a *breech presentation*). Though it is possible to have the baby present shoulder, face, or forehead first, these presentations make up a minority of all births. Most of the time, the crown of the baby's head finds its way to the cervix, opening the cervix much the same as when you pull a tight turtleneck sweater over your head.

Try to picture putting on such a sweater. Though you may observe that its opening for your head is thickly knitted and not very large, you already know your head will be able to pass through, and you try several strategies. With both hands you begin to pull it flat down over the top, but immediately discover that it is more difficult this way. You tilt your head forward, sliding your chin down onto your chest for additional leverage. Then you pull the sweater over the crown of your head, and the rest of your head presses through the neck of the sweater quite smoothly until it is almost all the way through. You discover this last bit of stretching requires extra effort and a more determined tug. Finally the sweater is over your head. The uterus works in much the same way as this during childbirth.

Cervix is the Latin word for neck.The cervix reacts to the firm, sporadic action of uterine muscles as the force of the fundus presses the baby's head through the cervix and into the birth canal. What happens is a dual action of stretching in response to pressing. This activity is called the *first stage of labor.*

These things, good Lord, that we pray for, give us Thy grace to labor for.

THOMAS MORE

SECOND STAGE: GIVING BIRTH

Contractions of the uterus usually increase in strength and length as the cervix opens and "thins out." Each contraction, or period of work done by the uterus, is followed by a period of rest. As the first stage of labor progresses, the rest periods become increasingly shorter, since the uterus must work more actively in a sustained effort to open the cervix all the way. Once the cervix opens to ten centimeters, or about four and a half inches, it is said to be completely effaced and dilated. It is at this point that the mother may begin voluntarily to use her abdominal muscles to help the uterus push the baby down through the birth canal to be born.

The pushing phase is called the *second stage of labor*. Contractions are long and strong to sustain the baby's descent through the pelvis, but usually not as close together as during the final stretching of the cervix in the first stage of labor. Since the cervix is totally opened, all of the work done by the uterus comes from the thickly layered muscle bundles at the fundus that press down firmly on the baby in a dynamic, well-coordinated fashion. As the baby's head moves onto the pelvic floor, the muscles surrounding the vagina open and allow for the passage of the baby.

When the baby's head passes under the mother's pubic bone, or *pubis* , the head is said to be *crowning* and is visible both during and between contractions. With crowning, the mother feels a stretching and burning sensation around the vaginal outlet, similar to what the mouth feels when widely stretched.

When the head crowns, the mother's health-care provider advises her to push only at certain times, since continuous pushing might stretch the tissues in the pelvic floor too suddenly. Many health-care providers routinely make an incision called an *episiotomy* in the perineum between the mother's vaginal opening and the rectum. (See Appendix C for a discussion of the pros and cons of this common yet controversial obstetrical procedure.)

Through the last series of contractions, the baby is pressed from the mother's body and into the world. As the baby's head is released from the mother's pelvic floor, the mother experiences a sensation of relief. The baby's shoulders may immediately follow the birth of the head or may be delivered with the next contraction after a few moments' rest. When the shoulders come through, the rest of the body no longer exerts any resistance. In a sudden rush, the baby slides out in one tremendous, exhilarating moment. The mother feels the smooth skin of her child's back as her baby slips into sight for the first time.

In this instant, the baby takes his first breath and adjusts to an atmosphere of oxygen. Having lived within a fluid-filled environment for about nine months, the newborn infant switches over to breathing air and living in much cooler surroundings. The first breath is designed to close off the duct that allowed the baby to bypass respiration while in the uterus. With one breath a flap shuts, and the outside air begins to circulate through the baby's lungs.

> *What a wonder it is—this miracle [of birth] that happens every day and every hour! Only the unusual strikes us more. God is always doing wonders.*
>
> GEORGE MACDONALD

THIRD STAGE: THE PLACENTA

Within several minutes of birth, the umbilical cord through which the baby was nourished stops pulsating, signaling the end of the placenta's provision. The cord is clamped and cut, and shortly thereafter the placenta detaches from the wall of the uterus and slips down and out of the mother's body. Accompanied by a certain amount of blood, the placenta is delivered usually within fifteen minutes after the baby's birth. This is called the *third stage of labor.*

Meanwhile the baby is checked and may begin nursing at his mother's breast. The suckling of the infant stimulates the uterus to contract, diminishing the flow of blood from the open vessels where the placenta had previously been attached. Breastfeeding is a marvelous feat of engineering! There need be no lapse in the infant's source of nutrition.

FOURTH STAGE: THE EARLY RECOVERY PERIOD

During the *fourth stage of labor*, the mother's body begins to recover its "steady state." With the delivery of the placenta (which had supplied high levels of progesterone and estrogen to maintain the pregnancy), a rapid and immediate drop in hormone levels takes place. This decrease triggers the onset of lactation, although milk usually is not produced for thirty-six to seventy-two hours.

The fourth stage lasts two hours, during which time the mother must be closely attended. A nurse or midwife routinely checks the mother's blood pressure, pulse, and uterus, which is manually palpated by pressing on the fundus through the abdominal wall. If the uterus is not contracting well, the nurse will massage the fundus firmly. This helps to diminish bleeding. The flow of *lochia* (discharge of blood, mucus, and tissue) is checked every so often to be sure that it is not heavier than it should be.

FIFTH STAGE: THE TRANSITION PERIOD

The *fifth stage of labor* is the most neglected stage of childbirth in our culture. Because it lasts six full weeks, many women tend to think that once the birth is over, they should immediately feel "normal" again. It is important to understand that after nine full months of tremendous metabolic, hormonal, and anatomical changes, a woman does not instantly revert back to a pre-pregnant state. Instead, the mother's body readjusts over a forty-two-day span of time, during which she is likely to be spending a great deal of time resting and nurturing her baby at her breast.

In many cultures around the world, new mothers are tended by family members who provide them with complete respite from routine tasks. This is a wise practice, since it gives a woman the attention she deserves and allows her ample time to know her newborn baby.

Labor requires stamina and a willingness to work toward a goal without stopping every few minutes to exclaim, "This is hard!" Giving birth requires nothing less than your complete attention; it involves your whole being in a way unlike any other activity. A woman gains a deep appreciation of the value of life through this process; a baby newly born from her mother's womb is a wonderful reward for the work of childbirth. Jesus described this phenomenon perfectly when he said, "A woman giving birth to a child has pain because her time has come; but when her baby is born she forgets the anguish because of her joy that a child is born into the world" (John 16:21).

Stages of Labor

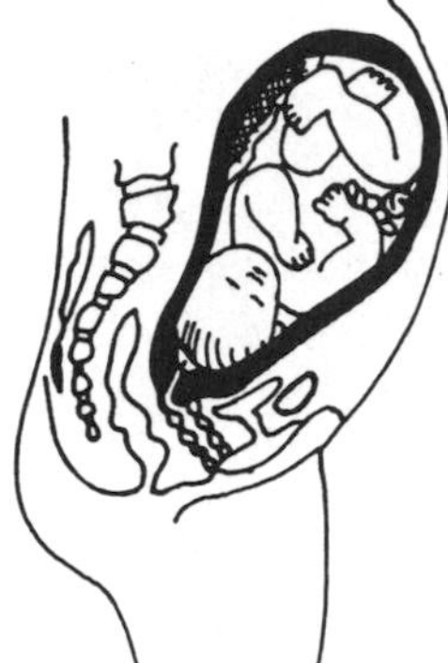

1. Before Labor

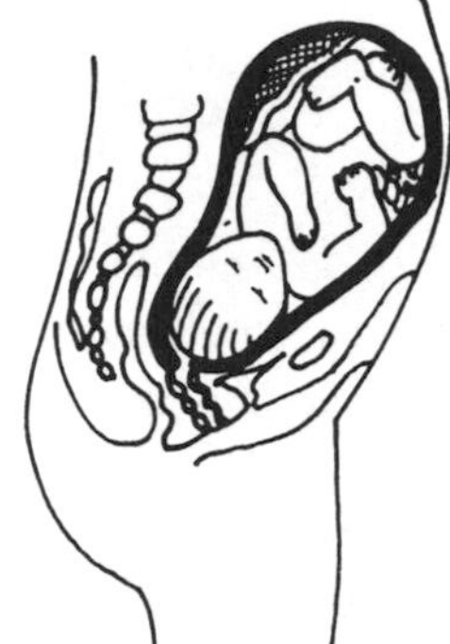

2. Cervix Effaced

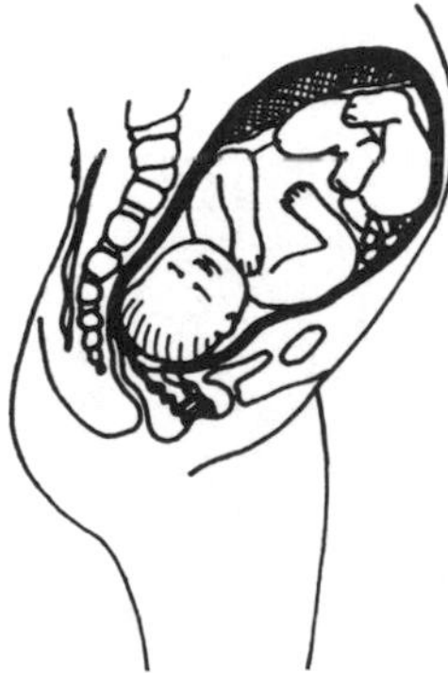

3. Early First Stage

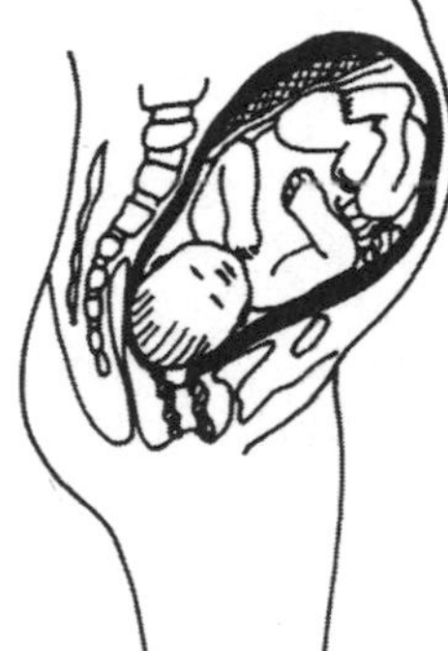

4. Late First Stage

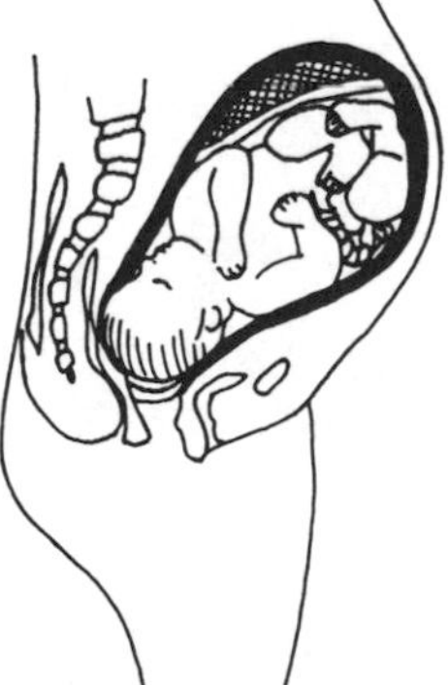

5. Early Second Stage

Stages of Labor — continued

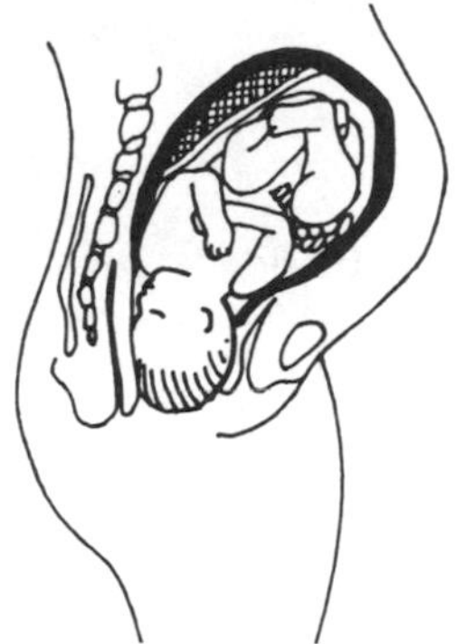

6. Late Second Stage

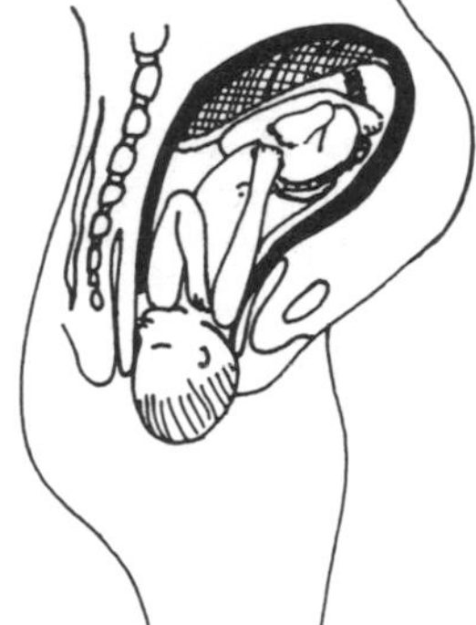

7. Birth of the Head

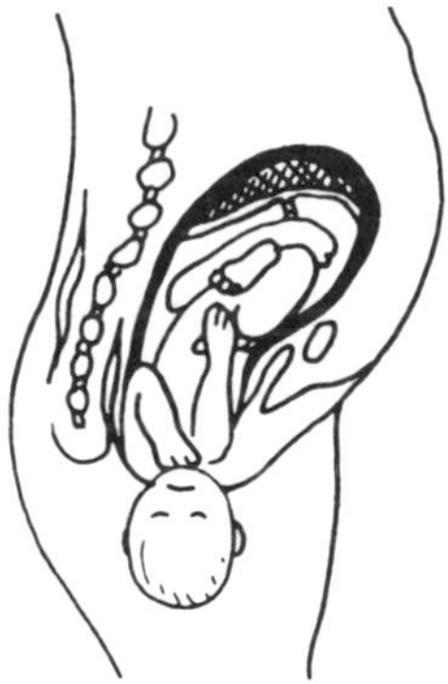

8. Birth of the Shoulders

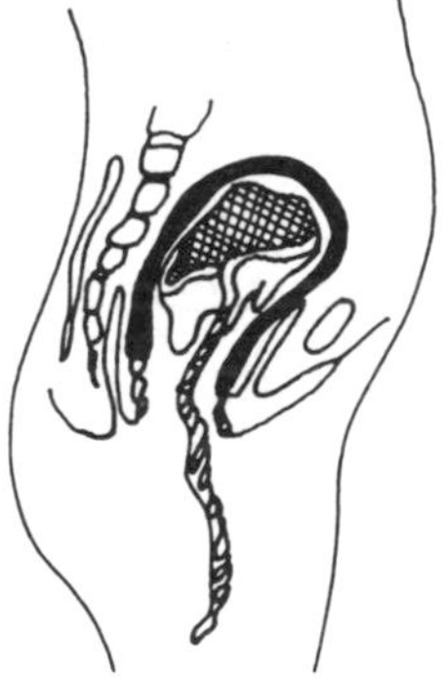

9. The Third Stage of Labor (birth of placenta, membranes, and cord)

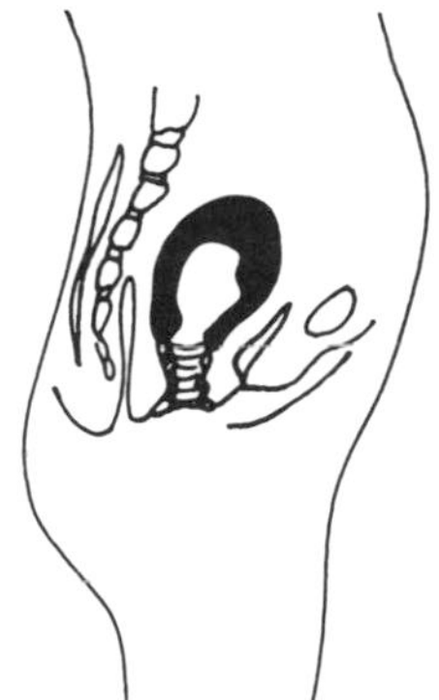

10. The Fourth Stage of Labor

AN OVERVIEW OF THE PROCESS OF CHILDBIRTH

Prelabor

- Body prepares itself to give birth
- Increased frequency of Braxton-Hicks contractions
- Increased vaginal discharge
- Changes in the cervix— softening, thinning, possible dilation
- Relaxation of pelvic joints and ligaments
- Beginning descent of the baby into the pelvis engagement
- Rectal pressure, backache
- Diarrhea
- Restlessness; emotional readiness to have the pregnancy over with

First Stage

- With cervical dilatation, uterine contractions typically become longer, stronger, closer together, more like menstrual cramps, and have associated backache
- Contractions thin and open cervix to ten centimeters and press baby deeper into pelvis
- Three phases in first stage of labor: (1) Early—1 to 3 centimeters; (2) Active—4 to 6 centimeters; (3) Transition—7 to 10 centimeters

Second Stage

- Begins when cervix is completely dilated to ten centimeters
- Following the completion of dilatation, uterine contractions typically become less crampy, more powerful in the area of the fundus, and further apart, with two- to five-minute intervals between
- Bag of waters, or amniotic sac, likely to break during this stage if it has not done so earlier
- Baby moves through pelvis and into birth canal, finally stretching open the pelvic floor muscles and entering the world

Third Stage

- Placental structure detaches from uterus lining and is delivered
- Baby checked and reunited with mother to begin breastfeeding if possible
- Process of lactation initiated as hormone levels drop

Fourth Stage

- Two-hour period during which the mother, father, and baby begin to adjust to post-pregnant life
- Uterus continues to contract (which typically feels menstrual-like); prevents excessive bleeding and begins process of involution (or return of uterus to normal size)

Fifth Stage

- Forty-two-day period following childbirth during which uterus completes process of involution; incisions associated with the pelvic floor or cesarean birth heal; lining of the uterus is sloughed away through a discharge called lochia, which persists for two to six weeks; breastfeeding is established, or suppressed if found undesirable to the mother; family adjusts to new baby; and baby's neuromuscular system, digestive tract, and sensory capabilities mature considerably

FACTORS INFLUENCING THE PROCESS OF LABOR

Though childbirth is a natural, basic biological function, it is also much more: Birth is a reflection of the culture in which we live, the means through which families perpetuate themselves, and the manner in which God expands his creation.

Each labor, each birth has its own special character, influenced by maternal, fetal/placental, cultural, environmental, and technological factors. Just as it is valuable to gain an understanding of the basic process of labor and birth, it is helpful to consider how specific variations in birth are shaped and influenced by the following factors.

Maternal Factors

Maternal factors involved in labor include the mother's state of health, age, and physical condition; number of previous pregnancies; number of babies carried to full term; size and shape of pelvis; attitudes, knowledge, and beliefs; her body's reaction to labor; structure of her uterus; elasticity of the perineum, pelvic floor muscles; inherited traits; stamina or ability to cope with stress; hormonal factors; effort expended; pain relief measures used during labor; pain threshold or ability to tolerate pain; choices in birth arrangements (who, what, where, and when); type of birth (vaginal or cesarean) and types of previous births; and prenatal care.

Fetal/Placental Factors

Fetal/placental factors are those associated with the baby, placenta, umbilical cord, and amniotic sac. These include the baby's size (genetic inheritance); age in weeks (gestational age); position; physical condition; the number of babies in the uterus; when the amniotic sac, or bag of waters, breaks; and the condition and location of both the placenta and the umbilical cord.

Cultural Factors

Cultural factors are practices associated with childbirth. They include the birth attendant's identity, training, beliefs, and skills; the other people present (including family members, nursing staff, and friends) and their training, beliefs, and skills; cultural beliefs about pain and childbirth (view of pregnancy as a state of illness versus wellness); and the behavioral expectations of the mother, her birth attendant, and others present.

Environmental Factors

Environmental factors include the place of birth, positions used by the mother during labor and birth, cleanliness of the mother's surroundings, the routines used, the staff present, and the physical setting and layout.

Technological Factors

Technological factors are the tools, drugs, and techniques used to facilitate the birth. They include the obstetrical interventions employed, the monitoring of the baby's condition, and the cost factors.

Because of the interaction of all the factors that influence childbirth and its outcome, it is easy to understand why no two births are alike. Not even the most skilled health-care practitioner can predict with 100 percent accuracy what will take place during a birth experience.

Yet one vital factor—the most important of all—is missing from those previously discussed. That is the Lord, who not only determines the course of our lives, but in whose hands all these other factors lie. Our heavenly Father takes everything into consideration. Our lives are conducted under his watchful eye. Will you trust his design for your life?

David, a man close to the heart of God, tells us, "The Lord is gracious and compassionate, slow to anger and rich in love. The Lord is good to all; he has compassion on all he has made" (Ps. 145:9). And in 1 Timothy 2:15 we find the promise that women will be kept safe through childbirth "if they continue in faith, love and holiness with propriety."

Does this mean that "bad" things can't happen to a good Christian woman? Or is it something more—that the Lord will preserve your life no matter what the circumstances?

God is with you. He will not forsake you. Trust him and commit your life, your labor, and your baby to him. Regardless of the outcome, the Lord will direct your path and will not allow your feet to slip.

SCRIPTURAL REFLECTIONS AND PROMISES

Trust in the Lord with all your heart and lean not on your own understanding; in all your ways acknowledge him, and he will make your paths straight.

PROVERBS 3:5-6

I lift up my eyes to the hills—where does my help come from? My help comes from the Lord, the Maker of heaven and earth. He will not let your foot slip—he who watches over you will not slumber; indeed, he who watches over Israel will neither slumber nor sleep. The Lord watches over you—the Lord is your shade at your right hand; the sun will not harm you by day, nor the moon by night. The Lord will keep you from all harm—he will watch over your life; the Lord will watch over your coming and going both now and forevermore.

PSALM 121

Humble yourselves, therefore, under God's mighty hand, that he may lift you up in due time. Cast all your anxiety on him because he cares for you.

1 PETER 5:6-7

TWO

Preparing Your Heart, Mind, and Spirit

Peace I leave with you; my peace I give you. I do not give to you as the world gives. Do not let your hearts be troubled and do not be afraid.

JOHN 14:27

Something marvelous occurred the day you were conceived. Within your mother's body, a single sperm cell penetrated the outer covering of the egg produced by her ovary. This ovum had been waiting to be released since it was created while your mother was in *her* mother's womb. For some reason, this single sperm cell—out of the millions upon millions your father had previously produced—and that one particular egg were the bundles of DNA the Lord brought together to become you. Though your conception required your parents' collaboration, your creation did not happen merely by chance. David affirms this amazing truth in Psalm 139:13-16:

> *For you created my inmost being; you knit me together in my mother's womb. I praise you because I am fearfully and wonderfully made; your works are wonderful, I know that full well. My frame was not hidden from you when I was made in the secret place. When I was woven together in the depths of the earth, your eyes saw my unformed body. All the days ordained for me were written in your book before one of them came to be.*

Before these two cells joined, God had ordained "all the days" of your life. He saw you before anyone else even knew you existed. This high view of the special nature of each individual to the Lord is immensely encouraging. How uniquely loved we are!

As the Lord watched over the merging cells, a beautiful radiance called the *corona radiata* surrounded you. A biologist once told me that he had watched this phenomenon under the magnification of a microscope in a laboratory using animal cells. His face broke into a smile as he described what he had seen: "It was so colorful! One of the most beautiful things I've ever seen!" My friend viewed conception as a delightful moment to be celebrated, even on a microscopic level.

Your life began with the joining of two half cells, since sex cells contain only half the number of chromosomes found in all other cells in the human body. Once fused together, they became a single complete cell that contained all of the genetic information necessary for your development. Like a scripted code, your genes helped to direct each phase of your growth, step by step, as the cells divided at an incredibly rapid pace, differentiating into the structures that became your skin, eyes, nose, ears, and heart. Bit by bit you were "knit together" within your mother's body. She finally could feel you kicking sometime around the twentieth week of her pregnancy.

Until she felt your first motion, you may have been more of a nuisance than anything else. All sorts of changes took place within her body as you, and then your placenta, secreted the various hormones that enabled her body to nurture you. Perhaps she was tired and nauseated, and her breasts grew tender as they began to prepare for nursing. She may have planned for you, or perhaps you were a real surprise—a factor that changed her life as nothing else could.

Your father only knew what your mother told him about your presence; his physical participation in your development was limited to one brief moment in time. Their relationship may have been sweet, steady, strained, or stagnant; but they were your parents just the same.

The Lord brought you forth from your mother's womb, as David expresses it in Psalm 22:9. Whatever the circumstances of your birth and throughout all the years that followed, the Lord has loved, protected, and guarded you. Your experiences—coupled with your God-given talents, personality, and genetic traits—all have fitted together to shape you into the unique person you are.

Your individuality is expressed in many different ways. Yet regardless of your financial, physical, or emotional circumstances, the Lord knows what motivates you, quiets you, or disheartens you. He has been with you through every day of your life. Consider Psalm 139:1-6:

> *O Lord, you have searched me and you know me. You know when I sit and when I rise; you perceive my thoughts from afar. You discern my going out and my lying down; you are familiar with all my ways. Before a word is on my tongue you know it completely, O Lord. You hem me in—behind and before; you have laid your hand upon me. Such knowledge is too wonderful for me, too lofty for me to attain.*

If you are expecting a child of your own, the poignancy of your own beginnings and the Lord's careful tending of your life may encourage you. By relating your own experience to that of your growing baby's, you may discover a greater depth of the Lord's love for you. Thanking God for the gift of his life within you, as well as for your baby's life, is an excellent place for your birth preparation to begin.

A baby is God's opinion that the world should continue.

ANONYMOUS

PREPARING YOUR HEART

The divinely orchestrated details of pregnancy—the various changes your body goes through from the moment of your baby's conception—are absolutely, positively amazing. They can give you confidence in God's design for your life. The emotional ups and downs, though, are considerably less predictable.

After all, Adam and Eve weren't technologically created as robots, but were magnificently and miraculously formed in God's own image. And within their God-created bodies, their Maker placed minds that substantially differed from all other animals' minds. Man was created to think and feel by *choice* rather than by instinct. As a result, Christian expectant parents can choose in faith to rely upon the same Creator who made the first man and woman so long ago—and find true emotional and spiritual strength for their childbearing journey in the process.

God has created you to be able to joyously choose to love and serve him, to find your heart's delight in his love. As you prepare for your baby's arrival, there will likely be moments when you may feel pulled in many different directions as various people offer well-meaning advice or when you face the reality of what it means not to have the answers to some of your biggest questions about the upcoming birth. There is real reassurance to be found in the Bible at such times.

By "seeking and pursuing peace," as Scripture advises, and by keeping close to God, you can find relief from much of the stress and strain typically associated with childbearing in our culture today. As the Lord reassures you of his love through his Word, you will be strengthened and renewed daily. Positive changes in your lifestyle will be less difficult to make as you create an atmosphere within your home in which family relationships can be nurtured and made fruitful. This doesn't mean that your experiences won't be difficult and frustrating at times. It means that your foundation in Christ will never fall apart or crumble.

Heartfelt Peace

A heart at peace comes from knowing and reflecting on who you are in relationship to the Lord. Remember, you are:

- A precious child of your heavenly Father (Matt. 7:11).
- A coheir with Christ (Rom. 8:17).
- A person granted the protection of angels (Ps. 91:11).
- God's servant, not the world's slave (Rom. 6:22).
- A temple of the living God (2 Cor. 6:16).

You also are redeemed, justified, cleansed, guarded, forgiven, blessed, saved from condemnation, and loved beyond measure! God's unshakable love, mercy, and grace are the solid source of your self-esteem. As you learn to see yourself the way he sees you, you will find peace.

Exercises

1. Read Romans 8 together and discuss how the concepts in the following verses apply to you: Verses 1, 2, 3-16, 17-18, 19-23, 24-25, 26-27, 28, 29-30, 31, 32-34, 35-38, and 37.
2. Make a list of conclusions you reached from this study of Romans 8. For instance, you might start your list with: "I am in Christ Jesus (v. 1); I am free from the law of sin and death (v. 2)," and so on. Place the list in a prominent place until you have it memorized.
3. In the following weeks, make an effort to put some of your conclusions into practice. Seek to live "according to the Spirit" rather than according to the flesh, and encourage others to do so. Be positive and supportive. Avoid comparing yourself to others. Instead, turn frequently to the Lord in prayer.

PREPARING FAMILY RELATIONSHIPS

One of the most important things you can do to prepare for your baby's arrival is to make peace within your family, forgiving those who have hurt you. There are no "perfect" families and no "perfect" people. As your baby grows and you prepare to give birth, look for opportunities to say "I forgive you." Seek God's wisdom concerning family relationships that have caused you pain. Allow your pregnancy to bring you into a more intimate relationship with God as he addresses past wounds. Reflect often—and deeply—on the unchanging reality of the Lord's love for you, your parents, your siblings, your spouse, your spouse's family, and your baby.

God is able to heal your hurts and restore relationships that may be distressing to you. Pray for his strength and wisdom, through the power of the Holy Spirit, to enable you to discover, discern, and forgive, thereby helping you build a loving atmosphere within the home he is helping you create.

> *I see this baby leading me back to my beginnings, reopening rooms I'd locked and forgotten, stirring the dust in my mind by re-asking the big questions.*
>
> LAURIE LEE

Exercises

1. What was your reaction to this chapter's description of your conception? As you relate this to your own baby's existence, what is your reaction?
2. Is it easy or difficult for you to relate to your parents, siblings, or in-laws? Are there things for which you need to forgive them? Do either you or your husband have any family history of abuse of addiction? Pray with one another or with a trusted friend that God will begin to heal the hurts in your past; seek wise counsel according to the Lord's direction.
3. Consider writing a note to your mother or father, a grandparent, sister or brother—someone who has known you throughout your life and to whom you can return some encouragement. Use this time, while your baby is waiting to become a part of your family, to "clean house."

PREPARING YOUR MIND

Because childbearing is a great responsibility filled with many unknown factors, it is perfectly normal to sometimes wonder what sex your baby will be, whether your child will be healthy, what labor will feel like, how your life will change as a result of giving birth, and other pregnancy-related concerns.

Think for a moment about the differences between worry, anxiety, and fear. How would you define these words? Are you fairly prone to any of these emotional states?

Being human makes it easy to hug our concerns close to ourselves, pondering over the myriad possibilities facing us. Learning to trust the Lord takes effort; we must walk with him day by day, getting to know him better. Pregnancy, childbirth, and parenthood will provide you with unparalleled opportunities to experience firsthand the Lord's ability to take care of your needs. You will become increasingly aware that his Word is true.

During a difficult time in my life, I found that by breaking down Philippians 4:4-9 and meditating on each portion of the verses, I could put into practice what I now believe is one of the Lord's most potent prescriptions for the maintenance of our mental health. As you read through these verses, consider how you can follow your Counselor's plan for promoting a sound mind and how you can apply each verse in your own life.

> *Rejoice in the Lord always. I will say it again: Rejoice! Let your gentleness be evident to all. The Lord is near. Do not be anxious about anything, but in everything, by prayer and petition, with thanksgiving, present your requests to God. And the peace of God, which transcends all understanding, will guard your hearts and your minds in Christ Jesus. Finally, brothers, whatever is true, whatever is noble, whatever is right, whatever is pure, whatever is lovely, whatever is admirable—if anything is excellent or praiseworthy—think about such things. Whatever you have learned or received or heard from me, or seen in me—put it into practice. And the God of peace will be with you.*

Write down what these words bring to mind. How can you change your thought patterns for the better? The Lord is able to strengthen us, but we must be willing to do our part. It may help to copy this passage—or another personal favorite—down and display it in a prominent location (your bathroom mirror perhaps?) as a frequent reminder.

Take my life and let it be / Consecrated, Lord, to Thee.

FRANCES RIDLEY HAVERGAL

SPIRITUAL STRENGTH BUILDERS

Make cards with the following Scripture verses on them, memorizing each passage to use when needed.

Psalm 34:17-18; Psalm 91:11; Isaiah 43:1-2; John 14:1; Philippians 4:13; Hebrews 12:2-3; James 4:7-8; 1 Peter 5:7.

PREPARING YOUR SPIRIT

We choose moment by moment what we focus on, ponder, think about. When we experience worry, fear, doubt, or anxiety, we can cling to our emotional pain—or turn our thoughts to God and surrender our burdens at the foot of the cross.

Relinquishing our heavy burdens and consciously trusting God to cover our weakness with his strength requires self-control and spiritual discipline. We can be thankful that the Lord tenderly longs for our cooperation with the Holy Spirit's appointed ministrations and blesses even our tiniest efforts. Many passages in Scripture encourage us to trust in the Lord's perfect protection.

The Lord's part in your pregnancy and birth experience—in your whole life, for that matter—can't be known fully this side of heaven. But we *can* state with confidence, based on what the Bible says, that *God knows your baby and he knows you*. Tell him your fears. Share your worries with him. Believe in his ability to bless you throughout your life. Trust him to direct your path, even when you may not understand why certain things happen.

If your pregnancy or birth is difficult, if your baby isn't what you expected, if your life plans must change, if your family relationships are painful—even if, in your opinion, "the worst" happens—realize that the Lord's grace *is* sufficient for you. You will never be separated from his unfailing love, compassion, and goodness.

God's will hath no why.

MARIA VON TRAPP

Exercises

In a journal write freely about any specific concerns, fears, worries, or anxieties you may have. If possible, ask your husband to do the same and discuss your responses with one another after considering the following questions:

1. Are your concerns realistic—based on real, possible, or probable events? If realistic, to what extent are they likely to happen?
2. What steps will you take, either alone or together, to diminish any anxiety you have? How can you encourage one another in the days ahead to base your confidence upon God's protection and provision?
3. How will you prevent or cope with the tendency to withdraw emotionally and physically from each other when you are tired or anxious?
4. In what practical ways will you relieve the fatigue and physical stress you're experiencing? How will you support one another in this area?
5. Given that spiritual warfare is an ongoing reality every Christian faces, how will you arm and protect yourselves from the enemy's attacks?
6. Who will you ask to support you—in prayer as well as in practical ways—during this pregnancy, birth, and recovery?

SCRIPTURAL REFLECTIONS AND PROMISES

And we know that in all things God works for the good of those who love him, who have been called according to his purpose.

ROMANS 8:28

My soul finds rest in God alone; my salvation comes from him. He alone is my rock and my salvation; he is my fortress, I will never be shaken. . . . Find rest, O my soul, in God alone; my hope comes from him. He alone is my rock and my salvation; he is my fortress, I will not be shaken. My salvation and my honor depend on God; he is my mighty rock, my refuge. Trust in him at all times, O people; pour out your hearts to him, for God is our refuge.

PSALM 62:1, 2, 5-8

Thou will keep him in perfect peace, whose mind is stayed on thee.

ISAIAH 26:3 KJV

Come to me, all you who are weary and burdened, and I will give you rest. Take my yoke upon you and learn from me, for I am gentle and humble in heart, and you will find rest for your souls. For my yoke is easy and my burden is light.

MATTHEW 11:28-30

THREE

PREPARING YOUR LIFESTYLE

I can do everything through him who gives me strength.

PHILIPPIANS 4:13

Childbearing requires an adjustment of priorities. Adequate rest, regular meals, suitable working hours, and safe exercise become important factors in promoting your health and the growth of the child within you. The quality of your pregnancy can be improved by eating and drinking that which will provide your baby with the nutrients needed for optimal development, and by easing the strains you may have previously placed on your body (overworking, skipping meals, smoking, etc.).

It's best if you can discuss with your husband the changes you need to make and learn about the special needs of pregnancy together. In this way, he can help you to take care of yourself, encourage you to stick to whatever plan you adopt, and protect you from undue stress and overwork. Hopefully, the changes you make during your pregnancy will be fairly permanent so that your child will learn sound habits by your example as she grows older.

The following lifestyle evaluation consists of three corresponding sections—questions about your lifestyle as it is now, information that will help you to know what changes to make to improve the quality of your pregnancy, and suggested ways to make these changes together.

> *In a higher world it is otherwise, but here below to live is to change, and to be perfect is to have changed often.*
>
> JOHN HENRY NEWMAN

PART 1: YOUR CURRENT LIFESTYLE

Answer these questions separately. Then, after completing the evaluation, discuss your replies together and proceed to Part 2.

1. How many days a week do you usually eat breakfast?
2. Do you normally eat balanced meals consisting of the "Basic Four" (breads and cereals, fruits and vegetables, dairy products, and high-protein foods)?
3. How much water and other beverages do you drink per day?
4. How many hours of sleep do you usually get per night?

5. Are you taking any prescribed or over-the-counter medication on a regular basis? List any medications you currently take and why you are taking them. Make sure also to include vitamins, aspirin, and simple cold remedies.
6. What is your current weight?
7. Are you working outside the home, or are you in school? How many hours a week does your job/school demand, including side trips, business-related activities, take-home work, etc.?
8. Do you participate in a fitness program or exercise regularly? What activities do you enjoy, and how long have you been doing them?
9. Have you moved recently, or do you plan to move within the next twelve months?
10. List any traumatic events that have occurred within your family or closest friendships during the past year (e.g., deaths, major illnesses, financial crises, etc.). Describe what effect, if any, the event(s) you listed have had upon you.
11. Do either of you plan to quit your job, switch employment, stop or begin school, or otherwise change your financial picture within the next year? What impact will this have on your lifestyle?
12. List any illnesses or injuries you have had during the past year, as well as ongoing health concerns (such as high blood pressure, anemia, obesity, or diabetes).
13. What is your health insurance coverage?
14. Do you smoke cigarettes or drink alcoholic beverages? If so, how often? Do you plan to continue to do so while you are pregnant (or while your wife is pregnant)?
15. How many previous pregnancies have you had? How many were carried full term?
16. Have you ever had a sexually transmitted disease?
17. Do you regularly wear seat belts?
18. Are you fairly calm, stable, and even-tempered, or are you tense, moody, and sometimes temperamental?
19. Do you find it easy or difficult to fully relax, other than when sleeping?
20. Are you satisfied with the sexual relationship you have with your spouse? If so, why? If not, how would you change it?
21. What is your current level of involvement in volunteer work?
22. How active would you say you are in your church or fellowship?
23. How often do you have a regular quiet time with the Lord? With your spouse? How often do you pray together, other than at meals?
24. How do you view this pregnancy? Is it a nuisance, a blessing, or a challenge? Do you see it as an illness or as a healthy event?
25. How satisfied are you with your marriage?

I avoid looking downward or backward, and try to keep looking upward.

CHARLOTTE BRONTË

PART 2: IDEAS FOR PROMOTION OF FAMILY WELLNESS

After discussing your responses to the above evaluation, read through the following recommendations for a healthful lifestyle. Discuss how these ideas coincide or conflict with your answers; then move on to Part 3.

1. A balanced breakfast is still considered to be the single most important meal of the day and should be a regular part of your daily schedule.

2., 3. The following is the recommended daily food intake (see Appendix A for serving sizes and suggestions) for women during pregnancy and while breastfeeding.
   - Calcium-rich foods: 4 servings
   - Eggs/high-fat foods: 4 full or 8 half servings
   - Protein: 4 servings
   - Yellow fruit, yellow and green leafy vegetables: 3 or more servings
   - Other fruit and vegetables: 2 servings
   - Whole grains and legumes: 5 or more servings
   - Foods high in vitamin C: 2 servings
   - Iron-rich foods: some every day
   - Water: minimum of 8 eight-ounce glasses, more while nursing

   Restrict your intake of foods and beverages high in calories, fats (especially saturated fats), salt, caffeine, alcohol, additives, sugars, artificial sweeteners, and preservatives. Many of these substances have been shown to increase symptoms of stress and to lower pain tolerance.

4. In spite of the opinions of various people, eight hours of sleep is still the recommended amount. During late pregnancy, two or three twenty-minute rest periods per day while lying on your left side will help your circulation and metabolism. In addition, you may find that you need more than eight hours of sleep at night while you are pregnant and several naps per day while your baby has you up at night.
5. Discuss all medications you take while you are pregnant and during lactation, even vitamins (if taken in large doses), with your health-care provider.
6. The recommended weight gain for women during pregnancy is twenty-five to forty pounds, depending on weight before pregnancy and frame size. A diet during pregnancy that restricts caloric intake to under 2,500 calories per day may not meet the RDA for nutrients. The time for focusing on weight loss is after the birth and weaning of your baby.
7. There are no specific time-management guidelines for pregnant women as long as things are going well. Certain jobs, however, are inappropriate. If environmental hazards exist at your workplace, you will need to consider what effect they will have on your developing baby. During the last four to six weeks of pregnancy, a job that demands heavy exertion or too much time on your feet is not advisable. My suggestion is that you and your husband pray for God's direction.

8. Generally, it's not advisable to begin any type of strenuous fitness program or engage in any new physical activity that might be harmful while you are pregnant. Fitness experts recommend participating in a program suited to the special needs of pregnancy, which protects the lower back and abdominal and pelvic floor muscles from strain. With your health-care provider's approval, walking, swimming, cycling, modified aerobic dance, and running activities can promote cardiovascular endurance, while certain stretching and strengthening exercises will enable your body to adapt more easily and recover more readily from the stresses of childbearing. (Walking and swimming are preferable if you are not currently engaged in any of the other activities listed. See Appendix B for specific suggestions.)
9. It doesn't take an expert to tell you that moving is stressful. Times to avoid it for expectant and new parents—the last two months of pregnancy and the first three months of your baby's life.
10. Regardless of what brought about any of the events you listed, their impact on your life is inescapable. Healing of the body or the mind takes time. Staying busy may only exhaust you, if that is how you are coping. On the other hand, withdrawal and inactivity can bring about stagnation or even self-destructive behavior. God wants you whole again. Please be patient with his way of bringing it about. Remember that "the one who calls you is faithful . . ." (1 Thess. 5:24) and he will take care of you.
11. Money and sex are the two most significant sources of conflict within marriage, as you may already know. Finances become an even greater concern with the advent of parenthood. However, many expenses in our culture are exaggerated, if not unnecessary. There are basic needs, and then there are wants. Matthew 6 reassures us that our heavenly Father knows our needs and teaches us how we ought to pray. He warns us not to worry because "each day has enough trouble of its own." Perhaps this is a time in your life when the Lord would have you simplify your lifestyle and learn to trust him more fully.
12. Since childbearing aggravates many conditions that could be harmful to your health and that of the baby, it's vital for someone qualified to attend to your health concerns now and throughout your pregnancy. Prenatal care plays an important role in the outcome of any pregnancy, whether it's complicated or not.
13. Be sure you understand what expenses your health insurance covers. It is easier to plan possible ways to pay for the costs not covered by your insurance if you know what they are early in the pregnancy. Also, most hospitals will allow you to bring in things to help you save money, such as disposable diapers, sanitary napkins, and similar items. Check all your options. Generally, birthing centers are much less expensive than hospitals for maternity care, as they are based on an outpatient model and do not require the same type of staff and equipment as hospitals.

14. Cigarette smoking and inhaling secondhand smoke is to be avoided during pregnancy. If you smoke now, it is worth it to your baby to quit because:
    - blood flow to the baby is restricted if the mother is a smoker, impairing the ability of the placenta to nourish the baby and often resulting in premature birth and/or a low-birth-weight baby;
    - children of smokers have a higher incidence of upper respiratory infections;
    - parents set the example for their children, who love to imitate their parents' behavior.

    God can set you free from this addiction if you sincerely want to quit. Alcohol consumption during pregnancy should be discontinued altogether. Though recent research suggests that fetal alcohol syndrome is dependent on genetic factors rather than on the level of alcohol intake, why take a chance?
15. Make sure your health-care provider has your complete medical history recorded correctly. This is an important tool used for planning the medical management of your pregnancy. A history of miscarriage may suggest certain precautions at different times during your pregnancy.
16. You will most likely be tested for both gonorrhea and syphilis at your first prenatal visit. Herpes Simplex II (genital herpes) is of concern as well. If an active case of herpes is present at the onset of labor, a cesarean birth would be indicated to avoid transmission of the infection to your baby.
17. It has been estimated that only about 14 percent of the adult population in the United States wears seat belts regularly. Many states now require that children be placed in a safety restraint until the age of four. Again your child will learn by example.

18., 19. Pregnancy is an ideal time to seek God's will for your life together and pursue a closer walk with him. Many passages in the New Testament make it clear what "fruit" the Lord expects us to bear. In becoming parents, we can learn to be less self-centered through being directly responsible for the needs of another human being who is dependent upon us for protection, sustenance, and love.

If you are struggling with anger, depression, guilt, covetousness, ambition, or anything from which the Lord desires to set you free, don't be surprised. It's by God's grace we are saved, not by our worth or virtues. As parents preparing in Christ for parenthood, you have a wonderful opportunity to learn to be less anxious about your life as a result of drawing closer to God during your pregnancy and birth. Those who look to God in humility to achieve self-control and freedom from stress find real solutions to life's toughest challenges.

20. As mentioned earlier, money and sex are not always easy subjects of discussion for husbands and wives. Communication, "speaking the truth in love," and a willingness to learn how to be sensitive to one another's needs are important for every couple.

Be honest about what you would change if you could, and discuss this together. Keep an open mind that allows you to really "hear" what your partner is saying. God created men and women with strikingly different sexual designs. While masculine reproductive function involves one primary aspect, a woman has five expressions within her body's design. In addition to the act of intercourse, these are ovulation, menstruation, pregnancy, and breastfeeding. Each of these expressions of female sexuality are uniquely controlled by a variety of combinations and levels of hormones. A healthy sexual relationship within marriage allows men and women to appreciate the differences our Creator designed into our bodies.

21., 22., 23. Many believers spend little time with their families. This should not be the case, except for specific and limited periods of time. As a wife and a mother of four, I'm just beginning to scratch the surface of what it means to serve my family in love. Love takes time, time spent together. The time spent with God in his Word and in prayer (both individually and together as a family) will yield a lasting harvest. Weigh the needs of your family and yourself against your other commitments. The church can always find another volunteer. Your family can't replace you as easily.

24. An important question, don't you agree? Not all babies are completely planned or wanted by both partners. Even when they are, the whole process can be exasperating at times, making you wonder if it's worth it or not. In my own life, I've found that being a mother has required me to make more changes in myself and in my life than any other role that I fill.

Children may be viewed as a liability by some in our society, but we read in Psalm 127:3 (KJV) that "children are a heritage of the Lord: and the fruit of the womb is his reward." Yet today abortion destroys millions of "unwanted" lives. Our society has placed a comparative value on human life, the afflicted and genetically different becoming objects of fear rather than human beings who deserve compassion and understanding.

Your life came into being under God's watchful eye. Because your parents did not prevent your conception, you possess a life that is everlasting. If you are pregnant, praise God for the life you carry in your womb! The Lord has blessed you and your child with *life*. If you view the value of this event from an eternal perspective, you will feel true satisfaction in participating together in the Lord's plan for your child's life.

25. Marriage relationships are diverse and challenging. As you consider the following "one anothers" of the New Testament, reflect on how they are being expressed in your marriage, and keep in mind that one thing never changes—the truth of God's Word.

- Have peace one with another (Mark 9:50 KJV).
- Love one another (John 13:34).
- Be devoted to one another (Rom. 12:10).
- Be likeminded one toward another (Rom. 15:5 KJV).
- Instruct one another (Rom. 15:14).
- Greet one another (Rom. 16:16).
- Serve one another (Gal. 5:13).
- Be patient, bearing with one another (Eph. 4:2).
- Be kind to one another, forgiving each other (Eph. 4:32).
- Submit to one another (Eph. 5:21).
- Lie not one to another (Col. 3:9 KJV).
- Admonish one another (Col. 3:16).
- Abound in love one toward another (1 Thess. 3:12 KJV).

Also consider the "one anothers" found in the following Scripture references: 1 Thessalonians 4:18; 5:11; Hebrews 3:13; 10:24; James 4:11-12; 5:9, 16; 1 Peter 1:22; 3:8; 4:10; 5:5; and 1 John 1:7.

Each of these guidelines, if practiced within the Christian home, blesses the entire family. The Golden Rule of "do unto others" begins with our closest neighbor—our spouse.

The art of being wise is the art of knowing what to overlook.

WILLIAM JAMES

PART 3: DEVELOP A PLAN

Now that you have read through the previous suggestions for a healthful lifestyle during and after pregnancy, you may wish to use the next section for ideas in developing a plan of action in making your lifestyle less stressful, healthier, and more enjoyable.

1., 2., 3. Suggestions for improved eating habits:
- Keep track of your food intake and try to stay close to the Daily Food Guide and suggestions in Appendix A.
- Make menus that appeal to you and shop only for items for which *you* have planned ahead.
- Clean out your cupboards. Remove all inappropriate foods.
- Don't condemn yourself if you slip and eat a hot fudge sundae rather than a cup of cottage cheese! The Lord loves you and will help you to improve your eating habits. Just seek his guidance next time.

4. Changes I can make to get sufficient rest (ways that I can help my wife to get the rest she needs):

5. List of drugs and vitamins I've taken so far during my pregnancy (show this to your physician if you haven't discussed this yet):

6. Refer to 1.-3.
7. Plans for work or school activity during pregnancy and afterward (what we will continue and what we can eliminate):

HOUSEHOLD TASKS

Who will:

Vacuum ____________________

Make the bed/change linens ____________________

Wash dishes ____________________

Cook (which meals?) ____________________

Clean the bathroom(s) ____________________

Take out the garbage ____________________

Wash the floor(s) ____________________

Mow the lawn ____________________

Do grocery shopping ____________________

Pay the bills ____________________

Do laundry ____________________

Take care of the pet(s) ____________________

Four questions to ask about all household tasks: Can this task (a) be eliminated? (b) be done less often? (c) be done at the same time as another task or activity? (d) be done by another household member?

8. Our current level of physical activity:

   Type of fitness program we will participate in with our doctor's approval:

9. We can make moving easier by:

10. The events that still bother me (husband and wife should each answer):

    My plan for coping:

    Scriptural references to help put these events in perspective:

11. Additional scriptural references concerning money:

    Debts that can be avoided or eliminated before the baby is born or within the next six months:

    Expenses associated with this pregnancy and early infancy (minimum):

    Worries we have about meeting expenses:

    Reassurances from God's Word about his provision for us:

12. Current health-care plan regarding existing health concerns:

13. Our plan for reducing health-care expenses if our coverage is not sufficient:

14. What I desire to change about smoking or drinking during pregnancy and afterward:

    Plan for support:

15. Special recommendations to follow:

16. Our health-care provider's suggestions concerning any of these conditions:

17. Plan for changing bad habits related to wearing seat belts or driving:

18., 19. Two areas of our life in which we desire the Lord's help:

    Plan of action (such as prayer, regular fellowship, quiet time with the Lord, etc.):

20. Ways we can improve our communication and our sexual relationship during pregnancy so that we can be relatively free of resentment, frustration, and guilt in this area:

21. Current volunteer involvement that can be reduced, phased out, or eliminated before the baby is born:

22. Current church commitments (committees, Bible studies, small group meetings, ministries, etc.) that can be phased out until our child is older, or that can be entirely

eliminated (seek guidance from the Lord and your pastor, remembering that your decision needs to be based on what's best for *you* and your family):

23. Changes we can make in our prayer and Bible study habits:

24. Scriptural references on the value of children:

25. A list of five "one anothers" we want to put into practice in our marriage now:

It is an old custom of the servants of God to have some little prayer ready and to be frequently darting them up to Heaven during the day, lifting their minds to God out of the mire of this world. He who adopts this plan will get great fruits with little pains.

PHILIP NERI

ENCOURAGEMENT FROM GOD'S WORD

Some of the changes that you need to make in your lifestyle may take time, while others need to begin as soon as possible for the sake of promoting the well-being of the mother and baby. Prioritize the changes you desire to make. Remember, you need not depend on your own willpower or strength alone to change. The Lord is your shepherd and will give you the things you ask for. See especially Psalm 121:1-2; Psalm 18:31-32; Proverbs 3:5-6; Isaiah 40:30-31; Colossians 3:23-24.

SCRIPTURAL REFLECTIONS AND PROMISES

Wisdom is at home in a discerning mind.

PROVERBS 14:33A NEB

Search me, O God, and know my heart; test me and know my anxious thoughts. See if there is any offensive way in me, and lead me in the way everlasting.

PSALM 139:23-24

When the way is rough, your patience has a chance to grow. So let it grow. . . . For when your patience is finally in full bloom, then you will be ready for anything, strong in character, full and complete.

JAMES 1:3-4 TLB

My grace is sufficient for you, for my power is made perfect in weakness.

2 CORINTHIANS 12:9

Keep your feet on a steady path, so that the limping foot does not collapse but recovers strength.

HEBREWS 12:13 PHILLIPS

FOUR

PREPARING YOUR BODY

The fruit of your womb will be blessed.

DEUTERONOMY 28:4

As you prepare your body for its birth-giving role, an important element in late pregnancy will be your willingness to "let God be God" in your life as the changes associated with your growing baby become more evident. This chapter presents ideas you can use to help your body adapt during the final months of waiting.

The physical discomforts of late pregnancy can be divided into four major categories—musculoskeletal, circulatory, digestive, and breast changes. Learning how your body prepares itself to give birth will help you understand the sensations and inconveniences during the last trimester of your pregnancy.

YOUR MUSCULOSKELETAL SYSTEM

Until the fifth or sixth month of pregnancy you may have felt minimal changes taking place within the muscles and bones that surround your baby. But as your baby grows, a variety of muscles must stretch to a greater degree to accommodate your unborn child. Many muscles attached to your skeletal system must bear the extra weight. The bones in your lower back and pelvis shift from their usual placement due to hormonal influences on the ligaments that maintain your posture and the framework of your bone structure.

The Lord designed your body for these changes. There may be days when you wonder what his plan actually was, but if you're willing to change certain habits and movements temporarily, you'll find the going a bit easier.

A labor of love is never lost in heaven's eyes.

ANONYMOUS

Your Abdominal Muscles

The corset-like structure that comprises your abdominal wall may be strengthened in a variety of ways. The best exercises protect your lower back while at the same time providing your abdominal muscles the opportunity to do some work, helping them become stronger and more supportive. Before you begin, learn how each exercise is to be done and check the condition of your abdominal wall.

Abdominal Muscle Evaluation. Lie on your back with your knees bent and your feet flat on the floor, about hip-width apart. While placing one hand on the floor for stability, lift your head up until you feel your abdominal muscles tighten. Keep your head lifted forward until the check is completed.

With your free hand, feel down the midline of your abdomen with two fingers, from your breastbone to your navel. You should feel an indentation that can be less than half an inch to over an inch wide. On either side of this indentation, you will feel two firm ridges of muscle. These vertical bands are called your *recti* muscles. Measure the size of the indentation between the recti muscles by the number of fingertip widths you can place between them. Then relax your head and place it back on the floor.

If the gap between the muscles is one fingertip wide or less, you should do variation A of the following exercise. If the gap is wider or bulges up like a long bubble when you lift your head, do variation B. The wider gap simply means that your recti muscles have become separated to a degree. This is especially likely if you have been doing sit-ups or have been pregnant before. Don't worry—just protect this weakened area when you exercise and avoid activities that cause you to bear down excessively with these muscles.

Modified Sit-ups. Variation A: Lie on your back with your head supported by the floor. Your knees should be up with your feet flat on the floor about hip-width apart. Press your lower back onto the floor (this helps to protect your back). Inhale through your nose. As you exhale slowly through your mouth, lift your head and reach forward with your arms toward your thighs. Lift only enough to curl your shoulders forward. Notice how the muscles of your abdomen press together and tighten. Hold for three counts, then relax back as you inhale. Repeat. Begin with a sequence of five, increasing to ten or fifteen daily.

Variation B: Before beginning the exercise described above, cross your arms over your abdomen and support both sides of it. This is done by gently pressing your hands against your recti muscles, instead of reaching forward with your arms, as you lift your head up.

Abdominal Breathing. This exercise is easy to do at various times throughout your day and is a simple way to strengthen these muscles. It is particularly good to do this exercise after a cesarean birth (while gently supporting the incision) as a means of relieving gas buildup. Start in a sitting, standing, or reclining position. Take a deep breath in through your nose, placing one of your hands over your lower abdomen just beneath your navel, and expand your abdomen out toward your hand as you inhale. Exhale through your mouth slowly, pulling your abdominal muscles in firmly. Feel them move and become tighter underneath your hand. Repeat three to five times at least once daily.

Pelvic Tilt. This basic exercise helps to strengthen lower back and abdominal muscles while easing tension and pain. (See illustration below.) There are three variations of this exercise:

PELVIC TILT

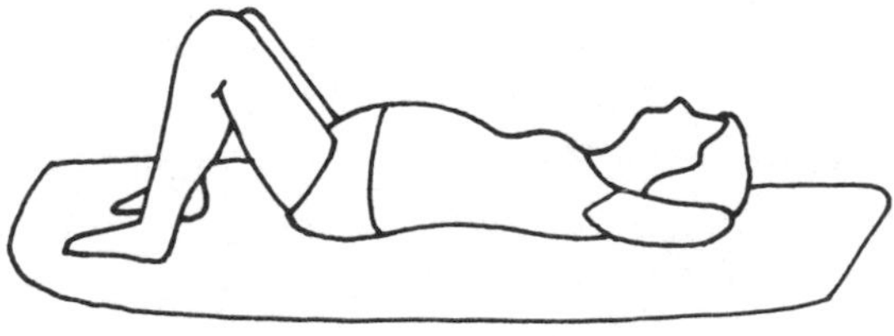

1. At Rest.

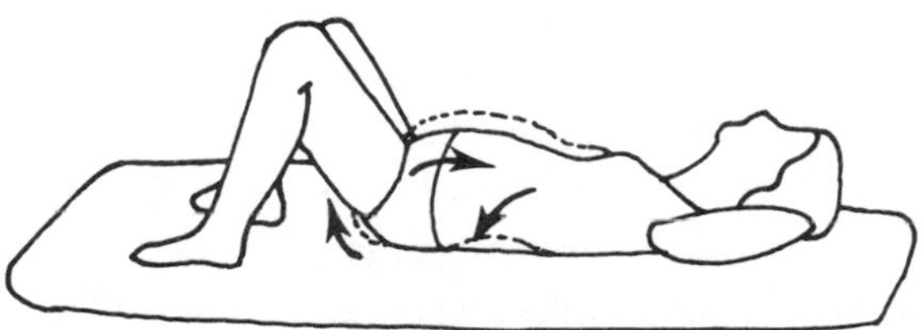

2. Pelvis is tilted as back is pressed onto the mat. Dots represent position when at rest.

Variation A: Back Press—Lie on your back with knees up and feet flat on the floor, about hip-width apart. Place your arms on the floor on either side of your body for stability. As you breathe in through your nose, note the curve of your lower back. Mentally determine how far this part of your back is off the floor. Exhale slowly through your nose, pressing your back against the floor firmly and erasing the space that was there when you were relaxed. (Notice that when you tilt your pelvis back firmly, your abdominal muscles tighten and your buttocks move slightly upward.) Hold three to five seconds. Inhale as you relax back into your original position, making sure not to exaggerate the curve and space (this could cause strain to your back).

Repeat five times, building up to fifteen times at least once daily or whenever your back aches.

Variation B: Feline Stretch—Get into a hands-and-knees position, as if you were imitating a cat. Keep your back flat between tilts; don't let it sag down. Inhale, feeling the normal curve of your spine; exhale and tilt your pelvis by pulling down with your buttock muscles and up with your abdominal muscles. Imagine that your pelvis is connected by a hinge at the level of the back of your waist. Tilt down from this point; hold three to five seconds. Inhale and relax, but don't become swaybacked. Repeat five times, building up to fifteen daily.

Variation C: Passive Pelvic Tilt—While lying on your left side with your knees bent and a pillow under your head, have your husband support your pelvis by placing his right hand on your hip and left hand against the back of your pelvis, pointing toward your tailbone. As you tilt your pelvis, he presses down on your lower back and back on your hip. This movement may ease lower back pain during labor as well as during late pregnancy.

Pelvic Floor

During pregnancy the muscles that form the "floor" of your pelvis serve several functions. They must support the contents of your abdominal cavity (including your baby), the enlarged uterus, fluid surrounding the baby, and the placenta; withstand pressures exerted against the pelvic floor muscles caused by laughing or coughing; and provide sphincter control of the openings to your bladder and rectum.

In late pregnancy it is not uncommon to inadvertently leak urine due to the pressure placed upon these supportive muscles. Simple exercises may be done to strengthen the pelvic floor and, as a result, provide greater control of these muscles. You may also strengthen this area of your body so that it will be more elastic during the birth process and aid in the recovery of muscles that have been stretched during the birth of your baby.

Evaluating the Strength of Your Pelvic Floor. Sit comfortably in a cross-legged position. Imagine your pelvic floor muscles as a hammock attached from the front of your pelvis to your pubic bone, in back at your tailbone, and sideways between your thighs within your pelvis. This "hammock" has three openings—your urethra, vagina, and anus. Around these openings are two strong bands of muscles. (See illustration.) These are called sphincter muscles. One surrounds your rectum, and the other surrounds both the urethra and the vagina. These sphincters are separate muscles that form an integrated structure. As you lift the pelvic floor up, the sphincters are designed to tighten and close firmly. Your buttocks and lower abdominal muscles should remain relaxed while you contract your pelvic floor muscles.

LIGAMENTS OF THE UTERUS

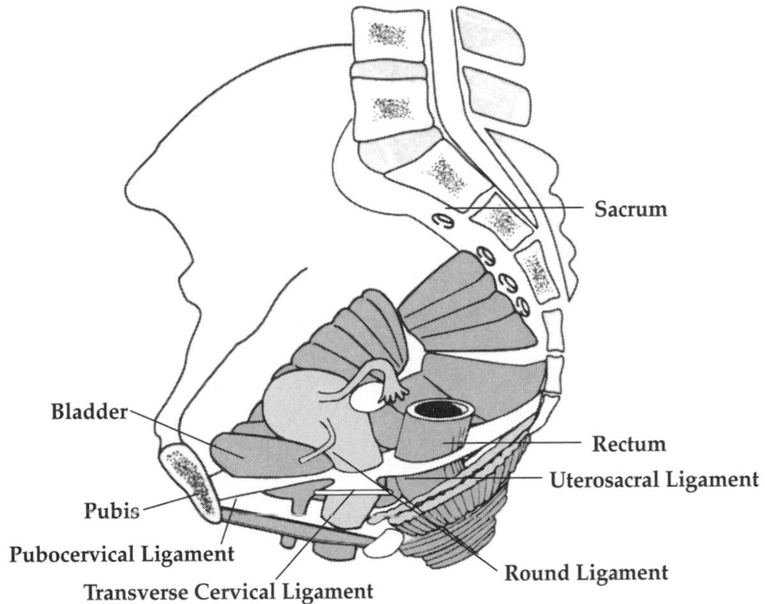

To evaluate the strength of this important area of your body, tighten the pelvic floor by lifting it as "high" as you can while at the same time closing the sphincters. Hold this position. Once the pelvic floor is lifted and the sphincters are tightened, slowly count to ten. As soon as you feel your pelvic floor muscles start to drop, note the number at which these muscles began to relax. Use the following exercise daily to strengthen the pelvic floor so that you can hold this lift for a full ten seconds.

The Kegel Exercise. Dr. Arnold Kegel has the unique distinction of having these unusual exercises named in his honor because of his research on the effect of exercise on pelvic floor relaxation. Dr. Kegel found that while the vagina has relatively few responsive nerve endings, pelvic floor muscles are sensitive during lovemaking and play a key role in a woman's sexual response. He also discovered that exercising the pelvic floor through a series of fifteen to twenty-five contractions several times daily could correct many cases of pelvic floor relaxation, as well as improve sexual response. This work suggests that *prevention* of pelvic floor dysfunction is even more important than the treatment of problems after they arise.

The Kegel exercise can be done anywhere without anyone being aware of it. It is best not to do Kegels while urinating, because stopping and starting the flow of urine can cause urine that has come into contact with bacteria lower in the urethra to move back up toward the normally sterile contents of your bladder.

As in the pelvic floor evaluation, contract the muscles of the pelvic floor by lifting them upward. At the same time, press the openings closed. You may breathe out as you lift if you find you have a tendency to tense any other areas of your body. Lift slowly and purposefully until you reach the "top" of the level you are able to attain. Hold for counts of three to five. Inhale and lower slowly. Repeat ten times, building up to twenty-five repetitions done at least once daily.

Posture and Body Mechanics

The way you move changes during late pregnancy. The tendency is for the curve in your lower back to become greater, so you need to pay special attention to your posture and movements while lifting objects, lying down, rising out of a chair or your bed, and climbing stairs. The following changes in daily habits will help you to prevent lower back strain.

LIFTING

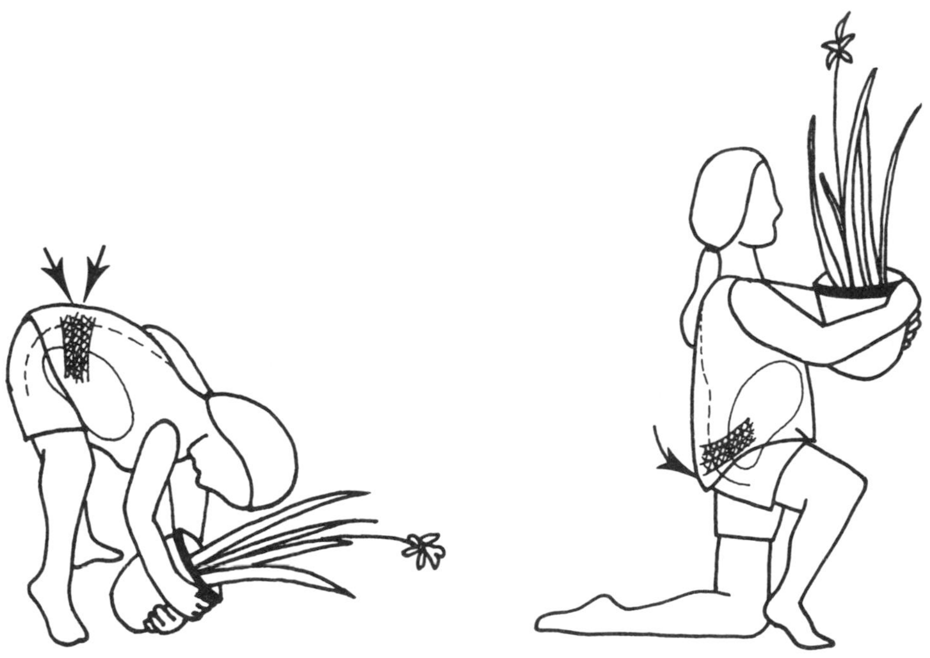

1. Avoid bending at the waist when lifting objects.
2. Instead, kneel and raise yourself and what you are lifting by using your legs.

Standing. Slightly tuck under your pelvis by pulling down on your buttock muscles and upward with your abdominal muscles. Consciously think of straightening your back when standing. Wear shoes that allow for this posture. Raise your head up and try not to slump your shoulders forward. This will enable you to feel and look better.

Sitting. To lower yourself into a chair or to stand up, use your legs more than the central part of your body. Grasp something to hold onto. While sitting, avoid crossing your legs since this impairs blood circulation. Also, become aware of keeping your back straight and squaring your shoulders as you sit.

Lying Down. Sitting at the edge of your bed, swing your legs onto the bed while stabilizing your upper body with your hands placed on the mattress. Using your arms, lower your body onto the bed into a side position. If you wish to lie on your back, roll over from your side instead of dropping straight backward from a sitting position. Reverse this process to get out of bed.

The Uterus and Pelvis

It is not unusual to feel aching on occasion in your groin on one or both sides just above the pubic bones. This sensation is due to the stretching of the round ligaments that attach the front sides of your uterus to your pelvis. (See Ligaments of the Uterus illustration.) Rubbing firmly with your hand in a slow, circular motion at the point of strain may help to ease the tension.

As further preparation for the birth process, the uterus will contract at regular intervals throughout pregnancy to strengthen itself. These contractions, called Braxton-Hicks contractions after the British physician who "discovered" them, are involuntary. They are more noticeable during and after physical exertion, following orgasm, or when a woman is frightened, fatigued, surprised, or angry. Women who have borne several children generally begin to notice these contractions earlier and more frequently than in previous pregnancies. Since Braxton-Hicks contractions are not associated with changes in the cervix or with the opening of the uterus, they are not true labor contractions.

Also, the joints in your pelvis will become somewhat looser due to the influence of a hormone called *relaxin*. This is the Lord's way of making the bone structure through which your baby passes a bit more flexible.

Worry doesn't empty tomorrow of its sorrows; it empties today of its strength.

CORRIE TEN BOOM

YOUR CIRCULATORY SYSTEM

By late pregnancy your total blood volume (which includes that of your baby and placenta) is 30 to 40 percent greater than normal. At this time it is not unusual to have a lower percentage of iron or hemoglobin in your bloodstream. If that is the case, your health-care provider may recommend that you take an iron supplement.

Since hemoglobin carries oxygen to all the cells in your body, it is important that you avoid becoming anemic. Oxygen is consumed in high quantities during labor. This is because the uterus requires oxygen for energy in order to function effectively. Anemia lowers your ability to carry oxygen in your blood. It can also decrease your resistance to infection, make you more prone to fatigue, and increase your sensitivity to pain.

The hormone progesterone relaxes certain muscles within your body. Although its main purpose is to keep the uterus relaxed until the appropriate time for labor to begin, the hormone acts on smooth muscles throughout your entire body. This means that the muscles within the walls of your veins are more relaxed, and varicose veins may result. In your legs it is more difficult for your blood to return to your heart because it must move "uphill" against gravity.

Wearing support hose, walking daily, raising your feet, and doing exercises with your feet all are ways to help the blood get back to your heart more easily, causing less pressure on the walls of your leg veins. Try to get your feet up during the day, and use the following two exercises to help stimulate leg circulation.

Foot Pumps. While sitting or lying down, pump your feet back and forth as if you were playing an old-fashioned organ. Be careful not to point your toes; you might get a "charley horse."

Foot Circles. While sitting or lying down, circle one or both feet outward and back to the center over and over again. After doing this for a minute or two, reverse the direction and circle inward. Do these frequently, especially if you have been sitting or lying down for a period of time.

Elevated blood pressure and swelling due to fluid retention are not unusual conditions during late pregnancy. By keeping your total protein intake at ten grams or more per day, restricting the amount of salty foods you eat, and resting on your left side for several hours per day, you may be able to alleviate these conditions.

Some of the sodium-rich foods you should limit include:

- pork products—ham,* bacon,* sausage,* hot dogs*
- cheese and meat products—processed cheese, cheese dips, snack spreads
- most canned meats,* soups, stews,* vegetables
- snacks—pretzels, popcorn, potato chips, many crackers
- seasonings—prepared mustard, catsup, Worcestershire sauce, steak sauce, soy sauce, pickles, relishes, meat tenderizers, many brands of peanut butter
- other—baking soda and many fast-food restaurant items

*These foods also contain high amounts of nitrites.

☙ YOUR DIGESTIVE SYSTEM

Your baby will press against your stomach and intestines as he grows, leaving less room for food and causing difficulties in digestion. The action of progesterone upon smooth muscle in your stomach and intestines also slows down the entire process considerably, sometimes causing heartburn and constipation.

Drinking an adequate amount of water and eating foods high in fiber will decrease strain on your bowels. Also, restricting your intake of greasy foods is wise since fat is the most difficult nutrient to digest. The exception to this recommendation is whole or 2-percent milk, which can help to alleviate heartburn by coating the lining of the stomach.

During the last six to eight weeks of pregnancy, it is particularly helpful to eat six smaller meals rather than three large meals per day. (Refer to Appendix A for food servings and menu suggestions.) Actually, this eating pattern is probably a more efficient way to eat throughout life. Avoiding spicy foods or bedtime snacks may promote comfort as well.

Frequency of urination is unavoidable during the last trimester due to the baby's growth and the settling of the baby into your lower pelvis. One of the nicest things about giving birth is that you get your bladder back. It's fairly typical during pregnancy to wake up several times a night to empty your bladder, which may be the Lord's way of helping you to prepare for night feedings.

☙ BREAST CHANGES

During late pregnancy your breasts are preparing for their role of nourishing your baby. Your veins will become more noticeable through your skin as the blood supply to the glands in your breasts increases. The little bumps on your areola (the dark ring around the nipple) become more prominent. These small bumps are called the "glands of Montgomery." They secrete a substance that moisturizes your nipples and kills bacteria. For this reason cleansing your nipples with soap is unnecessary.

The skin color of the areola also darkens, and the breasts themselves become larger as the glandular tissue develops. All of these changes serve to remind you of the special purpose the Lord had in mind when he created this part of your body.

Preparing Your Breasts for Lactation

Six to eight weeks before your due date is the ideal time to start preparing your breasts for lactation. However, even one or two weeks' worth of preparation will help. Use the following techniques in your preparation.

Breast Massage. During pregnancy the glands in your breasts become much larger, producing firmer breasts and occasionally feelings of heaviness. Massaging your breasts may help to encourage the flow of milk because it stimulates the ducts and glands by improving circulation and makes the ducts more elastic.

Simply place your hands at the base of the left breast where it is fullest, near the chest. Your hands are positioned with one hand on each side, with your thumbs above the breast and the remaining fingers below. Just slide your hands together gently and firmly in a smooth motion toward the nipple. Repeat this movement several times. Don't forget to massage both breasts in this manner.

Air Exposure. When possible, allow your nipples to be exposed to the air and avoid overprotecting them. One way this can be done is to wear a nursing bra with the flaps down while at home. In the shower let the water spray on the nipples. Avoid drying products such as soap or astringents. After bathing or showering, use a dry towel to lightly rub the nipples.

Check for Flat or Inverted Nipples

If you gently grasp your nipple, pull it out and let go, you will see the nipple react below the skin if the nipples are inverted. Flat nipples are simply those that do not stay firm and erect for long following this check.

If your nipples do not become erect easily, you may try nipple rolling more frequently to encourage the shaping of the nipples for breastfeeding. Grasp your nipple between your thumb and forefinger. Gently pull the nipple outward until you feel a slight discomfort and then slowly rotate the nipple. Continue this for about a minute and repeat on the opposite side. (NOTE: Do not use nipple rolling if you have experienced premature labor as nipple stimulation can provoke uterine contractions.)

If you have inverted nipples, a simple device called a breast shield can help. The shields are worn inside the bra and break down the inner adhesions around the nipples that pull them inward. Many women have found that these double-walled plastic shields are a useful, noninvasive treatment for flat nipples as well. Breast shields may be purchased from your local lactation consultant, La Leche League leader, or medical supply store.

OTHER CHANGES

In addition to the changes already mentioned, there are several other physical and emotional stages of late pregnancy:

- Increased clear-colored vaginal discharge due to hormonal activity. Try to remember that this prepares your vaginal tissue to become softer and more elastic. Wear breathable cotton underwear.
- Increased consumption of oxygen and need to breathe due to a greater demand

for air in your bloodstream. You don't have to apologize for being out of breath all the time. You really are breathing for two.

• Increased restlessness and decreased ability to sleep soundly. This is due to all the changes mentioned. Also it is possibly related to high levels of estrogen circulating throughout your system.

• Decreased ability to concentrate and remember things. I wonder why? Seriously, this is most likely the result of the constant involvement of your body in meeting all the demands of late pregnancy and nurturing your baby.

• Engagement of the baby into the pelvis as labor draws nearer. This can happen up to eight weeks ahead, but two to four weeks prior to labor is the average for a first-time mother. Engagement usually occurs later for a woman who has given birth previously. With the engagement of the baby, the diaphragm can move more freely, making breathing easier. Bladder space, however, is reduced considerably. Backache, rectal pressure, and hip discomfort are common with the additional weight of the baby pressing on the lower pelvis.

By the end of pregnancy your body will have readied itself and your baby for labor. Not surprisingly, you will be probably be quite thankful when labor finally begins.

COMMON PHYSICAL CONCERNS OF LATE PREGNANCY AND IDEAS FOR COMFORT

Complaint	Reason	How to Help
Fatigue, restlessness	Your ever-growing baby interferes with your need for rest. A decrease in bladder capacity requires frequent urination. Vivid dreams and anxiety can result in lack of rest. It may be difficult to find a comfortable resting position.	Accept the situation as temporary. Your pregnancy won't last much longer. Rest in a semi-sitting or left-side-lying position. Eliminate all unnecessary activities. Communicate your concerns that others help share the load. Short, frequent rest periods with music and relaxation techniques after emptying your bladder may help. Pray that the Lord will give you rest.
Constipation	This may be caused by iron supplements and sluggishness in your intestinal tract due to the effects of progesterone, a hormone secreted in high amounts during pregnancy. Progesterone relaxes smooth muscle.	Avoid caffeine. Drink weak, warm tea upon rising in the morning. Eat plenty of dried fruit, whole grains, and bran. Avoid eating too much cheese or too many bananas. Drink six to eight glasses of water daily.

Complaint	Reason	How to Help
Breathlessness	As your uterus grows upward, it presses against your diaphragm, making lung expansion more difficult. Also, your growing baby needs increasing amounts of oxygen so that the mother's oxygen consumption is 30 to 40 percent above normal.	Slow, deeper breathing helps. Avoid lying flat on your back since the weight of your baby on blood vessels beneath the uterus decreases the availability of oxygen. Stretch your arms overhead and reach with one arm at a time toward the ceiling while doing slow breathing.
Hemorrhoids	A combination of straining and the condition of relaxed walls of rectal veins (due to progesterone) leads to this problem.	Try to solve the constipation problem so that straining can be avoided. Prop feet on a stool while sitting on toilet. Tucks pads offer relief for discomfort.
Varicose veins	Also due to the effect of progesterone, which relaxes the muscle in leg veins, resulting in decreased blood flow. The weight of your uterus makes blood flow to your legs sluggish as well.	Foot Pumps, Foot Circles (see p. 52), and walking will help increase circulation. Resting with feet propped up makes it easier for blood to return to the heart.
Swelling of ankles, fingers	An alteration in your metabolism.	Increase protein intake. Rest lying on left side for one to three hours, three times per day. Do not restrict fluids or take "water pills" if at all possible.
Lower back pain	Your enlarged uterus is anchored to your lower back. When the uterus is pulled forward due to poor posture or failure to adjust body mechanics for late pregnancy, pain is more severe.	Use the Pelvic Tilt (see p. 47-48) to relax the broad ligament supporting your uterus. Rest with knees propped up when lying down. Roll onto side to get up. Lift and stand up with awareness of back and how to utilize posture and legs to decrease strain.
Groin ache	Round ligaments anchor the uterus to the pubic area on both sides. As the uterus grows, your ligaments are stretched.	Rub with heel of hand in a firm, circular motion. Apply warm compresses.

Complaint	Reason	How to Help
Braxton-Hicks contractions	This is a "warm-up" exercise involuntarily conducted by the uterus to tone and strengthen itself.	Try light massage, pubic stroking, slow breathing, and conscious release. Use these contractions to practice relaxation and breathing techniques.
Heartburn	Your enlarged uterus displaces your digestive tract, and the relaxing effect of progesterone on the cardiac sphincter of your stomach allows for the seepage of gastric juices into your esophagus.	Avoid large, heavy meals and greasy foods. Rest with your head elevated and try not to eat within four hours of retiring. Eat several smaller meals rather than three large ones.
Itchy Skin	Your skin is stretching over the growing breasts and uterus.	Wear nonirritating clothing. Lubricate skin; pure cocoa butter or vitamin E cream works well. Take warm showers.
Vaginal discharge	This can be considered normal unless there is foul odor or an inflamed, itching vulva.	Proper hygiene, mini-pads, and cotton-crotch panties help. Avoid feminine deodorants, powders, and bubble baths.
Leaking of urine	The weight of your baby on your pelvic floor weakens the contracting ability of the sphincter around the urethral opening.	Kegel exercises, frequent urination, mini-pads.
Anxiety, apprehension	Major changes are taking place involving shifts in lifestyle and priorities. The health and condition of the baby is a cause of concern to many expectant parents.	Communicate your concerns; accept how you are feeling. Go to appropriate sources for reassurance, guidance, and information. Review "Preparing Your Heart, Mind, and Spirit," chapter 2.
"Charley horses," leg cramps	Excessive potassium or insufficient amounts of calcium in the bloodstream may cause this problem.	Do not massage the cramped muscle. Stretch out cramps by pulling toes up while pressing heel down.

☙ SCRIPTURAL REFLECTIONS AND PROMISES

For who is God besides the Lord? And who is the Rock except our God? It is God who arms me with strength and makes my way perfect.

PSALM 18:31-32

Do not be wise in your own eyes; fear the Lord and shun evil. This will bring health to your body and nourishment to your bones.

PROVERBS 3:7-8

Even the sparrow has found a home, and the swallow a nest for herself, where she may have her young—a place near your altar, O Lord Almighty, my King and my God. Blessed are those who dwell in your house; they are ever praising you. Blessed are those whose strength is in you, who have set their hearts on pilgrimage. As they pass through the Valley of Baca, they make it a place of springs; the autumn rains also cover it with pools. They go from strength to strength, till each appears before God in Zion.

PSALM 84:3-7

Let your eyes look straight ahead, fix your gaze directly before you. Make level paths for your feet and take only ways that are firm.

PROVERBS 4:25-26

Surely God is my salvation; I will trust and not be afraid. The Lord, the Lord, is my strength and my song; he has become my salvation.

ISAIAH 12:2

But we have this treasure in jars of clay to show that this all-surpassing power is from God and not from us

2 CORINTHIANS 4:7

May God himself, the God of peace, sanctify you through and through. May your whole spirit, soul and body be kept blameless at the coming of our Lord Jesus Christ. The one who calls you is faithful and he will do it.

1 THESSALONIANS 5:23-24

FIVE

PLANNING YOUR BABY'S BIRTH DAY

Trust in the Lord and do good; dwell in the land and enjoy safe pasture. Delight yourself in the Lord and he will give you the desires of your heart.

PSALM 37:3-4

In our culture today, there is no one right way to give birth. Expectant parents usually can choose who will deliver their baby, where their baby will be born, who will accompany the mother through labor, and what things can be done to make their baby's birth special. As I mentioned earlier, planning your baby's birthday is a lot like planning a wedding. Although a traditional model exists, there are many things you can do to make your baby's birth a unique, safe, and joyous experience.

During pregnancy, a waiting period extends from confirmation of the pregnancy to the onset of labor and the baby's birth. The length of this period is typically seven or eight months—much like a premarital engagement period. Once the date is known, the preparing and planning begin. Where will the event take place? Who will perform the ceremony? What about guests? What things will be done to make this moment one of a kind? In most cases, there is ample time to prepare for the event and to find out the answers to each of these key questions.

Simplicity is the secret of seeing things clearly.

OSWALD CHAMBERS

CHOOSING YOUR HEALTH-CARE PROVIDER

Prenatal care primarily involves three people—the mother, her unborn child, and the mother's health-care provider. The baby's father also plays an important role in protecting his wife by helping her adapt her lifestyle to promote the well-being of herself and their baby.

Your choice of a health-care provider who will attend the birth in a way that fits your needs will be one of the most important decisions you make. Find out which of the following professionals are available in your community and then determine who can best meet your health-care needs.

Obstetrician

An obstetrician is a medical doctor (M.D.) or doctor of osteopathy (D.O.) who attended medical school for a period of four years and has completed a three-year residency in the area of his or her specialization of obstetrics. This type of physician is usually a practicing gynecologist as well, and therefore is a trained surgeon. The ability to treat the complications of pregnancy and childbirth makes an obstetrician the most skilled (and therefore the most expensive) maternity health-care provider.

If your pregnancy or birth requires expert medical care, you will want to consider an obstetrician. Select one with whom you feel compatible. If you want to be cared for by an obstetrician who practices medicine from a coherent life-affirming perspective, call your local crisis pregnancy center for a referral.

Family Practitioner

A family practitioner is also either a medical doctor (M.D.) or a doctor of osteopathy (D.O.). Family practice physicians certified since the late sixties have been required to complete a three-year residency program after graduating from medical school. Family practitioners can treat a variety of complications, but are unable to perform cesarean births. For this reason, family practitioners work closely with obstetricians so that an obstetrician would be available if necessary.

Many family practice physicians use fewer routine types of obstetrical intervention and are more conservative about the use of anesthetics during labor. GPs, or general practitioners, are usually doctors who have not completed a three-year residency in family practice or any other specialty, but they may provide excellent care due to years of experience.

Nurse-Midwife

Nearly all states provide for the practice of nurse-midwifery and have laws that determine the level of schooling a nurse-midwife must complete before being allowed to practice professionally. This type of health-care provider is a registered nurse who has studied normal gynecology and obstetrics for a one- to two-year period beyond nurse's training.

Nurse-midwives are typically women, whereas many obstetricians and family practitioners are men. Some women consider gender to be an important factor in their selection of a health-care provider. Nurse-midwives are qualified to practice normal obstetrics and "well-woman" gynecological care (pap tests, family planning, and regular exams). They must work in conjunction with physicians who serve as backups if complications arise. A nurse-midwife remains with her client throughout the entire labor, whereas physicians are available only as needed.

Direct-entry, Traditional, or "Lay" Midwives

This profession provided most of the obstetrical care available to childbearing women until the early 1900s. Direct-entry midwives practice independently, usually attending births in the home, and may or may not be working directly with a physician. Their training varies from having attended relatively few births to being part of a family tradition that extends back through many generations.

A number of midwives practice their art from a spiritual viewpoint; a certain percentage of direct-entry midwives attending home births are Christians, and they vary widely in their philosophies. Only a few states have licensure and certification laws that regulate the practice of direct-entry midwifery. In some states this practice is considered either illegal or "outside the law."

In considering your health-care provider, it is important to think about who is available in your area. Choose whomever you are most comfortable with as a couple. Pray together and do your best to evaluate the skills of the person you are considering by finding out about his or her training, scope of practice, location, philosophy of practice, availability, and costs. (See chart.)

POINTS TO PONDER WHEN DECIDING ON A HEALTH-CARE PROVIDER

Training
Certification, place of education, years of experience

Scope of Practice
Which situations must be referred to a specialist

Philosophy of Practice
Routine recommendations for use of drugs, surgery, and technology during labor; attitudes concerning birth alternatives; view of pregnancy and birth (primarily as inherently dangerous or normally uncomplicated), and basis of practice (traditional or an alternative approach)

Availability
On-call schedule; office hours; length of wait for an appointment or during an office visit; who does the backup if doctor is unavailable?

Costs
Fee; what is included; third-party or Medicaid reimbursement; how payment is made (must you pay and wait to be reimbursed through your insurance company?)

Locations of Practice
Office location; hospital(s) used (family-centered maternity care; size; neonatal intensive care unit; availability of alternative birth settings such as birthing rooms, birthing

chairs, and birthing centers); rules regarding father's involvement (extent of Dad's involvement during both vaginal and cesarean birth)

Other Questions to Ask
Is it important to you that your health-care provider be a Christian? Do you feel at ease with this person? Does he or she seem responsive to your concerns and able to answer your questions adequately? Does this provider perform abortions, or does he or she practice at a hospital where abortions are done? Does this provider's philosophy of practice support your childbearing preferences?

Basically, there are two approaches to providing maternity care. With the "traditional" approach, the emphasis is on risk factors. Institutionalized settings (labor and birth in separate rooms, centralized nursery, no home support) are used. Care is routinized. The economic and legal considerations are from the medical team's view; the education, philosophy, and personal values considered are those of the medical team; beliefs and attitudes are traditional. There is a lack of involvement from nonmedical disciplines.

The alternative model or approach to maternity care involves an emphasis on pregnancy and birth as normal life processes; a desire for alternative settings (birthing rooms and centers, decentralized nurseries, and home care); individualized care with the economic and legal considerations taken from the consumer's view; the education, philosophy, and personal values of the parents are the determinants; the beliefs and attitudes are not necessarily traditional; there is multidisciplinary involvement.

Health care is expensive in America. Services differ from place to place, and practices vary among health-care providers. It's wise to look around before you "buy," especially if your community offers a variety of maternity care services. The numerous options available can be confusing, but they also allow for a greater freedom to choose the type of medical care best suited to one's physical needs, lifestyle, personal values, and budget. Parents can now be more discriminating as to where they spend their health-care dollars if they consider the options carefully.

Given the changes in childbirth practices that have taken place in the space of just one generation in the United States, it isn't surprising that expectant parents sometimes find themselves placed in an awkward position between a hospital or health-care provider who offers traditional obstetric care and a writer or childbirth educator who introduces readers or students to alternative birth practices.

Physicians, midwives, authors, nurses, and childbirth educators seek to enhance the childbearing experience of the couples they serve by providing professional services based upon their well-reasoned viewpoints. Yet the proliferation of books, classes, theories, childbirth methods, and obstetric practices proves that we have yet to arrive at one "right" way of approaching childbirth.

Fortunately we are living at a time in history when mothers and babies have the greatest chance of surviving childbirth. In the midst of today's controversies in obstetrics, I believe it's possible to give birth with joy and dignity by looking to the Lord for direction in our lives. The number of choices available to us can be a blessing as we pray for discernment in deciding what is best in our own situation.

Too much and too little education hinder the mind.

BLAISE PASCAL

THREE COUPLES' EXPERIENCES

Theresa and Tom Stephenson, members of one of my childbirth classes, had their first child in the birthing room at a small community hospital in Georgia. Theresa had an uncomplicated birth with an ideal outcome—healthy baby, healthy mother, happy father.

After working with contractions without medication for a while, Theresa requested pain relief and was given a small dose of analgesia in her IV. Several hours later she asked for an epidural block—the regional anesthetic used during childbirth to numb the area between the knees and navel—and an anesthesiologist quickly arrived to administer the medication.

Although the baby showed signs of distress briefly, the difficulty proved to be temporary. When Theresa received some oxygen and switched to a side-lying position, the baby's heart rate rapidly returned to normal. Throughout the night, labor progressed smoothly, and she gave birth to an eight-pound baby girl just seven hours after her admission to the hospital.

"I was very pleased with the way everything went," she told me later. "The doctor and nurses were great. It was a lot easier than I expected—especially when I consider the way things might have gone. There really isn't anything that we would choose to do differently the next time around."

Unlike Theresa and Tom, another couple I knew chose a nontraditional setting for the birth of their third baby. Dissatisfied with the lack of personal attention they had received during previous labors, Nancy and Jim Bennett wanted to avoid routine medical interventions such as IVs and an episiotomy, and they elected to have the baby in a birth center instead of the hospital.

"The Family Birthing Center, located forty-five minutes from where we live, offered a homelike setting with little interference in the birthing process," explains Nancy. "They encouraged parents to determine what they want, but a doctor or nurse-midwife was there to supervise.

"The birth center turned out to be a good compromise between home and hospital. We had written down all the reasons why we should and shouldn't have a home birth and seriously considered doing that for a while," Nancy shared. "The more we pursued it, however, the more we realized how much there was to overcome. I wanted good prenatal care and medical backup in case an emergency arose, thinking, *How could I handle it if anything happens?* But since I knew several people who had had home births, I kept going back and forth on it."

Nancy's husband, Jim, commented, "There was a marked difference in our birthing experience the third time around. I was very much involved with Stacie's birth. I was the one who 'caught' her—the doctor primarily watched. Also, Nancy had an episiotomy with our first two children, and this time she didn't, which we both appreciated."

Yet another couple I taught, Stephanie and Chuck Ehrlinger, decided a home birth might be right for them after having two children in a traditional hospital setting. Both previous labors had proved upsetting.

"They kept doing things to me that I didn't want and didn't need," Stephanie noted, "and at the time I certainly wasn't in any condition to argue with anyone about it."

Dick was initially skeptical even though Stephanie wanted to look into the possibility of having a home birth after reading a book about the advantages of having a baby in a non-hospital setting.

"I have good insurance that pays for everything done in a hospital," he said. "I felt the safest way to have a baby is in a hospital with expert resources available in case something goes wrong. Yet when I met with our midwife Diane, I realized that a home birth can be safer in some ways than a hospital birth. But, let me tell you, prayer played a *major* role in our decision to plan a home birth."

While it was difficult to find someone who would serve as their medical backup in case hospitalization proved necessary, the Ehrlingers eventually found a doctor who was willing to offer them medical care. The baby arrived right on schedule—exactly on his due date—with friends and family gathered in the living room to share the Ehrlingers' joy.

"When Isaac was born, he was put on my tummy right away, and I nursed him immediately," Stephanie explained. "One of the women there sang a song and played her guitar to welcome Isaac into the world, and later I was served breakfast in bed. It was a wonderful experience being in the privacy of our own home."

CHANGING TRENDS IN CHILDBIRTH

The preceding examples of three couples' birthplace preferences demonstrate how wide the range of birthplace options and medical care choices have become in recent years. This is good news for childbearing families today. As health-care professionals respond to their clients' expectations and increasing pressure from insurance companies to lower health-care costs, the list of available choices will continue to expand.

The twentieth century brought as many changes to childbirth practices as it did to all other aspects of life. Until the discovery of antiseptic techniques and anesthetics in the mid-1800s, childbearing was routinely accomplished without them, and infection was common. As physicians began to assume greater control over birth practices through childbirth technologies, deliveries took place in hospitals with greater frequency. Medical intervention in the birth process became common practice in the United States, and women sought pain relief in greater numbers with each passing year.

Women expected modern medicine to bring about a higher number of safe deliveries with less pain, but these changes in birthing practices did not satisfy everyone. From the 1930s onward, people began to speak out against this trend toward the medicalization of childbirth, creating a movement that has become popularly accepted and that now encompasses many different views and organizations.

Looking back, I find it hard to believe we've come so far so fast. In 1972, the year our first child was born, there were no birthing rooms; Labor, Delivery, Recovery, & Postpartum (LDRP) rooms; or birth centers in the United States. Hospital birth in a delivery room—often without one's husband or labor partner in attendance—was the only safe choice presented to most women.

I clearly remember being dismayed to think that in order to have a baby I would have to be admitted to a hospital, endure a twenty-four hour separation from my newborn, and not be able to breastfeed on demand (all were common hospital policies at that time). I sought out the services of a physician who still attended home births in our community—perhaps the only remaining physician in Michigan who offered this option.

By the time I was pregnant with our second daughter, our family had moved to a different city. While discussing what I wanted our hospital birth to be like with my obstetrician, he agreed to allow the baby to be born in the labor room instead of the delivery room. I also asked to be discharged from the hospital after twelve hours if everything was going well. It must have been an unheard-of request in those days from the way the nurses looked at me so incredulously when it finally came time to go home.

Later our third child was born at home with an obstetrical nurse and my husband in attendance, but complications immediately following the birth encouraged me to try the hospital again when our fourth child was ready to be born in 1980. A comfortable birthing room replete with rocking chair, plants, and colorful posters greeted me upon admission. In addition, no interventions were used unnecessarily during the birth.

Rooming-in and family visitors were easily accommodated, and breastfeeding on demand was a common practice.

Since training to become a childbirth educator in 1973, I've witnessed a virtual explosion in maternity care options across the United States. The changes have proved remarkable as well as dramatic. Most hospitals now incorporate the kind of family-centered maternity care I could only dream about two decades ago. Birthing and LDRP rooms are available almost everywhere; babies and mothers are no longer routinely separated for long periods following birth; and early hospital discharge is increasingly common due to escalating health-care costs.

In an effort to stem the rising tide of home births and provide less expensive alternatives to traditional hospital settings, medical organizations now actively support the incorporation of new nontraditional birth options. The home-birth movement protested the cold, sterile surroundings and routine interventions used in most hospitals—but home births pose risks as well: Last-minute emergencies can take place in the blink of an eye in even the most "normal" labors.

Out of this controversy has come a wider array of birth settings than ever before, with health-care recipients reaping the benefits. What "fits" one woman isn't at all what another might prefer or need. The choice of where a baby will be born ultimately rests with the childbearing woman and her family.

Recently freestanding birth centers have become the latest alternative to be added to this ever-expanding array of maternity services. One birth center director explains why: "In the birth center we view pregnancy and birth as normal, healthy events in the life of a family. We promote wellness and positive attitudes about birth and parenting. At our center we pamper new mothers by offering at-home follow-up care, homemaker services, new parent support groups. . . . We want our center to be a place that [people] can turn to as new parents."

A study of delivery outcomes in birthing centers reported in the *New England Journal of Medicine* showed a significant reduction in risk to the more than 10,000 mothers and babies cared for in this type of obstetrical setting. Considering the reduced cost and reduced length of away-from-home stays associated with freestanding birth centers, this newest option in maternity care is an excellent choice for many families, where available.

While birth centers continue to increase in national popularity, most women in the United States and Canada today give birth in hospitals. But hospital birth experiences differ considerably from location to location—and not all of these differences can be ascribed to the ease or difficulty of labor and delivery alone.

Because current birthplace options vary widely in philosophy, types of services offered, fees charged, and attitudes toward patients, it's important to learn as much as possible about maternity care choices in your community before making a final decision. To get the kind of care you need—and deserve—it's wise not to wait until the last minute to conduct your search.

When preexisting medical conditions rule out options that cannot accommodate a higher degree of risk, flexibility is essential. For this reason it helps to view the birthplace location as a preferred selection rather than an absolute goal. The availability of emergency medical treatments and equipment is a blessing when technology is used appropriately to save lives and treat birth-related complications.

Whereas Theresa selected an epidural anesthetic in a birthing room setting, Nancy chose to have her child in a birthing center, and Stephanie planned a home birth. In working with expectant parents such as the Stephensons, the Bennetts, and the Ehrlingers, I encourage this decision-making process by providing information about birth alternatives available locally. I support their right to make an informed choice based on what they think is best for them.

For a majority of parents, the greater variety of birthplace choices available today makes it possible to achieve a safe outcome to labor and also meet families' personal needs. The type of birth style may vary considerably from one family to the next, but for most couples, the primary factor in their choice is the desire for the birth to have a positive impact on their child's development. A healthy baby received into the arms of thankful parents is everyone's main objective, regardless of the means used to achieve it.

Thinking It Through: Today's Birthplace Options

TRADITIONAL HOSPITAL SETTING

Advantages:

Any woman may use this setting regardless of medical condition; mother moves to delivery suite for vaginal or cesarean birth; many types of emergency equipment are available; anesthesia and other obstetrical interventions are widely used; staff consists of nurses, nurse clinicians, OB aides, physicians, and may include nurse-midwives; medical personnel are liable for the mother's and baby's health care; comprehensive insurance coverage is available; recovery is medically supervised throughout hospital stay.

Disadvantages:

Hospital setting can seem unfamiliar and cause maternal anxiety and apprehension; maternity care is often high-tech and routinized; transfer to delivery suite may be disorienting and uncomfortable; hospital staff stipulates who accompanies mother through the birth process; foreign bacteria increase the chance of infection for mother and baby; traditional hospital care is the most expensive type of maternity service, typically costing over $4,000.

IN-HOSPITAL BIRTHING ROOM

Advantages:

The normality of birth is emphasized; most obstetrical interventions used in a traditional hospital setting—including pain relief medication—are available, but often fewer routine procedures are used; transfer to delivery suite for birth is often unnecessary; emergency equipment is usually stored out of sight; insurance coverage is widely available; medical liability is assumed by physician and hospital staff.

Disadvantages:

Birthing in this setting may include many routine interventions (see "Common Obstetrical Interventions" box following) and may not substantially differ from a traditional in-hospital approach; staff controls who is present and what roles they must play; unfamiliar bacteria are present; birthing rooms may cost the same as traditional care unless the mother and baby are discharged early.

LDRP (LABOR, DELIVERY, RECOVERY, & POSTPARTUM) ROOM

Advantages:

LDRPs offer most of the same advantages and disadvantages as birthing rooms, but often cost less because mother and baby stay in the same room until hospital discharge, often leaving sooner; if the baby rooms-in with mom without leaving the LDRP, the chance of picking up an infection in a centralized nursery is greatly reduced; staff is shared with the nursery, enhancing continuity of mother-baby care; insurance companies cover—and actually prefer—the lower cost of LDRPs; hospital personnel are legally responsible for all medical treatment provided.

Disadvantages:

The disadvantages are primarily the same as those listed for birthing rooms, with the exception of infection risk related to use of centralized nursery.

FREESTANDING BIRTH CENTER

Advantages:

Birth is seen as a normal physiological process requiring little intervention in low-risk labors. Considerable emphasis is placed on promoting mother's comfort in labor—close-by kitchens supply nutritious foods and beverages; large bathtubs accommodate a variety of labor positions, and regular beds with plenty of pillows are used. Few routine procedures are used; cost of care is significantly lower; setting is designed to be homelike to reduce anxiety and thus feels warmer, friendlier, and more secure; family decides who is present at the birth and what roles they assume in conjunction with health-care providers; personnel may consist of a widely varied team including nurse-midwives, direct-entry midwives, OB nurses, birth assistants, childbirth educators, pediatric specialists, lactation consultants, family practitioners, and on-call physicians; insurance coverage usually covers center's charges; emphasis on early return home after the birth promotes family's involvement and responsibility in mother-baby care; liability varies from center to center.

Disadvantages:

Certain medical conditions require the mother's and/or baby's transfer to an in-hospital birth setting; the center may place restrictions on what obstetrical drugs may be administered (epidural anesthesia, for example, is usually not available); location of the setting may make hospital transfer difficult.

HOME BIRTH

Advantages:

Birth is viewed as a nonmedical family event; due to associated risks little, if any, intervention is used; the family controls who is present and what they do; the home provides a familiar setting, with familiar bacteria, significantly reducing the chance of infection for mother and baby; parents assume legal responsibility for the outcome of the birth; home birth is the least expensive place for a baby to be born.

Disadvantages:

Emergency medical treatment is not readily available in most cases; there may be a lack of medical backup to provide ongoing care, if needed; there is no access to pain-relieving drugs; most health-care professionals are strongly opposed to home birth and may make any necessary care unpleasant; parents must coordinate and pay for all health care and at-home support services, with little likelihood of third-party reimbursement in most places. For more information on childbirth alternatives in your area, contact the International Childbirth Education Association (ICEA), P. O. Box 20048, Minneapolis, MN 55420; (612) 854-8660.

COMMON OBSTETRICAL INTERVENTIONS ASSOCIATED WITH HOSPITAL BIRTHS

- restriction of food and fluids
- shaving mother's pubic hair
- restricted movement due to IVs and monitors
- enemas
- labor analgesia and anesthesia
- continuous electronic fetal monitoring
- chemically stimulated and induced labor
- artificial rupture of bag of waters
- assisted birth—forceps/vacuum extraction
- surgical birth—cesarean section
- interrupted parent-baby interaction
- water/formula supplemented infant feeding
- restricted visitation—separation from friends and family

A vision without a task is a dream;
A task without a vision is drudgery;
A vision and a task is the hope of the world.
ANONYMOUS

QUESTIONS TO AID HOSPITAL SELECTION

- Are there birthing rooms? LDRP rooms? When is the delivery room used?
- What supports are provided for women's comfort in labor (rocking chairs, padded recliners, bean bags, Jacuzzi tubs, dimmed lighting, extra pillows, squatting bars, music, showers, food and beverages, birthing chairs/beds)?
- What is your current cesarean rate?
- Is an IV or continuous electronic fetal monitoring required by the hospital, or does my doctor or nurse-midwife decide when these should be used? (Due to the current malpractice crisis, some hospitals' insurance companies demand that these interventions be used routinely.)
- Who stays with a woman throughout labor? Is there a limit to the number of people allowed? Are labor nurses skilled in teaching and applying noninvasive pain relief and active labor techniques (back massage, breathing, thermal stimulation, water therapy, physical movement, and positions to promote progress)?
- How long does the baby stay with the family after the birth takes place? Is a stay in the nursery required? How often and for how long? May all of the baby's care take place at the mother's bedside, if requested?
- What are your visitation policies? Are visitors allowed to hold and care for the baby? What rules govern sibling visits?
- Does this hospital employ a specially trained lactation specialist to assist mothers with breastfeeding? Are water supplements and pacifiers routinely used?
- Is this a teaching hospital? (If so, you may be examined and treated by medical students, interns, or residents unless you request otherwise.)
- Is a neonatal intensive care unit (N.I.C.U.) located in this hospital? If not, where are babies sent who require special care?

DETERMINING THE PLACE OF BIRTH

When planning where your baby's birth will take place, it is helpful to think about the services available near where you live. In some areas of the country, alternative settings for birth benefit from a degree of medical support that may not be as available in other locations. For a specific comparison of health-care options, visit the settings that appeal to you and inquire about their policies. It is best not to wait until the seventh or eighth month of pregnancy to do this, since you may find that your health-care provider does not utilize the service that suits your needs. If possible, explore all available settings early and then find a health-care provider that works at the place you have chosen.

While all of this "shopping around" may seem complicated or just plain unnecessary, there is an incredible freedom to select what is best for your own situation. Living in America provides us with real abundance in all areas of our lives, including maternity care. No one else can say what is ultimately going to be the best for you. That is between you and God. By being informed, you can utilize the mind the Lord has given to you to make the decisions relative to your care. Compare what's available; then make your plans with God's blessing by committing what you are doing to him. Trust him to direct your steps and be open to changes that may become necessary as the circumstances of your pregnancy and birth unfold.

SELECTING YOUR LABOR COMPANIONS

As the time of your baby's birth draws near, thoughts of who will accompany you through labor and birth will increase. This person, or group of people, will be important to you. You will be sharing one of the most important and intimate events of your life with whoever is present!

Until the late sixties, fathers were unwelcome at the births of their babies in most hospitals across the United States. With the popularization of prepared childbirth, a movement developed due to the efforts of a large number of parents and other professionals. These people brought about consumer demand for the inclusion of the husband in his wife's labor and birth. Within a relatively brief period of time, most hospitals changed their policies and began allowing father participation throughout the entire process of childbirth.

There are very few hospitals today that do not include fathers in this experience, with the majority actually encouraging the involvement of dads in labor and in the care of the baby after birth. A large number of hospitals do not restrict father participation to just "natural" or vaginal births, but also recognize the value of having the husband present during cesarean birth. The concept of the father's involvement throughout the childbearing cycle is called "family-centered maternity care."

But not every man is comfortable being a labor companion to his wife. And not every childbearing woman is married. In such cases, a woman benefits from choosing a labor companion whom she trusts and knows well, such as a friend or a relative. (It's actually not a bad idea to have two labor companions, since it may be necessary for one to take a break, and they can provide emotional support for one another as well as for the mother during the busiest times of labor.)

A labor companion is someone who deeply cares about your well-being and shares your commitment to the Lord; has an ongoing interest in you and your baby; is able to be gentle, aggressive, and straightforward with you; can recognize his or her limitations and is comfortable asking for help and advice; is able to interpret your ideas, concerns, and wishes to your health-care providers if you are too involved in labor to do so; will support you to the extent that he or she will not depend on you to determine what to do during difficult moments but will be prepared enough to offer you help as needed, and will remain sensitive to your nonverbal as well as your verbal requests; is available to listen to you relive your birth experience afterward, whether it takes days, weeks, or months of actual sharing as you assimilate it into your life.

When I'm asked what the most important factors were that enabled me to cope during my four labors, I always reply that it was a combination of God's support and my husband's help. I can't imagine giving birth without the presence of either! Somehow my husband's masculinity gave me extra strength; he was a broad chest to lean on, strong arms to hold me, and large hands to rub my back. His protectiveness and gentleness conveyed the Lord's love to me in a very tangible way. Also, the bond between us grew with each baby that we birthed together as we shared the pain and joy of each delivery.

I also have had friends or family members present for extra help at each of my children's births. These were people with whom I could be myself and express my strongest emotions freely. That is not to say that they were there every minute—emphatically not! Instead, these were people who could be called on to relieve my husband, provide prayer support, or help in other ways when needed. This has always been a source of comfort to me, to know that I would never be left alone and that I was being prayed for by those who love me.

Laugh and grow strong.

IGNATIUS OF LOYOLA

MAKING YOUR BIRTH EXPERIENCE ONE OF A KIND

There may be aspects of your baby's birth that are important to you to personalize. The birth attendant, place of birth, and labor companions you select will have an impact on how your labor goes. Beyond these, there are many ways to make each childbirth unique. Some ideas follow.

Music. Cassette tapes can be picked out ahead of time and played throughout labor. What music relaxes you? Some women even sing during labor!

Clothing. You need not wear a hospital gown that ties in the back and is impossible for nursing discreetly. Simply bring a gown or two of your own to wear. Don't forget to bring some socks or slippers.

Recording the Birth. Photographs, tape recordings, home movies, and videotaping are all commonly used today by parents who wish to make a lasting record of their baby's birth. Check with the staff if you would like to gauge the light level ahead of time or if you need permission to use unusual types of cameras or equipment. Or you might wish to make a journal or written account of the baby's birth.

Objects of Visual Interest. It helps to look at things other than a clock at the foot of your bed during labor. An extensive list of ideas can be found in chapter 7. Or you may discover that you prefer to keep your eyes closed.

Activity and Labor Position. Walking, bathing, showering, and rocking in a rocking chair may all be ways to help you feel more like yourself during labor, unless there is a specific reason for you to be in bed.

Prayer and Scripture. Use posters, cassette tapes, or handmade items to remind you of those prayers in the Scriptures that are especially meaningful to you. Your labor companion may read aloud or hold the Bible for you to read to yourself. Constant prayer is very helpful in keeping your mind off any fear that you may feel. Or you may wish to choose a personalized "my" passage from Scripture to meditate on and use as your "word picture," such as: "I love you, O Lord, my strength. The Lord is my rock, my fortress and my deliverer; my God is my rock, in whom I take refuge. He is my shield and the horn of my salvation, my stronghold" (Ps. 18:1-2).

Drawing Near to the Lord. The Bible is full of word pictures that describe the many attributes of God. You might find it helpful to picture the Lord as several of these "I ams" from the Bible, for example: "I am your shield, your very great reward" (Gen. 15:1); "I am God Almighty" (Gen. 17:1); "I am with you; I will bless you" (Gen. 26:24), and many others. See Exodus 15:26; 16:12; 22:27; 31:13; Leviticus 11:45; Numbers 18:20; Song of Solomon 2:1; Isaiah 44:6; 45:22; 49:26; 51:12; Jeremiah 1:8; Matthew 11:29; 17:5; 28:20 KJV; Luke 22:27; John 6:48, 51; 8:12, 23; 10:11; 11:25; 14:6; 15:1; and Revelation 1:8, 18.

Remember, your birth experience will be significantly influenced by the what, who, and where of your choosing. Planning your baby's birth day, like planning your wedding, is a reflection of your personal needs, tastes, and preferences. Learn what is available in your community and make the decisions that will allow you to labor and give birth in an environment where you feel safe. No matter what you choose, the Lord will be right by your side as you look to him for protection, strength, and guidance.

A HEALTHY MODEL OF MATERNITY CARE:

Excerpts from The Mother-Friendly Childbirth Initiative

Principles

We believe the philosophical cornerstones of mother-friendly care to be as follows:

Normalcy of the Birthing Process

- Birth is a normal, natural, healthy process.
- Breastfeeding provides the optimum nourishment for newborns and infants.
- Birth can safely take place in hospitals, birth centers, and homes.
- The midwifery model of care, which supports and protects the normal birth

process, is the most appropriate for the majority of women during pregnancy and childbirth.

Support

- A woman's confidence and her ability to give birth and to care for her baby are enhanced or diminished by every person who gives her care, and by the environment in which she gives birth.
- A mother and baby are distinct yet interdependent during pregnancy, birth, and infancy. Their interconnectedness is vital and must be respected.
- Pregnancy, birth, and the postpartum period are milestone events. These experiences profoundly affect women, babies, fathers, and families, and have important and long-lasting effects on society.

Autonomy

Every woman should have the opportunity to:

- Have a healthy and joyous birth experience for herself and her family, regardless of her age or circumstances;
- Give birth as she wishes in an environment in which she feels nurtured and secure, and her emotional well-being, privacy, and personal preferences are respected;
- Have access to the full range of options for pregnancy, birth, and nurturing her baby, and to accurate information on all available birthing sites, caregivers, and practices;
- Receive accurate and up-to-date information about the benefits and risks of all procedures, drugs, and tests suggested for use during pregnancy, birth, and the postpartum period, with the rights to informed consent and informed refusal;
- Receive support for making informed choices about what is best for her and her baby based on her individual values and beliefs.

Do No Harm

- Interventions should not be applied routinely during pregnancy, birth, and the postpartum period. Many standard medical tests, procedures, technologies, and drugs carry risks to both mother and baby, and should be avoided in the absence of specific scientific indications for their use.
- If complications arise during pregnancy, birth, or the postpartum period, medical treatments should be evidence-based.

Responsibility

- Each caregiver is responsible for the quality of care she or he provides.

- Maternity care practice should be based not on the needs of the caregiver or provider, but solely on the needs of the mother and child.
- Each hospital and birth center is responsible for the periodic review and evaluation, according to current scientific evidence, of the effectiveness, risks, and rates of use of its medical procedures for mothers and babies.
- Society, through both its government and the public health establishment, is responsible for ensuring access to maternity services for all women and for monitoring the quality of those services.
- Individuals are ultimately responsible for making informed choices about the health care they and their babies receive.

Ten Steps of the Mother-Friendly Childbirth Initiative

To receive CIMS (Coalition for Improving Maternity Services) designation as "mother-friendly" a hospital, birth center, or home-birth service:

1. Offers all birthing mothers:

   —Unrestricted access to the birth companions of her choice, including fathers, children, family members, and friends;

   —Unrestricted access to continuous emotional and physical support from a skilled woman—for example, a doula, or labor support professional;

   —Access to professional midwifery care.
2. Provides accurate descriptive and statistical information to the public about its practices and procedures for birth care, including measures of interventions and outcomes.
3. Provides culturally competent care—that is, care that is sensitive to the beliefs, values, and customs of the mother's ethnicity and religion.
4. Provides the birthing woman with the freedom to walk, move about, and assume positions of her choice during labor and birth (unless restriction is specifically required to correct a complication), and discourages the use of the lithotomy (flat on the back with legs elevated) position;
5. Has clearly defined policies and procedures for:

   —collaborating and consulting throughout the perinatal period with other maternity services, including communicating with the original caregiver when transfer from one birth site to another is necessary;

   —linking the mother and baby to appropriate community resources, including prenatal and post-discharge follow-up and breastfeeding support.
6. Does not routinely employ practices and procedures that are not supported by scientific evidence, including but not limited to the following:

   —shaving;

   —enemas;

   —IVs (intravenous drip);

—withholding nourishment;

—early rupture of membranes;

—electronic fetal monitoring.

Other interventions are limited as follows (statistics based on recent research studies):

—An oxytocin use rate of 10% or less for labor induction and augmentation;

—An episiotomy rate of 20% or less, with a goal of 5% or less;

—A total cesarean rate of 10% or less in community hospitals, and 15% or less in tertiary care (high-risk) hospitals;

—A VBAC (vaginal birth after cesarean) rate of 60% or more, with a goal of 75% or more.

7. Educates staff in non-drug methods of pain relief and does not promote the use of analgesic or anesthetic drugs not specifically required to correct a complication.
8. Encourages all mothers and families, including those with sick or premature newborns or infants with congenital problems, to touch, hold, breastfeed, and care for their babies to the extent compatible with their conditions.
9. Discourages nonreligious circumcision of the newborn.
10. Strives to achieve the WHO-UNICEF "Ten Steps of the Baby-Friendly Hospital Initiative" to promote successful breastfeeding, which are:

—Have a written breastfeeding policy communicated to all health care staff;

—Train all health care staff in skills necessary to implement this policy;

—Inform all pregnant women about the benefits and management of breastfeeding;

—Help mothers initiate breastfeeding within half an hour of birth;

—Show mothers how to breastfeed and how to maintain lactation even if they should be separated from their infants;

—Give newborn infants no food or drink other than breast milk unless medically indicated;

—Practice rooming-in: allow mothers and infants to remain together twenty-four hours a day;

—Encourage breastfeeding on demand;

—Give no artificial teat or pacifiers (also called dummies or soothers) to breastfeeding infants;

—Foster the establishment of breastfeeding support groups and refer mothers to them on discharge from hospitals or clinics.

SOURCE: Coalition for Improving Maternity Services, 1996. Permission granted.

SCRIPTURAL REFLECTIONS AND PROMISES

I will extol the Lord at all times; his praise will always be on my lips. My soul will boast in the Lord; let the afflicted hear and rejoice. Glorify the Lord with me; let us exalt his name together. I sought the Lord, and he answered me; he delivered me from all my fears. Those who look to him are radiant; their faces are never covered with shame. This poor man called, and the Lord heard him; he saved him out of all his troubles. The angel of the Lord encamps around those who fear him, and he delivers them.

PSALM 34:1-7

The eternal God is your refuge and underneath are the everlasting arms.

DEUTERONOMY 33:27

Then you will go on your way in safety, and your foot will not stumble; when you lie down, you will not be afraid; when you lie down, your sleep will be sweet. Have no fear of sudden disaster or of the ruin that overtakes the wicked, for the Lord will be your confidence and will keep your foot from being snared.

PROVERBS 3:23-26

In his heart a man plans his course, but the Lord determines his steps.

PROVERBS 16:9

SIX

LEARNING TO LABOR TOGETHER

Two are better than one, because they have a good return for their work. . . .
A cord of three strands is not quickly broken.

ECCLESIASTES 4:9, 12

When a woman labors to bring forth a child, she must travel a road that has been negotiated many times before by countless women through the ages. Yet for each woman, the journey is different. Because of this, it's a journey that benefits from the companionship of a friend. When the going gets rough, the one can lift the other up. Also interwoven into this cord of friendship is a relationship with the Lord. He forms the third part of a friendship strand that is "not quickly broken."

Throughout this chapter the primary labor companion is referred to as the husband, because this has now become common practice. However, the activities and duties described here can be performed by whomever you choose to accompany you through labor.

There are three phases in your childbearing experience in which your labor companion should ideally be involved. These include prenatal preparation for labor, the birth itself, and the first six weeks after the baby's birth. (This last stage, called the postpartum phase, is discussed in chapters 9 and 13.)

PRENATAL PREPARATION

Since you and your companion will function as a team during childbirth, it's best to prepare for the experience together. As you read the rest of this chapter, remember that these prenatal preparations will help strengthen both of you and ready you for a very special, unique time. (Chapter 9 covers what to do during labor and the birth.)

Talking to Experienced Parents

Develop a relationship with a couple with whom you feel comfortable, who care for their child or children as you would like to raise your child. This person-to-person contact is invaluable, even if it is fairly short term.

This sharing relationship enables the more experienced couple to teach by example and to include the couple expecting a baby in many family activities. Having close friends with whom you can learn the ins and outs of childbearing and child-rearing will be an invaluable experience when your child is ready to be born.

Praying Together

Surprisingly enough, many Christian couples do not pray together regularly other than at mealtimes. Yet the Lord clearly promised that "where two or three come together in my name, there I am with them" (Matt. 18:20). I can remember when the impact of this promise hit home with my husband and myself, and we realized how Christ strengthened our marital bond when we prayed together.

We all have a lot to pray for. With each new child born into a family comes additional responsibilities and relationships. There are numerous concerns and needs to be brought before the Lord. Scriptures such as 1 Thessalonians 5:17, James 5:16, Colossians 4:2, Romans 12:12, and Ephesians 6:18 encourage us to pray continually.

Season all your preparations for your new baby with prayer. Share your concerns with the Lord together, and your union in him will reap the harvest of the prayers you sow.

> *The best prayers are often more groans than words.*
>
> JOHN BUNYAN

Seeking Spiritual Guidance

There may be situations during your pregnancy when you find it beyond your ability to cope. Within the body of Christ you may find those who can offer you the help you need. If you experience marital conflict (not uncommon during pregnancy), financial crisis, poor health, or any other difficulty that seems too much to handle, consider sharing your concerns with your pastor or another qualified person in your church.

Those in leadership roles in the church desire to serve others. By their example, our faith is increased. This is a wonderful benefit of fellowship with the body of Christ, and it is the means through which we may experience God's love for us and serve one another in practical ways.

In Paul's first letter to the church in Corinth, he wrote: "If one part suffers, every part suffers with it; if one part is honored, every part rejoices with it. Now you are the body of Christ, and each one of you is a part of it" (1 Cor. 12:26-27).

BENEFITS OF HUSBANDS AS LABOR COMPANIONS

When a husband is willing to support his wife through pregnancy and childbirth, a number of benefits result:

- The husband's compassion for his wife and understanding of her nature deepen.

- The bond that was shared through the act of love that created their child will widen to include the husband's participation in the birth as well.
- His sense of attachment to his wife and baby will become more real to him as he participates in his baby's life from the very first breath.
- His involvement in caring for his wife during childbirth will reinforce their sense of oneness and belonging to each other.

Reading Books

The past decade has been termed the most explosive in the earth's history for the written word. Thousands of books and publications in every area, including that of maternal and child health, are printed around the world each day. Today's selection of books on pregnancy, childbirth, breastfeeding, and parenting is overwhelming. These books, as well as numerous magazines and journals, are written from a variety of perspectives, some based on secular philosophies or Eastern mysticism in one or several of its westernized forms. We need to follow 1 John 4:1-6, which cautions us to carefully consider the spirit behind what we are reading, hearing, seeing, or otherwise experiencing.

Christians should avoid condemning authors who hold a different view; at the same time, it's wise to realize that some books are more educational than others and do not include a strong anti-Christian or mystical viewpoint. Select books that clearly affirm the eternal value of human life and the beauty of God's creation and also offer an accurate account of childbearing or parenting. (A recommended reading list of helpful and informative materials is included in the back of this book. Also, most libraries now carry an excellent selection of books on these subjects.)

By reading good books about pregnancy, birth, and parenting, you will supplement your subjective, personal experience with sound information that enables you to better plan the birth and prepare your body for labor, teach you about breastfeeding, and discuss parenting strategies together. Books are an invaluable resource for expectant parents today, since practices pertaining to childbirth and parenting are now seldom passed from one generation to another.

There is a wisdom of the head . . . and a wisdom of the heart.

CHARLES DICKENS

Taking Classes

Taking the following types of classes can provide you with reinforcement, camaraderie, demonstrations, motivation, a variety of views, and, most importantly, *practice*. As you remember to pick and choose from the information presented, taking any class that fills your needs will help you become better prepared for the birth and beyond.

Be sure to inquire about prices, location, philosophy, the training of instructors, and the involvement of participants before enrolling. If a registered nurse is teaching, ask what additional training she has had to enable her to become an adult educator.

The availability of different types of childbirth classes varies widely among communities. The following types of programs may be offered where you live:

Early Pregnancy. Emphasis is placed on the prevention of birth defects and complications of pregnancy and childbirth. Discussions include nutrition, exercise, and the avoidance of substances harmful to the developing baby. Common complaints of the first six months are reviewed, and relief measures are offered. The emotional changes often related to the first months of pregnancy may also be presented.

Prenatal Fitness. Focuses on maintaining overall fitness, promoting relaxation habits, and strengthening the areas of the body most affected by pregnancy.

Infant Care Classes. Basic techniques of infant care are demonstrated and discussed, including bathing, diapering, comforting, feeding methods, and caring for a baby that is ill.

Preparation for Parenting. These programs may include the infant-care skills listed above, as well as infant development and the financial, emotional, and practical aspects of early parenting.

Childbirth Preparation Classes: The Lamaze Method. The Lamaze Method currently is the most popular preparation for childbirth. Though the Lamaze Method may be taught somewhat differently wherever Lamaze classes are offered, this approach to childbirth preparation comes from a viewpoint that emphasizes the active participation of both parents throughout the childbearing cycle. Most classes include use of visual aids (such as charts and movies), information on obstetrical procedures, and demonstrations of many types of relief measures. Breathing and relaxation techniques are central to all Lamaze Method instruction.

By the late seventies, few Lamaze instructors were teaching the "pure Lamaze" method of childbirth because it proved to be unrealistic. A diluted version of Lamaze's beliefs has been adopted over the years, and Lamaze's book *Painless Childbirth* is no longer widely read or recommended to Lamaze class members.

Childbirth Preparation Classes: The Dick-Read Method. Advocates of this method focus on the importance of relaxation and prenatal exercise in preparation for birth. The process of childbirth is fully explained to alleviate fear and dispel any misconceptions a couple may have about birth.

Childbirth Preparation Classes: The Bradley Method. The Bradley Method emphasizes the participation of the father during childbirth and stresses muscular relaxation. The dangers of obstetric drugs and interventions also are discussed. The Bradley Method is an extension of the Dick-Read Method, both of which hold the philosophy of "natural childbirth" as their central theme.

Childbirth Preparation Classes for Christian Parents. Taught from a biblical perspective, classes for Christian couples offer clear information about the childbearing experience, emphasize the role of prayer during pregnancy, encourage reliance on God's strength, advise dependency on the Holy Spirit's help and sustenance, and teach valuable coping skills. *Apple Tree Family Ministries* (A.T.F.M.), based in California, offers a comprehensive program based on the Dick-Read Method and includes information on sexuality, natural family planning, breastfeeding, and the Christian family, though most childbirth classes offered from a Christian perspective are available only on a community- or church-wide basis.

For many, the opportunity to prepare in Christ to give birth has had a remarkable impact. I have seen expectant mothers give their fears to God, drawing strength from him to cope with the challenges they faced during their pregnancies, labors, and the months afterward. Reluctant fathers-to-be have opened up in prayer on behalf of their wives and babies, assuming the responsibilities of protecting and providing for them.

These men and women, who have truly turned to God, have not come away empty. Every cup has been filled beyond measure. It's my hope that you also will find your lives enriched through the principles shared in this book as a supplement to whatever form of childbirth preparation class you decide to take—that you will draw ever nearer to our almighty Father as you prepare for your baby's birth together in Christ.

Prenatal Yoga Classes. Yoga is not a spiritually neutral form of physical exercise and stretching for stress relief. This practice is intimately connected to the ancient religion and philosophy of Hinduism. Consider using another method of relaxation that will not introduce the influence of Hinduism into your life.

Birthing Center and Home Birth Classes. If you are planning an out-of-hospital birth in a freestanding birthing center or in your home, it's a smart strategy to take whatever classes are offered by the center or your midwife. These will help prepare you for the experience you have chosen and inform you as to what to expect should any complications arise.

Breastfeeding Classes. Breastfeeding is a learned maternal activity that is not typically passed from mother to daughter in our culture. Understanding myths concerning breastfeeding and gaining accurate information are keys to successful lactation. Prenatal nipple preparation is demonstrated, and visual aids such as slides and movies may be used to aid the establishment of healthy lactation.

Cesarean Birth Classes. Since father participation in cesarean birth has increased, C-birth classes have helped prepare many couples for a surgical birth experience. Visual aids of the procedures involved are utilized, and pain relief measures, types of anesthesia, and emotional responses to having a baby by cesarean are discussed.

Vaginal Birth After Cesarean (VBAC). VBAC classes teach women who have had a cesarean how to cope with labor and prepare for a vaginal birth.

Many other types of classes are also available; those included here are represented on a nationwide basis. Classes may be available through a C.E.A. (a Childbirth Education Association run by a board of parents and professionals), your health-care providers, hospitals, clinics, birth centers, community colleges, the Red Cross, a YMCA or YWCA, independent childbirth educators, and many other organizations. For additional classes, consult the Yellow Pages in your phonebook under "Childbirth Education" or "Parents."

Going to Office Visits

Office visits during pregnancy increase in frequency during the last trimester. There are many times when you would rather not wait alone, so why not go together? It is wonderful to hear the baby's heartbeat and to discuss your birth plans with your health-care provider as a couple. This way you both will have a clear understanding of what to expect during labor. Most health-care providers welcome the father's presence at prenatal visits and are happy to discuss concerns with you both.

Touring the Baby's Birthplace

It's really beneficial to tour the setting where you plan to have your baby. This can be arranged through childbirth classes or directly through the hospital or center. During the tour, take notes and try to get a clear picture of what takes place where and what policies govern the maternity care offered.

Studying Scripture

Since this book is based on a Christian worldview, it contains encouraging passages from Scripture that I hope you can adopt into your own walk with God. However, this is not meant to be a substitute for Bible study. Rather, it is meant to stimulate a meaningful, independent study of God's Word.

Explore the Word for encouraging verses you can use during pregnancy and labor. Use what the Lord has so generously given to us for edification, strengthening, and instruction in his Scriptures. As Paul wrote in 2 Timothy 3:16-17: "All Scripture is God-breathed and is useful for teaching, rebuking, correcting and training in righteousness, so that the man of God may be thoroughly equipped for every good work."

We are not permitted to choose the frame of our destiny. But what we put into it is ours.

DAG HAMMARSKJÖLD

Learning and Practicing Pain Relief Measures

Noninvasive pain relief measures—measures you can use without physically invading or penetrating the body—are methods you can use yourself or that your labor companion can perform for you during labor to enhance your comfort. "Suffering through it" is a self-defeating birthing strategy when there are many safe, effective ways to alleviate pain during labor.

The use of drugs for pain relief is not an either/or question. There are advantages and disadvantages to every type of available pain relief. Plan on discussing with your health-care provider the types of medications generally used during labor and learn the benefits and risks of those drugs. Some specific times when anesthesia should be used include cesarean birth, a difficult forceps delivery, or when an episiotomy is necessary. These procedures represent additional trauma to the mother's body beyond the normal physiological process of birth. (See Appendix C for more information.)

Choose the forms of pain relief that you believe will be best for you. If you decide to use only noninvasive forms of pain relief, do so because that makes good sense and seems the safest for you.

WHAT TO ASK, TAKE, AND KNOW CHECKLIST

When you go on a tour of your baby's birthplace, talk to your health-care provider, and take birth preparation classes, you may use the following checklist to get ready for your baby's arrival.

1. *What to ask your physician or midwife about when she/he wishes to be contacted:*

I am to call ____________________ at (phone no.) ____________________ when my membranes rupture (yes or no), when contractions are lasting for _____ seconds and are _____ minutes apart. Other conditions about which I should notify my doctor/midwife:

____

____

____

____

2. *What your health-care provider will want to know:*

(Your name) __________________ . (I am in) (I think I am in) labor. The contractions I am having are _____ seconds long, occurring about every ____________________ minutes, and are (regular) (irregular). They started at (time)__________. My membranes (are not) (may be) (are) leaking. I feel (describe how the contractions are affecting you):

3. *What to know about admission procedures:*

(I am) (I am not) preregistered. If not, I can get a preregistration form from ____________
____

When in labor, I will go to ______________________________________ (hospital/center). During business hours, I will go to __________________________. After _____ P.M., I will go to ____________________________________. These areas are reached from ____ (street name). Parking will be available (location) ___________________________________ and costs ___________________________. I will be taken to labor and delivery on the ______________ floor, in the ______________________ wing.

4. *Labor aids to have with you (a possible list):*

- Bible
- two pairs of clean, warm socks
- sweet/sour lollipops for flavor
- items for attention diversion
- clean seven-inch paint roller or two tennis balls (for applying counter-pressure to the lower back
- watch with a second hand
- food for yourself and your labor partner
- thermos with beverage
- pocket change
- phone number list
- portable phone/pager
- corn oil or lotion for massage
- tape recorder
- cassette tapes of favorite music
- hot water bottle for back
- breath spray or mouthwash
- your own nightgown and pillow
- lip balm
- camera/film/flash/batteries/videotape
- birthday cake (freeze ahead) and candles

5. *What to pack in your suitcase:*

- toothbrush, toothpaste, brush, comb, etc.
- clean nursing bra for each day you will be in the hospital and nursing pads
- reading materials, especially about breastfeeding and early parenting
- birth announcements, stationery, pen

- clean underwear, night clothes, robe, slippers (be sure to select garments that will facilitate nursing if you'll be breastfeeding)
- outfit and blanket in which to take your baby home (your baby will be dressed in hospital clothing during your stay unless you desire otherwise)
- loose-fitting clothing for your return home
- tape recorder and cassettes
- packets of herbal teas, raisins, and other dried fruits to help alleviate constipation

6. *What to ask about hospital procedures and alternatives (check those procedures that apply after discussing them with your physician, or call your hospital):*

____ Hospital gown/own nightgown

____ Check weight

____ Check blood pressure

____ Take temperature

____ Electronic fetal monitor/amplified stethoscope/fetoscope

____ Blood specimen

____ Enema/natural bowel movements

____ Mini-prep/no shaving of perineum

____ IV/Heparin lock

____ Vaginal exam (When? How often?)

7. *As the labor companion, I:*

(will be able to remain with my wife/friend at all times) (may be asked to leave [under what circumstances?]) (will be filling out admitting forms until asked to join my wife/friend). If I am asked to leave, a reasonable amount of time to complete the procedures is ____________________ minutes. If they do not call me by this time, I can check my partner's progress by speaking to ____________________________. The time to put on a gown will be ______________. I will ask ____________________________, if necessary, when to put on my scrub suit and mask at the birth.

8. *Questions to ask about medications:*

If it becomes necessary for my health-care provider to administer medication, what does she/he prefer to use and why? (Include your doctor's comments on what she/he prefers to use for vaginal and cesarean birth.):

____

____

Record some of your feelings about using medication during labor and birth (What do you think will determine whether you use analgesia and/or anesthesia, if anything is used?):

Medication Checklist—What to Ask:

- What is it?
- Why would I need it?
- How long will it affect me or my baby?
- What are the possible side effects?
- Is the dosage flexible?

9. *Optional items to think about and discuss with health-care provider:*

If available, what are the criteria for use of the birthing room? Birthing center? How does she/he feel about it? Is she/he comfortable with its philosophy?

Health-care provider's comments:

Our preference:

Does your health-care provider do episiotomies frequently? How often (percentage)? If not, is she/he familiar with the technique of perineal massage? When does she/he consider episiotomy to be useful? What anesthesia will she/he use?

Comments:

Preferences: ______________________________

____

Does your health-care provider practice gentle birth techniques?

____

Comments: ______________________________

____

Preferences: ______________________________

____

Would she/he deliver your baby in a position other than the lithotomy (reclining) position? ____________ Under what circumstances:

____

Comments: ______________________________

____

Preferences: ______________________________

____

Other questions, comments, and preferences:

____

When do you hope to first breastfeed your baby?

____

Do you want uninterrupted contact with your baby?

____

What is the usual length of time for the baby to be in recovery before going to the nursery?

____

Will you be together as a family in the recovery room?

Comments: ____

____

Preferences: ____

____

Do you want rooming-in? ________ Around the clock? __________ When will it begin? __________ What is the procedure? ________________________
Can the father be with you overnight?____________

Comments: ____

____

Preferences: ____

____

Visiting hours at the hospital, and the people who may visit, are:

____

____

The typical length of stay after a vaginal birth is ______________________
After a cesarean birth: ______________________

Comments: ____

____

____

Preferences: ____

____

____

____

SCRIPTURAL REFLECTIONS AND PROMISES

Let the beloved of the Lord rest securely in him, for he shields him all the day long, and the one the Lord loves rests between his shoulders.

DEUTERONOMY 33:12

The Lord gives strength to his people; the Lord blesses his people with peace.

PSALM 29:11

Do not conform any longer to the pattern of this world, but be transformed by the renewing of your mind. Then you will be able to test and approve what God's will is—his good, pleasing and perfect will.

ROMANS 12:2

He who dwells in the shelter of the Most High will rest in the shadow of the Almighty. I will say of the Lord, "He is my refuge and my fortress, my God, in whom I trust."

PSALM 91:1-2

I can do all things through Christ which strengtheneth me.

PHILIPPIANS 4:13 KJV

For God hath not given us the spirit of fear; but of power, and of love, and of a sound mind.

2 TIMOTHY 1:7 KJV

We wait in hope for the Lord; he is our help and our shield. In him our hearts rejoice, for we trust in his holy name. May your unfailing love rest upon us, O Lord, even as we put our hope in you.

PSALM 33:20-22

SEVEN

CHILDBIRTH EDUCATION: PHILOSOPHIES AND PERSPECTIVES

Have I not commanded you? Be strong and courageous. Do not be terrified; do not be discouraged, for the Lord your God will be with you wherever you go.

JOSHUA 1:9

CHILDBIRTH IN THE BIBLE

The powerful images of creation, life, pain, work, and birth presented in the first three chapters of Genesis are familiar to Christians everywhere. Although there are many different views of the impact of these events, I believe that reflection on these chapters can uncover principles on which all can agree.

The first passages of Genesis explain that when man and woman were created, the Lord blessed them and said, "Be fruitful and increase in number; fill the earth and subdue it" (Gen. 1:28). The Creator of the first two human beings created them in a much different way than babies are conceived and birthed today. The man was formed out of the ground, and the woman was brought forth out of the flesh and bone of man's side (Gen. 3:19; 2:22). They were born fully grown and ready to be joined together in marriage.

At some later point, the crafty serpent asked the woman if the Lord really had commanded her not to eat from any tree in the garden. ("Crafty" is a good description of the serpent, who knew that the woman had not yet been created when the Lord had spoken to the man about the forbidden fruit!) This serpent then convinced the woman to eat the fruit that "was good for food and pleasing to the eye, and also desirable for gaining wisdom" (Gen. 3:6).

In what appears to be just a brief moment of history, the future of the human race was drastically altered. When the man disobeyed his God-given orders, "the eyes of both of them were opened" to the realization of their nakedness. It is in this way, we are told by God's Word, that sin entered the world—through the deception of one woman and the disobedience of one man.

What has this to do with childbirth in our time? The impact of the Fall upon the process of childbearing was significant and will continue to be so until the Lord returns. Though there is no way to know what the Lord had in mind as a design for human reproduction before the Fall, we're explicitly told that the actions of the serpent, the woman, and the man had consequences that affected all of their descendants (Gen. 3:14-19).

God determined what the outcome would be upon the lives of Adam and Eve when they disobeyed him, but he did not forsake them. In determining the consequences of their transgression, the Bible tells us that the Lord chose to make these activities physically stressful. Yet if we continue to read through the Bible, we're comforted repeatedly by the Lord's compassion for his people. Psalm 145:13 reminds us that "the Lord is faithful to all his promises and loving toward all he has made." His greatest gift of love to us was Jesus, through whom the Lord grants us everlasting life and restores sinners to eternal fellowship with himself. It is a *loving* Lord who decided what the consequences of the Fall would be.

I believe God did not arbitrarily mete out punishment in anger. He acted in accordance with his divine character. If we believe in God's love for his creation, we can view his response to Adam and Eve as one motivated by love and a desire to cause their descendants to continue to look to him for protection and sustenance after they had left the Garden of Eden.

In the fourth chapter of Genesis, the effect of childbirth on Eve shows God's design: "Adam lay with his wife Eve, and she became pregnant and gave birth to Cain. She said, 'With the help of the Lord I have brought forth a man'" (Gen. 4:1). According to this verse, it appears that the strenuous toil of giving birth turned Eve toward the Lord for help, and it was to him that she gave thanks for the safe delivery of her son.

As women giving birth today, we can acknowledge the reality of labor in childbirth, its biblical basis, and its role in drawing us closer to the Lord. The toil of labor still draws our eyes heavenward, often causing us to admit that we're not "as gods," sufficient in ourselves and able to exert complete control over our lives. In James 4:8, 10 we're given the promise that if we draw near to God, he will draw near to us; that if we humble ourselves before him, he will lift us up. We can openly declare our weakness before the Lord, for he has been with us from the beginning and has promised that he will never forsake us.

As Christians we're able to approach our Creator with assurance and confidence based on Christ's perfect sacrifice on Calvary. We can't alter the actions of Adam and Eve, but we can walk in the newness of life God gives through Jesus Christ.

PARENTS PREPARING IN CHRIST

The childbirth preparation method presented in this book is unique because it incorporates into its curriculum a biblical and moral view that the normal physical, emotional, and spiritual challenges of labor during childbirth are not evil. This book provides you with information that will help you eliminate unnecessary sources of discomfort that result from not understanding how your body functions during labor. It also shows you how it is possible to cope with the amount of "toil" you experience during childbirth if you cooperate with the process of labor rather than fighting it, and draw close to the Lord in prayer.

By combining the God-given resources of the Bible, the knowledge of the human body, and the methods of medical science in creating the Parents Preparing in Christ curriculum in 1979, I hoped to strike a balance between a biblical perspective on childbearing and valid scientific techniques. As our Western culture has become increasingly influenced by Eastern philosophies and pantheism in the two decades since I put together the curriculum, I believe this balance may be even more important today.

Because *The Christian Woman's Guide to Childbirth* is based on a Christian worldview, it contains many encouraging passages from Scripture that I hope you can adapt into your own walk with the Lord. This book is not intended to be a substitute for Bible study. Rather, it is meant to stimulate a meaningful, independent study of God's Word.

The value of personal, family, and corporate prayer cannot be overemphasized. In my classes, participants and I frequently read from the Psalms during relaxation practices and labor rehearsals. My goal in both my teaching and my writing is to motivate and challenge Christians to look to the Lord for strength during pregnancy and childbirth—as in all of life—through prayer, fellowship, and Bible study.

Describing the anatomy and physiology of childbirth by saying, "Nature intends" or "The organism determines," or similar terms, seems to me to label the process of childbearing a biological accident or evolutionary feat. In the Parents Preparing in Christ program, credit is given where credit is due through openly recognizing the Lord as our Maker, the one who designed the entire universe and created everything in it. Knowing that God is behind everything is tremendously reassuring and comforting.

Another aspect of this approach to childbirth education is the belief that God is sovereign. In basing our concept of human dignity on the truth of holy Scripture, we know that every child conceived is valued by the Lord. The Christian view of human life places a high value on all individuals, regardless of their age, sex, race, or ability.

The belief that our heavenly Father's love is unconditional also is incorporated into all aspects of this type of childbirth preparation by acknowledging the truths of such Scriptures as Psalm 139:15-16: "My frame was not hidden from you when I was made in the secret place. When I was woven together in the depths of the earth, your eyes saw my unformed body. All the days ordained for me were written in your book before one of them came to be," and Job 10:8: "Your hands shaped me and made me. Will you now turn and destroy me?"

The number of choices available in childbirth education today can be a blessing as you pray for discernment in deciding what's best and most useful in your own situation. I know you will also want to consider the philosophies upon which current methods are based and ponder how the theories behind them may complement—or conflict with—how childbirth is presented in the Bible.

THE LAMAZE METHOD

The Lamaze Method currently is the most popular way to prepare for childbirth. Yet many are unaware of its origin. Fernand Lamaze, an ardent socialist, based the method named in his honor on techniques he learned while visiting clinics in Russia. (Technically, Lamaze's method is called *the psychoprophylactic method*, or PPM. The name means "mind [psycho] in favor of [pro] prevention [phylaxis].") As the Communists took control of Russia following the revolution, the government developed the PPM as the solution to the age-old problem of childbirth pain.

In the thirties a massive propaganda campaign was conducted to convince Russian women that they could deliver their babies painlessly by using this method. Through this form of mind control, the propaganda stated, women could rid themselves of the "curse" of childbirth pain. Communists viewed the idea of a biblical curse on childbearing as an archaic religious doctrine.

By the time Dr. Lamaze visited the Soviet Union, the government's PPM program was in full swing. To his amazement, he saw that pain expression among laboring women in Russia was noticeably absent. Dr. Lamaze carried his discovery back to the socialist clinic where he worked in France and developed a program to teach women the method he had learned in Russia. He emphatically believed that childbirth pain exists merely in women's minds through the influence of their socialization and culture. His intense training program involved using prenatal education to refute the notions his students had acquired while growing up. By replacing these ideas with information based on "scientific knowledge," Lamaze believed childbirth pain could be erased completely

Yet pain *expression* and pain *experience* are two very different things. With the repression of personal and religious freedom in the Soviet Union following the advent of communism, few women would have chosen to refute government propaganda or give birth in a way other than what the "experts" recommended. Medical bills were no longer a consideration, and the majority of women were probably very grateful to be receiving care. *Thus I believe women may have felt labor pain while using PPM but most likely chose not to express it.*

As with others who have studied human labor and birth in various cultures, Lamaze confused the lack of pain expression with a lack of pain experience. Current anthropological research suggests that one's culture defines what types of pain experiences are acceptable, with different groups of people expressing pain in different ways. These studies also claim some degree of labor pain seems to be universal among all peoples and that our former belief that more "primitive" women give birth painlessly is a myth.

By the late seventies, few Lamaze instructors were teaching the "pure Lamaze" method of childbirth because it proved to be unrealistic. Consequently a diluted version of Dr. Lamaze's beliefs was eventually adopted, and his book *Painless Childbirth* is no longer widely read or recommended to Lamaze class members.

When I trained to be a Lamaze instructor in 1973, I didn't see any contradictions between the PPM method and my Christian beliefs. But as I began studying the subject of labor pain for academic reasons, my closer scrutiny of Lamaze's original statements revealed genuine discrepancies between his beliefs and my own.

Many Christians have been involved as students or instructors of Lamaze theory over the years without being aware of its atheistic orientation and dismissal of the book of Genesis. Dr. Lamaze's proponents originally believed that childbirth could be completely painless with PPM. Later research refuted this contention.

Dr. Ronald Melzack conducted an important study in Montreal on the use of the Lamaze method and its effect on labor pain. In an article he published in the *Canadian Medical Association Journal* (August 15, 1981, pp. 357-63), he concluded that even after Lamaze training, labor is still painful. What is especially significant about Melzack's study is that at the time, he was one of the most respected authorities on the subject of pain in the world. (Dr. Melzack is the developer, along with Patrick Wall, of the gate-control theory of pain, which revolutionized the field of pain research. See *Science*, November 19, 1965, pp. 971-79.)

Lamaze instructors have realized for at least as long as I've been involved in childbirth education that what Melzack stated is certainly true. Very few Lamaze teachers inform participants that labor can be absolutely painless if a woman performs the PPM techniques correctly. Though this man's beliefs are no longer held by those who teach his method, these classes continue to be called by the name "Lamaze." The reason for this may be that the name "Lamaze" has become synonymous with childbirth education itself. Even though Lamaze classes no longer teach much of Lamaze's personal philosophy, his name still sells the product.

For Christians who participate in Lamaze classes, it may be helpful to understand this change while remembering that some aspects of Lamaze's original theory are quite compatible with a biblical view of childbirth.

Aspects in Conflict with a Biblical View

- The concept that only *words* and *thoughts* create labor pain.
- The belief that labor pain is nothing more than the product of the fear of childbirth and consequently is *psychological* in origin.

- The view that this fear of childbirth originates in "ancient" religious teachings and that there is no truth in religious teachings concerning labor in childbirth.

Aspects Compatible with a Biblical View

- The desire to help women adapt to the process of childbearing.
- The value of noninvasive pain relief measures to decrease suffering during labor.
- The importance of understanding the physical events of childbirth.

THE DICK-READ METHOD

Another currently used method of childbirth was introduced by Grantly Dick-Read in his book *Childbirth Without Fear,* published in 1944 (Harper & Row). Dick-Read advocated a spiritualized view of childbirth. He essentially states that a loving Creator could not have intended childbirth to be painful. Instead Dr. Dick-Read believed that true, natural childbirth allows a woman to participate joyfully in giving birth according to God's design.

Research confirms that about 10 percent of all labors are relatively painless and uncomplicated, taking place fairly quickly and with a minimum of physical effort on the mother's part. On the other hand, another 10 percent are unusually long, complicated, or difficult. The remaining 80 percent involve a moderate amount of pain at various times, depending on the different factors present.

For the 10 percent of the women who experience relatively painless, uncomplicated labors, childbirth is understandably perceived to be more enjoyable and more gratifying than for the remaining 90 percent. Thus about one in ten women may say afterward, "It was easy," or "I was only in labor a couple hours and then pushed a few times. I'd do it again tomorrow," or "I thought I had a mild case of the flu, but fortunately I decided to go to the hospital to be checked and had the baby twenty minutes later." Women in this group seem ideally suited to the childbearing function of their bodies and may have anatomical and physiological traits that allow them to go through labor and birth with a minimum of disturbance.

But an "easy" birth is not necessarily a reflection of a close walk with the Lord. Longer or more complicated labors don't appear to me to be God's way of judging us for wrongdoing. Childbirth pain is present to varying degrees in most labors and is not the result of a lack of faith or the wrath of God.

It may have been a woman belonging to the uncomplicated 10 percent who caused Dr. Dick-Read to wonder why labor isn't always a good experience. In response to his consideration of the matter, Dick-Read developed a theory: *Fear creates labor pain*. He believed that in the absence of fear, pain experience in labor can be substantially reduced or eliminated altogether.

Once again I would like to point out that the source of labor pain is not only fear but instead can be traced to many other factors. Lacking modern research data, Dr. Dick-Read believed that in cultures around the world in which women aren't taught to fear childbirth, labor pain isn't prevalent. The imagined picture still held by many today of women who labor in the fields, squat to have the baby, and then return to work, is a simplistic and naive view of childbearing behavior.

Dr. Brigitte Jordan, the first anthropologist to conduct extensive field studies of childbirth in several societies, described labor pain in her book *Birth in Four Cultures* (Eden Press, 1978) as an expected part of the childbirth process. Maintaining the belief that nowhere in the world is birth purely a "natural" event, Jordan builds a convincing argument that birth practices are culturally produced, created by groups of people according to the values and beliefs shared by their tribe or group or community. To believe that birth takes place somewhere in the world without pain and free of cultural expectations is to believe in a fantasy about how "less civilized" humans act during childbirth, asserts Dr. Jordan.

Dr. Dick-Read believed that labor pain can *only* be the result of physical, functional, emotional, or medical interferences in the natural process of human labor and birth. He viewed labor pain as an abnormality or aberration of childbirth—an indication that something is wrong. Yet Dr. Dick-Read did not substantiate what percentage of all labors are free of any pain-producing abnormalities.

If a minority of all women experience little or no labor pain, they are then the exception instead of the norm. Clearly, childbirth pain is not due only to fear, a physical abnormality, or complications of labor. Rather, I believe the reverse is true: *Pain itself can create fear during birth.* Fear may then magnify painful sensations and/or stimulate adrenaline secretion.

Aspects in Conflict with a Biblical View

- The belief that the experience of labor pain is incongruent with a loving Creator's design for childbirth.
- The concept that fear creates bodily tension, which produces rather than intensifies labor pain.
- The idea that labor pain can be the product of only abnormal physical, functional, and/or emotional processes or of technical intervention in labor.
- The view that pain in childbirth is an avoidable evil that warps a woman's birthing experience.

Aspects Compatible with a Biblical View

- The belief that God is motivated by love.
- The theory that fear and tension can interfere with the process of labor.
- The importance of physical fitness through prenatal exercise.
- The value of learning how to relax during childbirth.

THE BRADLEY METHOD

While the methods of Robert Bradley (the initiator of husband-coached childbirth) are based on the same theories as the Lamaze and Dick-Read methods, they are animalistic rather than atheistic or naturalistic (*Husband-Coached Childbirth*, Harper & Row, 1965). Dr. Bradley suggests that animals such as sheep do not seem to experience pain during normal labors because they instinctively "know" how to cope with the birthing process. He concludes from this that if human females would imitate sheep, they, too, would find labor relatively painless.

We have the capacity to worry about future events and imagine all sorts of outcomes to situations. We are capable of an almost unbelievable range of emotions and expressions of feeling—embarrassment, pride, guilt, courage, crying, laughing, moaning, speaking, yelling, whispering, smiling, and grimacing. For a woman in labor, these

DIAGRAM OF HUMAN PAIN EXPERIENCE
Adapted from H. K. Beecher

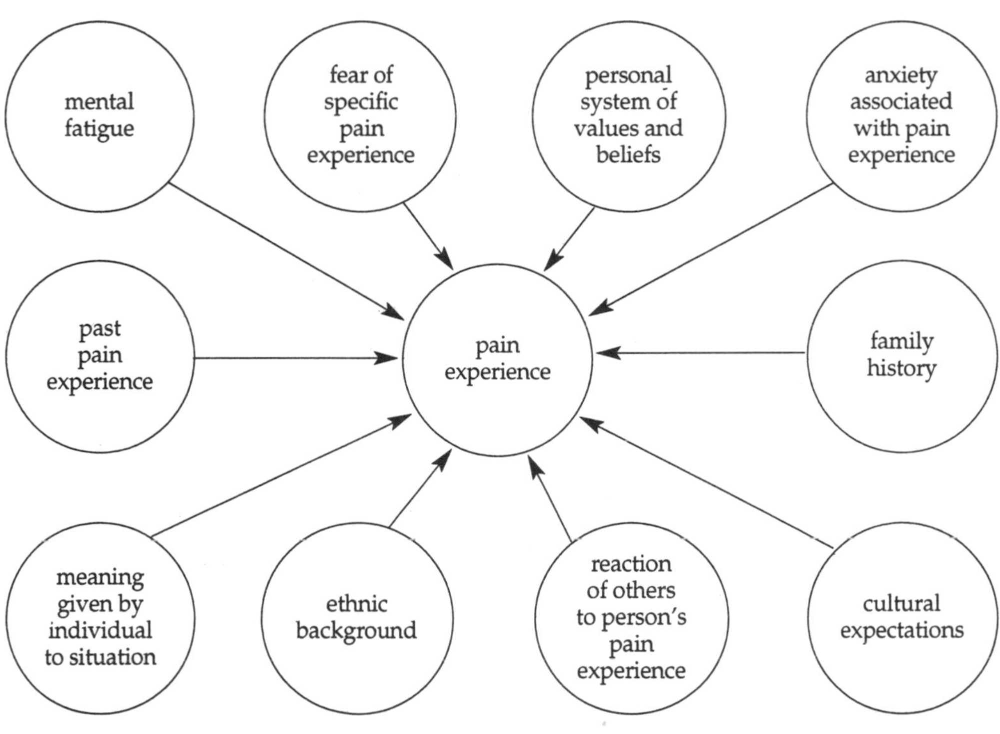

would disagree, I believe that free will, more than any other trait, differentiates our species from other species.

Just as we wouldn't wish to imitate other aspects of animal sexuality (no birth control, poor mate selection, etc.), it makes little sense to compare human labor and birth too closely with those functions in animals. This would deny that we are created in the image of God, that the value of human life differs from that of animal life, or that the Fall affected us in specific ways.

Aspects in Conflict with a Biblical View

- The belief that human pain experience can be exactly equated with the pain experience of animals.
- The view that labor pain is an unnatural phenomenon.
- The denial of the many differences between humans and animals.

Aspects Compatible with a Biblical View

- The concept that husbands and wives benefit from going through labor together. (See chapter 6.)
- The idea that husbands are capable of providing help and direction for their wives during pregnancy and childbirth.
- The emphasis placed upon allowing the body to function as it should in labor.
- The promotion of relaxation as a means to allow the body to adapt to the birth process.

> *Don't let controversy hurt your soul. Live near to God in prayer. Just fall down at his feet and open your very soul before him, and throw yourself right into his arms.*
>
> CATHERINE BOOTH

NEW AGE METHODS OF CHILDBIRTH

Though the methods of Drs. Lamaze, Dick-Read, and Bradley all contain fallacies of their own, another trend in childbirth has introduced spiritual perspectives that are decidedly anti-Christian. Within this pantheistic movement, the Judeo-Christian concepts of sin and atonement are replaced by a philosophy of self-perfection. While several books have been written about the possible implications of this movement upon Christianity as a whole, its specific impact upon methods of childbirth may be summarized briefly.

Before I was converted to Christianity in 1971, I explored Hinduism and Yoga, practicing dietary restrictions as well as breathing, relaxation, and meditation techniques. What especially appealed to me about Eastern mysticism was its lack of condemnation of sinners and the inclusion of evil into good. I was taught that the ultimate state that the Hindu or Buddhist strives to obtain through cycles of life and death, taking place during repeated "reincarnations," is Nirvana, or nothingness. This nihilistic view, as I found out after becoming a Christian, contradicts the biblical concept of heaven and hell and the sacredness of each created human life.

Because of my personal background, I am particularly sensitive to the childbirth books that have been appearing in the popular market based on philosophies and perspectives that spring from Eastern mysticism and pantheism. Paul's words in Colossians 2:8 seem especially applicable to the kind of thinking represented: "See to it that no one takes you captive through hollow and deceptive philosophy, which depends on human tradition and the basic principles of this world rather than on Christ."

In Psalm 131, David's words direct us to the only true source of strength and guidance: "My heart is not proud, O Lord, my eyes are not haughty; I do not concern myself with great matters or things too wonderful for me. But I have stilled and quieted my soul; like a weaned child with its mother, like a weaned child is my soul within me. O Israel, put your hope in the Lord both now and forevermore."

There are some things we must entrust to God alone. Some spiritual knowledge is beyond our comprehension. We must recognize God as our portion and provider and realize that self-help and self-perfection techniques based on Eastern mysticism and pantheism are incompatible with true Christian discipleship. In John 12:24-25, Christ bids us to die to ourselves that we might live more fully in him. Salvation comes only through the atoning sacrifice of Christ on Calvary; it cannot be earned. This cannot be more clear than when stated by Christ himself in John 14:6: "I am the way and the truth and the life. No one comes to the Father except through me."

NEW AGE TERMINOLOGY

- Altered states of consciousness
- Aquarian age
- Astral planes
- At-one-ment (three words as opposed to atonement)
- Auras
- Autogenic (self-source) training
- Bioenergetics
- Birth traumas or arias/chants
- Body-imaging
- Centering
- Christed hands
- Cosmic system
- Creative spirituality
- Guided imagery
- Haptonomic therapy
- Human potential movement
- Inner voice
- Life force
- Limbic system
- Mind power
- Networking
- Out-of-body experience
- Primal pain
- Psychology of being
- Re-birthing
- Shamanism
- Spirit-breathing
- Telepathy/telepathic
- Transcendance
- Transformation through birth
- Transpersonal psychology
- Universal energy/mind
- Visualization

When pain is to be borne, a little courage helps more than much knowledge, a little human sympathy more than much courage, and the least tincture of the love of God more than all.

C. S. Lewis

SUMMARY

When a method of childbirth denies women's experience of labor pain, labeling it psychologically created or evil, that method also denies the teaching of Scripture. The effects of the Lord's judicious wisdom as to the consequences of the Fall are carried in our bodies and in nature. These effects serve as a reminder to us to seek God's help and protection throughout our lives.

Some may consider this unfair, yet Jesus' death on the cross doesn't seem fair either, according to worldly logic. The first chapter of Paul's letter to the church at Corinth reassures us that "the message of the cross is foolishness to those who are perishing" (1 Cor. 1:18), and "the foolishness of God is wiser than man's wisdom, and the weakness of God is stronger than man's strength" (1:25).

Even more, we are told, "But God chose the foolish things of the world to shame the wise; God chose the weak things of the world to shame the strong. He chose the lowly things of this world and the despised things—and the things that are not—to nullify the things that are, so that no one may boast before him. It is because of him that you are in Christ Jesus, who has become for us wisdom from God—that is, our righteousness, holiness and redemption. Therefore, as it is written: 'Let him who boasts boast in the Lord'" (1 Cor. 1:27-31).

It is indeed the God of Abraham, Isaac, and Jacob who is able to lift us up. Parents who are preparing in Christ to give birth know that it is the Lord's strength, not their own, that enables them to face childbearing with peace and joy.

Drs. Lamaze, Dick-Read, and Bradley have each contributed to our knowledge of childbirth. They have helped return childbirth to the family and counteracted the impact of routine hospitalization upon those at the center of the childbearing experience—the mother, the father, their infant, and other family members. Yet none of their theories has been sufficiently proven through research, and the issue of labor pain remains.

We are living at a time when we can give birth in relative safety and select the conditions under which we will have our babies. Through prudent planning and preparation for childbirth from a biblical view of creation, bringing new life into the world can be one of the most rewarding experiences of our lives, drawing us even closer to the Lord as we look to him to lead us. How *very* blessed we are!

The true way to be humble is not to stoop until you are smaller than yourself, but to stand at your real height against some higher nature that will show you what the real smallness of your greatness is.

Phillips Brooks

✤ SCRIPTURAL REFLECTIONS AND PROMISES

Help us, O God our Savior, for the glory of your name; deliver us and forgive our sins for your name's sake.

PSALM 79:9

Stand firm then, with the belt of truth buckled around your waist, with the breastplate of righteousness in place, and with your feet fitted with the readiness that comes from the gospel of peace. In addition to all this, take up the shield of faith, with which you can extinguish all the flaming arrows of the evil one. Take the helmet of salvation and the sword of the Spirit, which is the word of God. And pray in the Spirit on all occasions with all kinds of prayers and requests. With this in mind, be alert and always keep on praying for all the saints.

EPHESIANS 6:14-18

The wise in heart are called discerning, and pleasant words promote instruction.

PROVERBS 16:21

EIGHT

COPING WITH LABOR

As the mountains surround Jerusalem, so the Lord surrounds his people both now and forevermore.

PSALM 125:2

Next to the fear of death, the fear of pain is the greatest fear we have. People do not enjoy hurting and will do whatever they can to avoid painful situations.

The function of pain during childbirth has challenged many researchers. Pain usually is a protective mechanism that guards the body from sustained injury. Birth is the one normal physiological event in the body that often is accompanied by various degrees of physical stress and discomfort.

I believe the Lord directly helps mothers as we give birth. The intense sensations of childbirth can result in a deepened relationship with God as we ask him for strength and comfort. Not only this, but the experience of giving birth also helps us better appreciate the fruits of our labor. A woman who plays an active role in the birth of her baby, who sees her baby come into the world, often finds that her ability to protect and nurture the child goes far beyond mere social expectations. The birthing process ties her to her baby in a special, inimitable manner.

STRESS MANAGEMENT IN LABOR

What exactly *is* stress, and how can it affect childbearing? It's helpful to define specific stressors by their source. *Thermal stress* is stress due to high or low temperatures; *physical stress* is due to vigorous bodily activity; *emotional stress* is due to personal situations and family life events; *mental stress* is due to the demand for a high level of mental performance; and *psychological stress* is due to a combination of factors associated with emotional and mental stress.

In childbearing a combination of both physical and psychological stress is experienced. Labor is physically, emotionally, mentally, and spiritually demanding. Yet it does not have to be stressful in a harmful way.

The Lord has built into our nervous system the capacity to go into action in a life-threatening or dangerous situation. This natural ability is called the "fight-or-flight" response. When we become fearful, our body secretes chemical substances that "turn on" this response. (See Nervous System chart.)

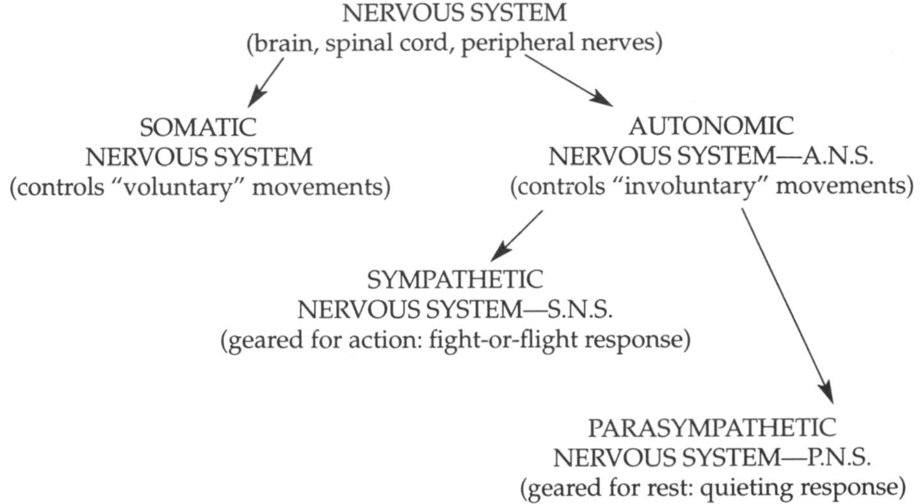

The *autonomic* (or "automatic") *nervous system* controls the large muscles in the fundus of the uterus during labor. The cervix, on the other hand, is influenced by the *sympathetic nervous system.* When fear stimulates the secretion of stress-related substances, the cervix may either stay closed or open very rapidly. This protective mechanism allows the mother to flee to a place of safety or quickly deliver her baby and then get away.

When no real danger exists, this mechanism can become a problem because labor may continue without progress or become so forceful that the baby is born too fast, not allowing the cervix and birth canal to stretch gradually. This is self-defeating, to say the least.

But be encouraged! The Lord also has built into our bodies a way to undo the effects of stress through the *parasympathetic nervous system.* When the P.N.S. is stimulated, we relax. Bodily processes slow down; energy is conserved. In labor, activation of the P.N.S. allows the body to function more normally and with greater efficiency.

For this reason, it is important to learn how to turn on this nullifier of the fight-or-flight syndrome, called the "quieting response." This response helps counteract the effects of stress on the body caused by labor, allowing uterine contractions to open the cervix more gradually. (See the following chart for the effects of adrenaline on the sympathetic nervous system.)

ADRENALINE: ITS EFFECTS

Body Function	Fight-or-Flight	Quieting Response
Heart rate	Faster	Slower
Breathing rate	Increased	Decreased
Blood pressure	Elevated	Lowered
Sweat production	Increased	Decreased
Metabolic processes	Speeded up	Slowed down
Circulation in large muscles	Greatly increased	Remains steady
S.N.S. activity	Increased	Decreased
P.N.S. activity	Decreased	Increased

ADDITIONAL FACTORS IN LABOR

Uterine contractions	May stop or become stronger	Occur more rhythmically with gradual increase in strength
Cervical dilation	Cervix may resist opening or may open very quickly	Cervix opens with less resistance, in a more gradual process

The Quieting Response

Read through Psalm 23. What a beautiful word picture David has painted for us! Shepherd . . . lacking nothing . . . lying down in green pastures . . . quiet waters . . . restoration . . . paths of righteousness . . . God's presence, protection, guidance, and comfort. This is as solid a guarantee as we could want that God will indeed help us through all we experience.

The quieting response is a God-given psychological phenomenon, and it's important to learn how to use it both properly and wisely. Stress management can take many forms. As a Christian, I choose to avoid any stress reduction exercise that places me in a suggestive state within a non-Christian context (hypnosis, guided trances, etc.). In my classes I am acutely aware of the power of suggestion as couples become physically and psychologically relaxed. For this reason, I use tapes recorded by Christian musicians, play soothing classical music, and read psalms to remind participants of the Lord's presence.

Let nothing disturb you.
Let nothing frighten you.
All things pass.
God is unchangeable.
Patience gains everything.
He who clings to God wants nothing.
God alone is sufficient.

TERESA OF JESUS

The "Natural" Response to Labor

Most people react to any type of abdominal tension by hunching forward, clutching their stomachs, and intermittently holding their breath. This is fairly automatic; it's a protective gesture made in response to intestinal upset.

Laboring women have a tendency to do the same thing when uterine contractions increase in intensity and duration in childbirth. It's challenging to voluntarily relax the muscles one does have control over while the uterus contracts involuntarily with great force. *Learning in advance what to expect and practicing relaxation regularly will help you cooperate with your body when labor actually begins.*

Why Relaxing Helps

Muscles require energy in the form of oxygen and a basic sugar called glucose in order to work properly. This energy is provided through the blood, which circulates through the cells that make up all muscle tissue within the human body. When oxygen intake, blood circulation, or energy absorption is impaired, a muscle cannot function effectively. Waste products build up in the muscle, causing discomfort; lack of oxygen results in cramping; overall fatigue sets in. This is the body's way of warning a person to slow down or completely stop the action causing overexertion.

During labor contractions, it's important to conserve energy in parts of the body not directly involved in the birth process. This way, the uterus doesn't have to compete for oxygen and glucose being used by other muscle groups or suffer from a lack of oxygen because you are holding your breath. This energy conservation can be accomplished by voluntarily relaxing those muscles you *can* control and by breathing slowly during labor.

All methods of childbirth are based on this physiological principle: "Contraction begins—I relax, I breathe." As a Christian, you will have an extra plus: You will be supported by God's strength and help as Christ himself accompanies and comforts you during labor. Rather than becoming fearful and panicky from the uncontrollable physical sensations and stress of labor, you can cooperate with the birth process by leaning on the Lord. This may take every ounce of determination you can muster at times, but it will be the most rewarding and challenging work you will ever do.

These, then, are the purposes of relaxing and breathing calmly in response to labor as you place your trust in God's help:

- To provide adequate energy to the working muscles of the uterus.
- To conserve energy by voluntarily relaxing all other muscles under your control.
- To avoid resisting the pressure of the uterus as it moves the baby through your body and out into the world.

• To avoid the stimulation of the fight-or-flight response and the secretion of adrenaline.

PREPARING TO RELAX DURING LABOR

All muscular activity taking place within the human body is mediated through the nervous system. Muscles cannot function independently under normal conditions. They can be moved only in response to signals sent to and from the brain along cable-like communication channels called nerves. When nervous impulses are blocked due to nerve damage or anesthesia, loss of sensation and decreased muscle activity result. (See Appendix C for common drugs used for pain intervention during labor and a description of their effects.)

In preparing your body to adapt to the process of childbirth, you are training your will to respond constructively to the stress of labor. Remember, the brain coordinates the behavior of the body; the will influences the brain. It is through the will that we direct the mind to inform parts of the body to relax.

Behavioral psychologists do not believe in the concept of the "will." Instead, they theorize that all behavior is the result of conditioning; human behavior is the result of genetic and environmental influences. While this theory may contain elements of truth, as Christians we know that people are more than just organisms that adapt to a "path of least resistance." We know we have choices.

The Christian view asserts that people are made up of body, mind, and spirit. Therefore, the first step in preparing yourself to relax during labor is to strengthen your will. This will enable you to choose what is beneficial for your body during labor.

God raises the level of the impossible.

CORRIE TEN BOOM

Strengthening Your Will

As you prepare for labor, acknowledge that it is the Lord who created you and the baby within you. Use your will to say, "I trust you, Lord. I belong to you; you are my God." Ask the Lord to help you relax. Find Scripture passages that give you confidence, and think about them often. Give thanks and praise to God for the many things he has done in your life.

It may help to picture yourself in one of these ways as you relax:

- Leaning on the everlasting arms.
- Lying down in green pastures.
- Walking beside the still waters.
- Resting under the shadow of his wings.

There are many other word pictures for you to choose from.

As you rest, comfort yourself by thinking of the Lord being with you. In class I read most of Psalm 139 as couples relax on floor mats or in chairs; I also use dim lighting and play soft praise songs in the background. Reading this psalm is deeply reassuring for childbearing women—and their husbands. What can possibly compare with the knowledge that the Lord is with you *always*?

Relaxing Your Body

In labor you won't be able to control the muscles of the uterus, which must forcibly contract to press your baby down against the cervix to open it, then push the baby through the soft, stretchy tissue of your vagina. Cervical dilation takes place during the first stage of labor. Your greatest challenge will be to allow your body to complete this task by itself. You must cooperate constructively by keeping as calm as possible, breathing or walking to help gravity bring your baby down into your pelvis.

In preparing for this event, it's helpful to relax once or twice daily in the following ways:

Choose a quiet environment. You may wish to dim the lights and play soothing music. Turn off the TV and unplug the phone to be free of interruptions.

Find a comfortable position. Upright positions are the best, such as sitting "Indian-style," semi-reclining with back support and pillows under your knees; straddling a chair with a pillow over its back and leaning into the back of the chair; or rocking in a rocking chair with your feet on a footstool.

Put aside your worries. This is the time to relax both your mind and body. You might try to spend an equivalent amount of time each day not worrying about anything.

Think about the Lord. Use whatever Bible verses, prayers, or poetry you wish. Spend these moments with God in appreciation for who he is and what he has done for you. This is not a time for intercessory prayer or petitioning. It is a time just to relax in God's presence and glorify him by being still before him.

Breathe slowly and evenly. As you relax, your breathing rate will slow to about half its normal rate. Check this, if you wish, by counting the number of breaths you take for twenty seconds and then multiplying that number by three. It is best to check your rate at the beginning of practice and toward the end, before you stretch and get up.

Relax your body. This can be done simply by "going limp," if relaxing comes naturally to you. Or you can use the method shown in the chart "Learning to Relax Your Body."

Learning to Relax Your Body

Step 1

Do each exercise slowly, with an awareness of varying sensations as you tense the muscle area and then relax it. After you have gone through the list a few times, go through it again, releasing each muscle group without using tension as a comparison. Practicing this will enable you to fully relax all muscle groups consciously. Once you are confident in your ability to consciously relax these areas, proceed to Step 2.

Area to Be Tensed	How to Tense
Toes	Curl toes
Feet	Stretch toes
Ankles and calves	Pull toes and feet toward leg
Knees	Pull back on knee caps
Thighs	Press thighs together or onto floor
Buttocks	Press together
Pelvic floor	Pull up, front to back
Lower abdomen	Pull muscles in
Lower back	Tilt pelvis back, erase curve
Abdomen	Bulge out
Chest	Take deep breath, using chest muscles
Upper back	Press shoulder blades back
Shoulders	Pull shoulder blades toward ears
Fingers	Spread fingers apart
Entire arm	Tighten all arm, hand, and finger muscles (To release, start with fingers, then wrist, lower arm, elbow, upper arm, and shoulder.)
Neck	Pull tight
Jaw	Drop jaw and stretch
Tongue	Press against roof of mouth
Lips	Press together
Cheeks	Smile
Eyes	Shut eyes tight
Forehead	Raise eyebrows

(Remember, the tension is to show you a contrast, helping you learn how to relax these muscle groups naturally. As you tense each area, release it slowly and deliberately.)

Step 2

Large Muscle Groups. In this exercise, replace tensing with relaxing, thinking toward large muscle groups. Release further by exhaling, until you can feel that you are fully released. The following large muscle groups are to be relaxed:

1. Right leg
2. Left leg
3. Both legs
4. Lower body
5. Right arm
6. Left arm
7. Both arms
8. Upper body
9. Entire body

Step 3

Relaxing with Distraction (flexibility games)

A. Tense one part of the body while relaxing tension in the rest of the body. For example: Tense your entire left leg. Have your labor companion check your arms and right leg to see if they are relaxed. Repeat this with your right leg and each arm. For a greater test, try tensing diagonally while relaxing opposite limbs (right leg, left arm).

B. Release with motion by tapping your finger or rotating your feet as you relax the rest of the body. Have your labor companion assess the level of muscular relaxation.

C. Relax in a public place, such as a shopping mall. Sit on a bench with your labor companion and have him discreetly check to see how relaxed you are.

D. Relax in tense situations, such as during prenatal exams or while driving.

Evaluating Your Progress

If you are able to relax your body by stimulating its parasympathetic nervous system's quieting reflex, you will find that, as you become more skilled, several changes will take place. Your heart rate should drop to eighty or below (sixty-five or below if you're not pregnant). This can be checked by placing your index and middle fingers against the bone on your wrist or pressing them lightly against the artery at the side of your neck.

As you relax, your breathing will become slower and deeper, reducing the rate to around half. Don't forget to check this rate both before you begin and after you have relaxed for about ten minutes, comparing the two figures.

Another noticeable change will be in your skin temperature, which lowers in response to stress and rises when you are relaxed. Check the temperature of your fingertips both before and after relaxing.

WORKING TOGETHER: THE LABOR PARTNER'S ROLE

As a labor companion, you will be watching for expressions of discomfort in your wife when she is in labor, determining what might be helpful and providing support in the use of pain relief measures.

Consider these questions: Does her back look tense? Is her breathing raspy? Is she grimacing or irritable? Patiently offer help as needed, remaining calm, quiet, and positive in your outlook.

Husbands usually are very responsive to any expression of pain from their wives. The better you know one another, the easier it becomes to read nonverbal signals. This is another reason why husbands can be ideal labor companions. The intimacy of a marital relationship fosters a private language and a unique way of communicating feelings.

On the negative side, some husbands may feel helpless or directly responsible for causing the physical stress their wives experience during labor. If this happens to you, it will be essential to keep in mind that you are not alone. The Lord is there to help *both* of you. Also, your health-care team is able to provide additional support when needed.

Being a labor companion, laboring together, means that you can "lift her up" because your body isn't laboring in the same way. But it also means that you should empathize with her and share in her feelings.

You can effectively evaluate how your wife is feeling during labor by:

- what she says
- what sounds she makes
- her facial expressions
- how she responds to her surroundings
- how she moves her body
- how she shows her feelings
- how she relates to people

After having our fourth child, I remember looking at my husband and thinking, *He looks as tired as I do!* Dave *was* tired. He labored with me, and we were very close throughout that birth. My love for him grew even greater because I was so thankful to have him caring for me during such a vulnerable time in my life. The presence of one's husband can be both reassuring and strengthening.

It will be helpful if you can assist your wife with relaxation, breathing, and comfort techniques within two contexts—during at-home practice and in labor. Prenatal practice enhances your ability to communicate nonverbally with one another and creates a foundation of cooperation, making labor support easier. In addition, your practices can be a special time when you convey your love and support.

When labor begins, try to stay calm and begin encouraging your wife to relax from the start by using a calm, supportive manner. Watch for expressions of emotional stress and physical discomfort, and be flexible in determining what comfort measures may be useful. When a technique isn't working or she isn't interested in trying it, use something else instead.

Where love is, there is God also.

LEO TOLSTOY

Easing Tension Through Touch

An effective way to stimulate the parasympathetic nervous system (P.N.S.) is by stroking the skin in a light, soothing manner. (See "Using Stroking During Pregnancy and Childbirth" chart.)

In our culture we often are inhibited about touching others. We tend to think of touch as something sexual or erotic. Yet if you consider the times when someone truly comforted you, it is likely that the person expressed concern and love in such practical ways as holding your hand, putting an arm around your shoulders, or embracing you.

During a visit to Mexico, I was pleasantly surprised by the warmth of the people there. Sisters walked arm in arm, and boys freely put their arms around the shoulders of their friends. Mexican family members seemed very close and expressed their affection in physical ways. To my North American eyes, this looked pleasant but foreign. When I returned home, I really missed seeing people expressing affection openly.

Nonsexual nurturing touch can be a positive way to support your partner in times of stress. At the end of a long day, a back rub can revive your spouse's sense of joy in living. In labor massage may be confined to areas of a woman's back, lower abdomen, and thighs. Determine what type of touch is the most soothing for her and don't give up using this relaxation method after the baby arrives—you'll need it to relax too.

Remember: Your touch and caring attention speak clearly to your wife—rely on your hands and eyes to convey tenderness, patience, and love. When she's in labor, be prepared for mood swings and stress reactions, realizing that it's perfectly normal for even the most cool, calm, and collected woman to express serious doubts about her birthing ability. By remaining calm and reassuring, you can provide a stable, soothing reference point during intense labor contractions.

USING STROKING DURING PREGNANCY AND CHILDBIRTH

Benefits

- Stroking provides a focal point toward which the mother can concentrate her relaxation.
- Stroking promotes the circulation of blood through the body, enabling toxic wastes produced through the muscular activity of the uterus to be removed more quickly.
- Massage stimulates the parasympathetic nervous system (P.N.S.), provoking the quieting reflex.
- Being touched by a loved one helps the mother feel cared for and provides a way for the labor companion to express affection and concern.
- The stimulation of the skin can raise a woman's tolerance to pain by sending impulses to the brain that interfere with other messages coming in regarding painful sensations.

Tips for Effective Stroking

Stroking should be mild and light since the mother's circulating blood volume is much higher than normal. In addition, any massage should be patterned, repetitive, rhythmical. Use corn oil or cornstarch to minimize friction against the skin and massage skin-to-skin when possible to promote relaxation. Make sure the mother is in a comfortable position.

A Simple Technique for Giving a Good Back Rub

This back rub technique is guaranteed to promote harmony in your home! It is especially nice when done at the end of a long day after showering or bathing.

- Circle sweeps: Lie on your side in a comfortable position. Have your labor partner place his/her hands at the base of your waist and begin stroking with small, upward, sweeping circles that meet on either side of the spine and become larger in diameter to cover the shoulders. Upon reaching the shoulders, the movements should resume again from the base of the spine. This stroking should be rhythmical and always in an upward and outward direction.
- See-saw: Now have your labor partner place his/her hands next to one another, over the tops of your buttocks, with the thumb of the upper hand touching the small finger of the lower hand. Following the contour of your body, your partner should firmly draw the hands outward, then inward, moving gradually up the back. Once the neck is reached, the stroking begins again at the bottom of the spine.
- Walking: Beginning at the base of the spine, your labor partner places his/her fingers on either side of the spine facing upward and slightly toward the spine. Alternating from left to right, your partner presses firmly and massages in a circular motion. This is continued in a "walking" motion up the back and begins again at the base of the back once the neck is reached.
- The harp: As a completion to these three types of stroking, have your labor partner begin at the neck, with fingertips at the right side of the spine, and draw his/her fingers quickly and lightly down the spine. As soon as the right hand begins, the left hand is placed at the left side of the neck, stroking downward in the same fashion as soon as the right hand completes its stroke. This should be a quick, rhythmical, alternating stroke.

Techniques for the Lower Back

- Figure eight: With you in a comfortable side-lying position, your labor partner uses the flat of one hand to broadly stroke across the back of the pelvis. This may be done vertically or horizontally across the lower back. Your labor partner should use his/her free hand to hold your hip bone, stabilizing the pelvis.
- Self-applied stroking: While lying on your side, you may stroke your own lower back by drawing the back of your hand firmly over that region. Firmer pressure may be applied if the thumb is hooked on the front of the hip, with the fingers reaching back in a broad circular motion over the lower back.

Other Areas of Focus

- The abdomen: Either you or your labor companion can do a light, rhythmical stroking with the fingertips on your bare abdomen over the area where a contraction is felt.
- Low massage for cramping: Position fingertips on either side of the center of your pubic bone. Slowly draw fingers up and over the groin to the hip bones (iliac).

Return hands to the original position, repeating rhythmically for the duration of the contraction. When in a sitting position, use both hands; when in a side-lying position, use one hand.

- Light massage (effleurage): Position fingertips on either side of the navel. Draw fingers up, outward, then downward. Draw large circles, always returning through the center point of the abdomen. Be sure to keep touch light.
- The thighs: Lie in a semi-reclining position, with your legs relaxed on pillows or the bed raised under the knees. While facing you, your labor companion can stroke the muscles of the inner thigh beginning with hands placed over the inside of the calf. Hands should be drawn firmly up over the inner thigh and toward the groin, if comfortable. Every third or fourth stroke is swept up over the top of the thigh and completed by a firm movement down the outside of the leg, to the feet, and over the toes. Concentrate on relaxing into the stroke of your support person and on keeping the perineum relaxed.

Easing Pain Through Attention Diversion

Since our minds can only interpret a limited amount of incoming information, looking at and listening to things that will hold your attention during labor can raise your pain threshold and help you feel less discomfort. The following are things you could use in this way. Some may seem extravagant or unusual, but if you select things that are meaningful to you, they won't seem so once you're in labor.

These are not tools to be used as a way of inducing hypnosis or a "mystical state." Instead, they simply distract your attention from the pain stimuli.

Two-dimensional Items. Posters, photographs, art prints, drawings, paintings, slides projected on the wall. (Select for appealing colors, diversity, and meaningful content.)

Textiles. Weavings, tapestries, needlepoint, embroidery, fabrics, quilts. (Select large, bright, attention-getting items. Handmade items are especially unique.)

Religious Objects. Statues, symbols, art, hand-lettered verses, hymns, songs, prayers. (Find things to remind you of your personal beliefs and to give you a greater perspective beyond the physical experience of labor.)

Baby Items. Stuffed animals, toys, garments. (Bring things that will help reinforce attachment to your coming child.)

Living Things. Plants, flowers, small aquarium, small pet, terrarium. (Pick those that have a pleasant odor and convey a sense of vitality.)

Light. Slides, diffused light, candles, kerosene lamp. (Be careful of eye strain—find sources of light that are attention-holding, fascinating.)

Small Objects. Silk flowers, statues, art objects, motion figures, Magic Sand, pine bough, or holiday ornaments. (Be creative in finding a few fun and interesting things.)

Surrounding Environment. Tiles, wallpaper, clock, draperies, window/view, hardware, architectural features, facial features or hands of people around you, garments or jewelry they are wearing. (Look at parts of room or people that are nonthreatening and reassuring.)

Thermal Stimulation

Many women have been helped by applying heat or cold to areas that become cramped or tense during labor. Any of the following relief measures can be used, but avoid extremes in temperature. Always be careful not to burn or damage the skin. Ideas for warm thermal stimulation include baths or showers, compresses (a slow cooker is ideal for keeping them warm), a hot water bottle, heating pads, warmed blankets, Mentholatum, and eucalyptus oil.

Cold thermal stimulation ideas include ice packs (commercial or self-sealing plastic bags), a hot water bottle filled with ice water (can also use a hollow rolling pin or empty detergent bottle), cold compresses soaked in ice water, a spray mist of cold water, or pads soaked in witch hazel.

EASING FIRST STAGE OF LABOR THROUGH BREATHING TECHNIQUES

Patterned breathing is useful during the process of birth for several reasons. It can bring a greater measure of control to our reactions to challenging situations. Rhythmical breathing is distracting and places our focus on a positive bodily response to stress rather than on the stress itself. Also, adequate breathing insures adequate oxygenation, enabling the uterus to perform its work more effectively and efficiently.

Patterned breathing will change your usual response to large muscle contractions. Rather than tensing and holding your breath during a cramp, you are conditioned by the breathing to think, *Contraction begins—I relax, I breathe.*

Finally, breathing techniques will keep your focus on coping with stress or pain. The attention is centered above the level of pelvic congestion and discomfort. Instead of passively observing what is happening, you will consciously interpret what's taking place within your body and actively participate with its increased demand for oxygen.

Practicing Breathing Patterns

The role of a labor companion begins during practice. As a labor companion you should learn and understand the patterns and techniques that will be useful during labor. During practice, work to develop ways of supporting your partner's breathing through verbal encouragement, eye contact, tapping, counting, or breathing in unison. Practice your signals so that you will not feel awkward using them during labor.

It's a good idea, while practicing, to periodically change roles, giving each of you a chance to be the supportive partner. Whoever is acting as the labor partner will call out the beginning, peak, and the end of each contraction to reinforce the use of breathing patterns. Be sure you both understand fully how each breathing pattern is done.

Another way to make these patterns a more natural response is to use them casually at times other than practice. Do the patterns several times per day, especially during tense or uncomfortable moments for maximum benefit. (The slow breathing pattern is particularly soothing when you feel irritable, frustrated, or stressed.)

As you consider the different patterns, be flexible in choosing which pattern to use at any certain point in labor. The patterns are interchangeable and need not be done in the order presented. Keep in mind the following key points:

1. Keep breathing as relaxed and slow as possible for as long as possible. This saves energy. Always begin and end a contraction with "cleansing breaths," using first a "greeting breath" and then signaling the end of a contraction with a "completion breath."
2. When you make your breathing faster, don't breathe as deeply as when it was slow. Remember, as the rate goes up, the depth goes down. Quicker breathing means shallower breathing.
3. Be confident in your ability to "listen to what your body is saying," and change your breathing accordingly. Use only the patterns and rates that make you feel more comfortable.
4. Try to breathe in and out in equal amounts.
5. Try different patterns and variations until you discover what helps you relax the most.

Avoiding Hyperventilation. Hyperventilation occurs when an excess of oxygen builds up in the bloodstream. In can happen to a woman in labor when:

- She has not practiced breathing techniques sufficiently before entering labor. When unsure of a breathing pattern, a woman in labor can easily breathe with too much force or too unevenly. She needs to practice often and be sure her instructor checks her progress.
- She increases her breathing rate without decreasing the depth of breathing during a contraction. The deeper and faster the breathing, the greater the oxygen consumption will be. Remember, as the rate goes up, the depth goes down.
- She gasps in air during a contraction due to anxiety, fatigue, or discomfort. Gasping results in a disruption of the oxygen balance in the bloodstream. Active labor support through the labor companion's tapping, counting, or singing out a rhythm to regulate breathing can help her achieve a more even exchange of air.

The symptoms of hyperventilation include tingling in the fingertips, lips, cheeks, and/or around the mouth; dizziness; numbness; and light-headedness. If you feel any of these symptoms during labor, you will need active labor support that will provide you with a restoration of carbon dioxide in your bloodstream. One way to achieve this is by breathing into a paper bag or cupped hands for one or more contractions or between contractions.

One thing you need to realize is that during labor your uterus will consume much more oxygen than it will during practice. Therefore, it is not uncommon for light-headedness to occur during practice of breathing patterns. If this does happen, simply take a break and then resume practice with mock contractions of no more than thirty seconds each. Be sure to rest between each "contraction" and avoid breathing too rapidly or deeply.

Faithfulness in carrying out our present duties is the best preparation for the future.
FRANÇOIS FÉNELON

BREATHING PATTERNS

Slow Breathing

Function: To slow the rate and increase the depth of breathing to produce relaxation and calmness. This helps combat nausea, anxiety, and fatigue.

Pattern: Breathe in through the mouth or nose slowly and exhale the air through the mouth in a controlled, slow breath, similar to a deep sigh. The breathing is continuous, beginning the next breath without any pause. Experiment with letting the air expand your chest (chest breathing) and then your abdomen (abdominal breathing). Decide which way brings you the most comfort and relaxation.

Rate: The rate should be about half your normal breathing rate.

Light Breathing

Function: By keeping the breath lighter, pressure on the uterus from the expansion of the abdominal wall is avoided.

Pattern: Basically a modified slow-breathing pattern. Bring air in through the nose, or mouth and nose, and exhale through the mouth. There may be a slight sound as the air is exhaled. This pattern, because it is more shallow, involves more of the upper chest, which can expand out to the sides, if desired.

Rate: Should not exceed thirty breaths per minute.

Counted Breathing

Function: To raise pain tolerance through an increased rate and decreased depth of breathing while encouraging concentration on a specific count. "Blow breaths" provide a break from the lighter pants.

Pattern: Breathe slowly in and out through the mouth, or in through the nose and out through the mouth. Shift rate and depth as you respond to the pressure of contractions.

Rate: Keep the rate as slow as possible, preferably less than thirty breaths per minute.

Blow-Blow

Function: To help relieve the urge to push if you are told that you cannot do so. It must be remembered that the urge to push is practically irresistible and that the breathing does not *eliminate* the desire—it helps you to cope with it.

Pattern: When the urge to push is felt, whether merely catching of the breath or a full-fledged desire to bear down, puff out air sharply and quickly. An extended blow can turn into a push, so make the puffs steady and fast.

SUMMARY

In this chapter you have learned a variety of useful pain relief techniques for coping with the physical stress of birth. Consider these suggestions simply as ideas to be used or discarded as you see fit. It's important to try out a variety to discover which work best for you. Then when labor begins, you can use those that make you feel better.

As you prepare together for your baby's birth, you can fill this time of preparation with pleasant words and joyful anticipation. Remember these wise words from Proverbs 16:24: "Pleasant words are a honeycomb, sweet to the soul and healing to the bones." Make this a time that you both will look back on with fondness.

SLOW BREATHING

Inhalation shaded area symbolizes a contraction

Exhalation

A. Contraction beings.
B. Greeting breath (deep inhalation, full exhalation).
C. Slow breathing at a rate or 6-10 or 12-18 breaths per minute.
D. Contraction ends.
E. Completion breath (deep inhalation, full exhalation) and thanksgiving that this contraction is gone forever!
F. Resume normal breathing rate.

LIGHT BREATHING

Inhalation   shaded area symbolizes a contraction

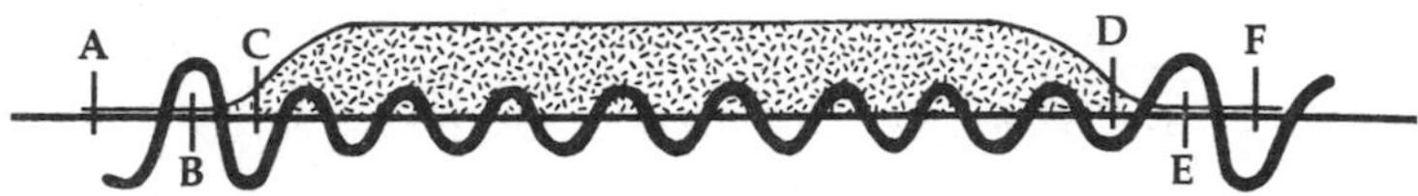

Exhalation

A. Contraction begins.
B. Greeting breath.
C. Light breathing at rate of 18-24 or 26-30 breaths per minute.
D. Contraction ends.
E. Completion breath and thanksgiving.
F. Resume normal rate.

45-second contraction: breathing rate and depth maintained throughout.
60-second contraction: breathing up at peak, down at depth.

COUNTED BREATHING 3:1

Inhalation   shaded area symbolizes a contraction

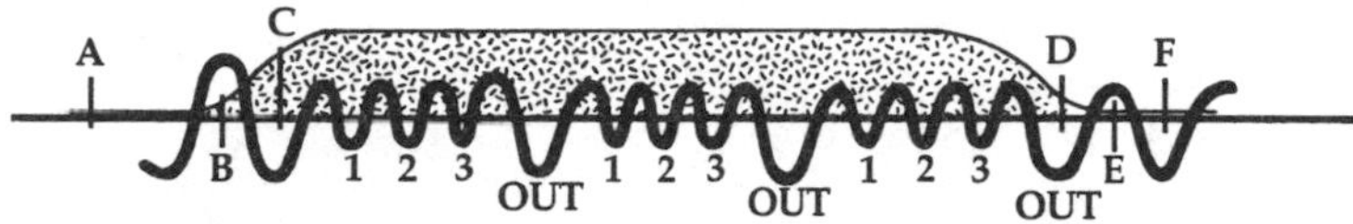

Exhalation

A. Contraction begins.
B. Greeting breath.
C. Count breathing with 3 lighter, more shallow breaths followed by 1 deeper, shorter breath. Try for about 24-30 breaths per minute.
D. Contraction ends.
E. Completion breath and thanksgiving.
F. Resume normal breathing.

60-second contraction: 3 to 1 breathing maintained throughout.

COUNTED BREATHING 4:1

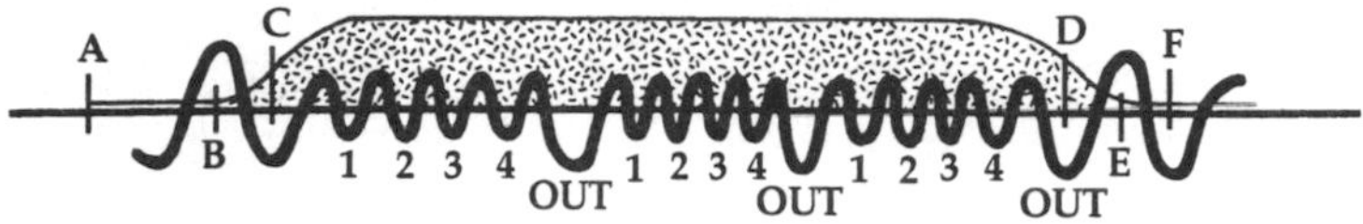

A. Contraction begins.
B. Greeting breath.
C. Counted breathing with 4 lighter breaths followed by 1 deeper, slower breath (about 32-36 breaths per minute).
D. Contraction ends.
E. Completion breath and thanksgiving.
F. Resume normal breathing rate.

90-second contraction: 4 to 1, except at peak; 2 to 1 during peak.

COUNTED BREATHING 2:1, 1:1 FOR PEAK

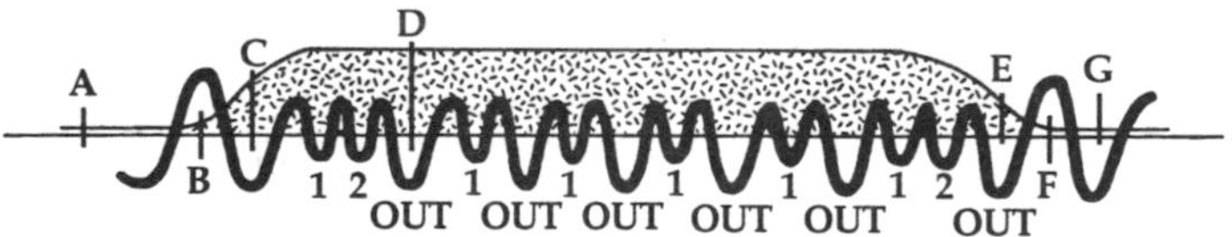

A. Contraction begins.
B. Greeting breath.
C. Counted breathing at a rate of 2 shallow to 1 deeper breath.
D. Counted breathing at a rate of 1 shallow to 1 deep breath—no faster than 40 breaths per minute.
E. Contraction ends.
F. Completion breath and thanksgiving.
G. Resume normal breathing rate.

90-second contraction: 2 to 1 except at peak; 1 to 1 during peak.

I. Blow-Blow Breathing with Urge to Push at Peak

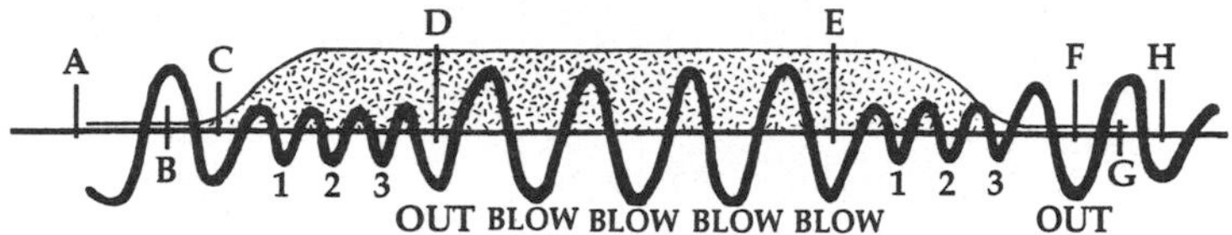

A. Contraction begins.
B. Greeting breath.
C. 3 to 1 counted breathing until urge to push develops.
D. Begin puffing air out after each inhalation.
E. Resume 3 to 1 counted breathing when urge to push subsides.
F. Contraction ends.
G. Completion breath and thanksgiving
H. Resume normal breathing rate.

II. Blow-Blow Breathing with Urge to Push During Entire Contraction

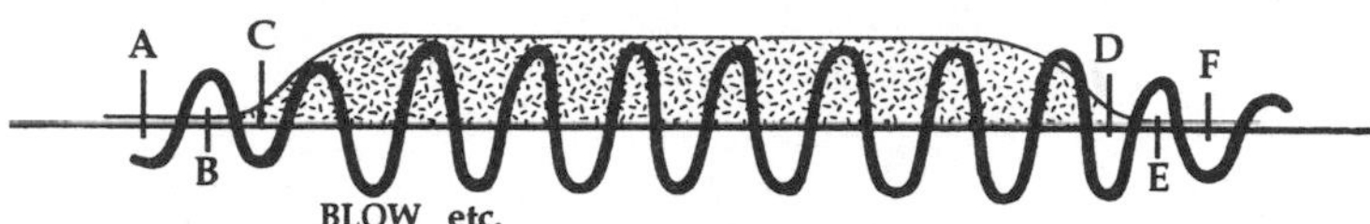

A. Contraction begins.
B. Greeting breath.
C. Begin blowing out continuously throughout contraction with light puff after adequate inhalations.
D. Contraction ends.
E. Completion breath with thanksgiving.
F. Resume normal breathing rate.

RELATIONSHIPS BETWEEN LABOR EVENTS AND PHYSICAL STRESS

Stage	Events	Possible Affected Areas
1 Opening of the cervix	Effacement and dilation of cervix Uterine contractions Movement of baby deeper into pelvis	Pubic to umbilical region Upper thighs Lower back Hip joints
2 Movement of baby through birth canal	Uterine contractions Stretching of vagina, pelvic floor, and perineum Passage of baby through pelvis	Abdomen (especially with urge to push) Hip joints Lower back, tailbone Perineum, pelvic floor, vagina, and rectum
3 Expulsion of placenta	Passage of placenta through cervix and vagina Uterine contractions Repair of lacerations or incision in pelvic floor and perineum (episiotomy)	Pubic to umbilical region Lower back Upper thighs Perineum, vagina, pelvic floor, and rectum
4 Two-hour recovery period following childbirth	Uterine contractions Beginning of involution of the uterus Fundal massage Aggravated hemorrhoids Beginning of healing process (of episiotomy)	Pubic to umbilical region Lower back Rectum Perineum, pelvic floor, vagina
5 Six weeks following childbirth	Uterine contractions (for first few days) Healing of perineum Breast engorgement with onset of lactation (48 hours, then diminishes) Adjustment of nipples to nursing	Pubic to umbilical region Lower back Perineum, vagina, pelvic floor Rectum Entire chest wall Nipples

Physical Causes of Pain in Childbirth

- "Referred" pain: messages sent from the pelvic area to other places in the body
- Fast or prolonged labor
- Uterine function
- Pressure on pelvic floor
- Stretching of cervix
- Poor physical condition
- Pelvis size
- Mother's position
- Baby's position in uterus
- Physical disease or disability
- Pull on supporting ligaments
- Cramping and waste buildup in muscles
- Procedures done to mother

Some Factors That Influence Pain Experience

- Your body's response and the cause of pain
- The meaning you give to pain
- The reaction of others
- What you've learned about this type of pain
- Your earlier experiences with pain
- Your age and personality
- The situation in which you experience pain
- The coping methods you choose
- Your ethnic and social background
- The accuracy of your expectations

Self-Statements During Labor

The following phrases contain suggestions that can help alleviate anxiety, fear, and worry before, during, and after your baby's birth. Review them, adapting them for your own use and keeping in mind that the things you think about during these three stress phases (anticipation, presence, aftermath) will influence your ability to cooperate with your body.

STATEMENTS TO AVOID	STATEMENTS TO USE
Anticipation Phase **Before Labor Begins**	
This is going to be impossible.	O, Lord, what must I do?
There is no way I can cope with labor.	I can cope with my labor with your help, Father. I can pray about this.

STATEMENTS TO AVOID	STATEMENTS TO USE
I'll just ignore this whole thing and deal with it when the time comes.	I will think and pray about what I have to do.
I'll probably panic when labor starts.	When I feel labor begin, the Lord will help me know what to do.
I feel better when I worry.	I won't worry—worrying is useless.
This whole thing depresses me. Why does it have to be this way?	I can deal with the pain; the relief measures I've learned will help, and the Lord will sustain me.
Nothing is going to help.	I have lots of ideas and strategies to call upon.
The Lord can't love me if this is what labor is. Pain means I lack faith.	I believe in God's love for me no matter how difficult things get.
I don't know how to relax. I've always been a tense person.	I'll take a few deep breaths now to relax, and remember Psalm 23.
The Bible can't help me.	Scripture passages are my best defense.
Presence Phase During Labor and Birth	
I hate this.	I can meet this challenge with God's help.
God can't be with me and allow me to feel this way.	God is with me; he is my strength and hope.
I've never been able to handle pain. This is awful.	I have dealt with pain before; I can deal with it now.
I can't deal with this.	I'll take just one contraction at a time; God's grace is sufficient for me.
I can't get my mind off how I feel.	I'm not going to think about the pain; I'll look to the Lord and use relief measures.
These contractions are terrible.	The tension in my uterus can be my ally, my cue to cope.
I can't get rid of this anxiety.	Anxiety is normal, but I can cast it on God.
No one will believe this—they'll think I'm exaggerating.	I don't need to prove myself to anyone or try to pretend my pain isn't real. The Lord knows how I feel.

STATEMENTS TO AVOID	STATEMENTS TO USE
I can't do anything but hold my breath and curl up into a ball.	I'll just lean on God and use my breathing patterns.
Something's wrong—I know it.	I won't assume the worst or jump to conclusions. God is in control.
This is a total waste.	There is something in this to feel good about; my child is coming into the world.
I don't care about doing anything right now. Leave me alone.	This feeling reminds me to use my relief measures and fix my eyes on Jesus.
I'm angry and I don't care.	Getting angry won't help this baby get born.
I'm really a failure.	Doubting myself is unnecessary; I know I can do this with God's help.

Coping with Sensations/Feelings at Critical Moments

I can't do this. I've got to get rid of this pain.	I can't eliminate this pain completely; I *can* deal with it with God's help.
Maybe if I complain, everyone will feel sorry for me, and that will make me feel better.	Complaining won't help; I will look to the God of my salvation instead.
This is completely out of control.	I can switch to a new relief measure at any point; it's my choice, something I can control.
There's nothing I can do to help.	What are the things I need to do?
The Lord has forgotten me.	Help me, Lord.
It helps to show my true feelings.	Feeling upset won't help; I know the Lord is with me.
If the pain gets worse, I'll ask them to knock me out. I can't stand it.	When the pain becomes intense, I will focus on Christ and on what I need to do.

Aftermath Phase After the Baby Is Born

I'm ashamed of myself.	Praise God, that contraction is gone forever! With God's help, I got through without getting upset.
Nothing works.	Alleluia! It worked!

STATEMENTS TO AVOID	STATEMENTS TO USE
I can't do anything right.	I knew I could do it through Christ who strengthens me.
I feel horrible.	That was hard, but I'm doing fine. Thanks, God.
I can't handle this.	I managed that pretty well, with God's help.
No one's going to know how badly I blew it.	I can't wait to tell everyone how the Lord helped me!
The Lord can't love me if he deserted me like this.	That was one of the most stressful things I've ever had to deal with, but the Lord was with me all the way.

SCRIPTURAL REFLECTIONS AND PROMISES

To thee I offer my outstretched hands, I thirst for thee in a thirsty land. . . . Show me the way that I must take; to thee I offer all my heart.

PSALM 143:6, 8 NEB

The Lord your God is with you, he is mighty to save. He will take great delight in you, he will quiet you with his love, he will rejoice over you with singing.

ZEPHANIAH 3:17

Lord, when doubts fill my mind, when my heart is in turmoil, quiet me and give me renewed hope and cheer.

PSALM 94:19 TLB

A friend loves at all times.

PROVERBS 17:17A

I am thy servant; give me insight to understand thy interaction.

PSALM 119:125 NEB

Since we live by the Spirit, let us keep in step with the Spirit.

GALATIANS 5:25

NINE

WORKING THROUGH LABOR

The eternal God is your refuge and underneath are the everlasting arms.

DEUTERONOMY 33:27

When labor begins, you will experience new physical sensations and emotions. The details of labor are presented in this chapter, along with possible variations and descriptions of the roles played by your labor companion and health-care provider. Consider this section of the book your practical labor guide. (You may even find it helpful to refer to these pages during labor, so don't forget to pack it in your things where it can be located conveniently.)

FIRST STAGE: EARLY, ACTIVE, AND TRANSITION PHASES

Early Phase: the Mother's Experience

During the early phase of the first stage of labor the mother's experiences may include:

- periodic menstrual-like cramps and backache that increase in strength, duration, and frequency over a relatively short time or over a number of days.
- the breaking of the bag of waters. (Check the color and odor and call health-care provider.)
- a blood-tinged mucus discharge as the cervix thins out. (This may take place in advance of labor or as labor progresses.)
- stomach-flu-type symptoms of intestinal upset and diarrhea.
- anxiety about whether or not labor is beginning.

Use the following chart to help you determine whether or not you are in true labor, and then seek your health-care provider's opinion.

To time a contraction, include the interval of rest until the next contraction begins. In other words, contractions are timed from the beginning of one to the beginning of the next. (See "Timing a Contraction" diagram.)

TIMING A CONTRACTION

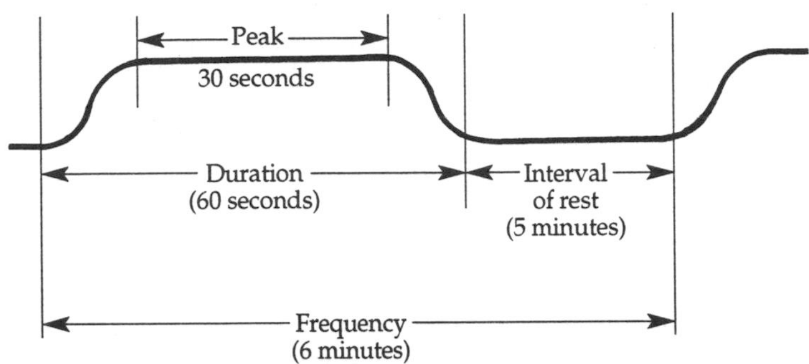

While in this early stage, you may find it easier to sleep if you're given a back rub. (Don't worry about sleeping too long; once you're in active labor, the contractions will definitely wake you up.) Also, a warm bath (if membranes are intact) or shower may help you relax. Eat and drink something that is easily digested and that will give you energy. Walking sometimes is beneficial, since the increased pressure on the cervix from gravity has a tendency to stimulate labor. With all the new sensations and feelings, you may be surprised by how labor feels and what happens. Try to accept it gracefully and give thanks!

TRUE AND FALSE LABOR

"TRUE" LABOR	"FALSE" LABOR
Contractions	
Get closer together Become more intense Feel crampy in front or achy in back	Average interval between contractions does not shorten Intensity and length stay the same
Discharge	
Thick mucus discharge from cervix—may be clear, though usually blood-tinged	None or clear but not copious
Changes in Cervix	
Effacement and dilation Process of birth resulting in baby's arrival	Little or no effacement or dilation Symptoms stop; baby does not arrive

Early Phase: Husband's/Labor Companion's Role

As the labor companion, you can help establish the right perspective regardless of circumstances. When the early phase begins, stay calm and help your wife get comfortable. Remind her that it often takes 40 to 50 percent of the time in labor to dilate three centimeters.

Provide your wife with loving reassurance. Time the contractions and call her health-care provider if she asks you to. Also, notify prayer partners or relatives and make arrangements for other children you have.

If you're leaving home for the birth, this would be the time to pack the suitcase and put it and your pillows in the car. Above all, be sure to tell your wife you love her, comforting her with your voice, touch, and presence.

Together you can recall God's promises, praising him for your wife and baby. Rejoice together in the way God has designed the process of labor. Pray for his help and protection, giving thanks even though you may be tired, confused, or excited.

Meditate on the Lord as your Shepherd, and read Scriptures or play music to remind you of his living presence. Cast your anxiety on him, believing that he will deliver you and will not allow you to undergo more than you can handle (1 Cor. 10:13). Ask the Lord to assist each of you, giving you strength and guiding your health-care providers.

Early Phase: Health-Care Provider's Role

Your health-care provider should be available as needed, provide assistance in determining the appropriate time for transfer to the place of birth, evaluate the progress of labor, and recommend what the mother can do to be more comfortable and to promote the health of herself and the baby.

Early Phase: Relief Measures

- Proper spiritual perspective (See husband's role.)
- Easily digested food and beverages
- Back rubs
- Shower; bath
- Thermal stimulation
- Walking; upright position
- Peaceful environment; dimmed lighting for resting
- Music
- Patience, forbearance; emotional support and encouragement
- Acceptance of how labor feels
- Surrender of your labor to God, remembering everything is in his hands

He [God] can see me—right there in His hand!

MOTHER TERESA

Active Phase: The Mother's Experience

Normally your cervix will have completed effacement (thinning out) and will have dilated from four to six centimeters. Your digestive processes slow down or stop, and you may be nauseated, burp frequently, or vomit. Your contractions become longer, often reaching peak strength and staying at peak longer, and the intervals between grow shorter (forty-five- to sixty-second contractions occurring every two to five minutes is normal).

You may want to be left alone and may feel like complaining. Try to be thankful instead! You will have to concentrate on pain relief measures and may want to change to a lighter, faster breathing pattern. You should remember to urinate every thirty to forty-five minutes.

You probably will go to your chosen place of birth at this time, and you may be given a synthetic hormone, Pitocin, to make the contractions stronger. Also, your membranes may be artificially ruptured to stimulate labor.

You'll find it more difficult to get comfortable, and it may become more uncomfortable to walk. (But remember, walking between contractions may stimulate the progress of labor.) You may talk less and need active labor support.

Active Phase: Husband's/Labor Companion's Role

At this point your wife may require your undivided attention. Encourage her to relax, especially between contractions. Support her through praise, encouragement, and firm direction.

Your wife may feel a need for privacy to work through this stage on her own; if so, respect that need. If she wants you there, have a comfortable chair near the bed so you can sit when possible. Consider starting relief measures such as back massages, offering ice chips, etc. Remind her to maintain breathing at the slowest rate possible (to save strength) and rhythmical (to prevent hyperventilation).

Keep her informed of her progress. Remember to ask for help from staff when needed. Keep the room as quiet as possible, minimizing distractions. Also, you may wish to ask a nurse or friend to step in for you if you need to take a break.

The pot knows the feel of the Potter's hands, but because it is not the Potter, it cannot fully fathom its Creator's mind.

JILL BRISCOE

Active Phase: Health-Care Provider's Role

The midwife will check fetal heart tones (baby's pulse); monitor the mother's blood pressure; perform vaginal checks to assess cervical effacement, dilation, and the descent of baby (station); help the mother and father relax; feel the fundus of the uterus through the abdominal wall (palpation of the fundus) to gauge the relative strength of contractions; recommend possible relief measures; keep the physician informed of the mother's progress, if applicable; inform parents of baby's condition and progress of labor; and make a record of the events taking place. The physician or midwife will evaluate the mother's condition and recommend and perform treatments as needed.

Active Phase: Relief Measures

- Prayer, music, Scripture verses
- Ice chips, cool washcloth
- Positive self-statements and affirmations; emotional support and encouragement
- Upright body position for gravity
- Frequent urination (every thirty to forty-five minutes)
- Massage of back, leg, pubic area, thighs, and/or abdomen; counter-pressure
- Change of position
- Extra pillows, blankets
- Quiet, soft music
- Thermal stimulation
- Use of focal point; auditory and visual distraction
- Clean bed linens and bed pad; clean, dry socks
- Lollipop; lip balm
- Fresh gown
- Quieting response; breathing techniques
- Analgesia (usually a low dosage of Demerol with Phenergan or Vistaril) or anesthesia (possibly a paracervical or epidural block)

Transition Phase

Transition is the term used to describe the third phase of the first stage of labor. This phase occurs between seven and ten centimeters dilation and involves the final stretching of the cervix over the baby's head (or presenting part).

Transition means to progress from one state to another. So in this phase you move from the first to the second stage of labor. Remember the example of pulling a tight turtleneck sweater over your head? At first your head enters the sweater easily, but as it nears the tight outlet, you must pull with greater sustained force.

During transition the uterus contracts for longer periods at shorter intervals to accomplish the final stretching. The contractions may be as long as ninety to one hundred twenty seconds with as little as twenty to thirty seconds between. You may well feel as though one contraction leads to another. Transition is completed when the cervix has stretched enough to allow the baby's head to pass through. The cervix width usually is about ten centimeters at this point.

For most women transition lasts for twenty to thirty contractions with their first baby and ten to twenty contractions for successive births. It's an especially difficult phase of labor due to the longer contractions and shorter rest periods and because the mother often is tired from the first two phases. Also, several other symptoms occur because of the tremendous physical effort needed in this stage. (See symptoms chart.)

COMMON TRANSITION PHASE SYMPTOMS

SYMPTOM	RELIEF MEASURES (for labor partners to perform)
Mood change (caused by fatigue, demands of accelerated pace of labor, little rest).	Remember the Lord's presence; play soothing music; give encouragement and reassurance; get help when needed; emphasize the goal; stay calm and be aggressive in offering help; read psalms aloud.
Withdrawal, resistance to helpers (caused by pain and lack of control).	Respect the effort involved in labor; stay positive; express acceptance of the mother's feelings; don't leave; just be more quiet; continue in prayer for wife and baby, out loud or in silence.
Trembling, shaking (caused by exertion of uterus, alteration of metabolism).	Gentle, firm, rhythmical massage; warm blanket; encouragement and reminders that this soon will subside.
Backache (caused by pressure of baby moving through pelvis, uterine activity, and position of mother).	Use warm or cool compresses; apply counter-pressure to affected area; use firm massage; help her assume appropriate position; offer reminders that the baby is approaching the birth canal.
Hot flashes (caused by increased activity of uterus and altered metabolism).	Remove clothing; close drapes and pull window blinds shut; place cool washcloths over body; lower room temperature if possible.
Cold extremities, chills (caused by decreased circulation to hands and feet due to uterine demand for increased blood circulation).	Provide clean, warm socks; fluff warm blanket over feet; raise room temperature if possible.

Dry mouth (caused by medication and/or breathing techniques).	Offer ice chips, lollipop, cool washcloth, lip balm; urge slower breathing—especially between contractions.
"I want to give up" attitude (caused by stresses, pain, and shorter rest periods in labor).	Use pain relief techniques; offer praise and prayer, active support, reassurance and encouragement; keep perspective—"not much longer"; administer analgesia in small doses, if desired, as long as the birth is not imminent.
Hyperventilation (caused by over-breathing or erratic patterned breathing).	Establish even rhythm to breathing by breathing with her; slow down breathing; have the mother breathe into a paper bag to restore her CO_2 level.
"Urge-to-push" reflex (caused by descent of baby into pelvis).	Have her do light breathing with quick puffs to release abdominals; ask physician to check dilation; have mother change to active pushing when given the okay.
Rectal pressure—similar to the urge to have a bowel movement (caused by baby's head compressing rectum while passing through pelvis).	Remind her that it's the baby, not a bowel movement; suggest that she fully release pelvic floor as pressure is felt; encourage by stating that the baby's birth is getting closer.
Pressure below pubic bone (caused by passage of baby under pubic bone.)	Massage over pubic bone area; apply warm or cool compresses; urge change of position; offer reassurance.
Cervical pain (caused by pressure of baby's head against cervix during last phase of stretching).	Urge conscious release of muscle tension; have her do faster, lighter breathing at peak of contractions; offer encouragement; possibly administer anesthesia to cervix (paracervical block).

NOTE: *While each of these symptoms is common, no one woman will experience them all!*

Promoting Labor Progress

Your labor may get off to a slow start, with intermittent menstrual- or flu-like abdominal cramping off and on for twenty-four hours or longer without really "kicking into gear." Or you may check into the hospital only to discover you are dilated to two or three centimeters, and then you labor for four hours or more with little or no change in the cervix.

To stimulate your labor's progress, try (or suggest your wife try) the following:

Relaxation. As much as possible, let go of your anxiety and tension; "give permission" to your uterus to do its work as you relax during and in between contractions.

Slow breathing. Slowing and deepening the breathing level supplies extra oxygen to working muscles and calms the central nervous system.

Quiet environment. Protect your privacy by asking others to minimize disruptions, play music softly, and turn overhead lights off. Keep things quiet with the lights dimmed for at least thirty minutes.

Warm bath or shower. If possible, soak in the tub or stand in the shower for a while to ease physical and/or emotional stress.

Walking. Walking is an excellent way to stimulate labor. It uses gravity in your favor by getting the baby's head down closer against the cervix, aiding dilation. Sitting upright on a bed or in a chair are also helpful labor positions for this reason.

Coping with Back Pain During Labor

Most women have at least some degree of backache sometime during labor. This pain may be temporary, or it may persist throughout labor. Often called "back labor," this back pain is caused by at least one of the following:

- The baby's head is large for your pelvis and exerts a great deal of pressure against the pelvis as it passes through.
- The back of the baby's head is toward your back and pressing against the back of the pelvis. This is a "posterior presentation."
- Your position is causing gravity to pull the baby's head down against your back.
- The baby's head is at an awkward angle as it comes through the pelvis.
- The wide ligaments anchoring the uterus to the lower back are stretched as the uterus contracts.

One way to help relieve back labor is through the mother's position. A side-lying position, in which the mother lies on either side propped with pillows, helps keep the weight of the baby off the back and makes the mother's back available for massage.

Standing, Indian-style sitting, and sitting upright have several advantages. An upright position in labor allows gravity to bring the baby's head closer to the cervix and can encourage dilation (see above). The baby's head is pulled into the pelvis rather than onto the back, and the mother can lean forward to receive back massage. Also, the bed can be raised to a ninety-degree angle for extra support.

In an all-fours position, the baby's weight is taken off the mother's back entirely. However, this position my be difficult to sustain with intense contractions.

Massage also may provide good relief from back pain during labor. A firm, low-back massage with steady rhythmical, repetitive movements can be done with contractions. Be sure to use oil, lotion, or cornstarch to reduce friction and ensure the smoothness of the massage.

If the baby's head is pressed against the mother's pelvis during contractions, it may help to provide counter-pressure by pressing inward against the pelvis at the place where the baby is pressing outward. Do this with the hand, forearm, a clean paint roller, or the foot (when you're too exhausted to use your hand or arm). A constant pressure exerted during contractions may help greatly.

Some women find that passive pelvic rock, rocking the pelvis between and/or during contractions while it is supported by a labor partner, provides relief. This technique mainly promotes relaxation of muscles connected to the pelvis. With the mother on her right side, the labor partner grasps the mother's hip bone with his left hand and places his right hand over the back of her pelvis, fingers pointing downward as they touch the tip of the mom's spine. As the mother gently rocks her pelvis, the labor partner presses downward when the pelvis tilts forward and relaxes his hand as the pelvis returns to its normal position.

Something the labor partner should keep in mind is that he needs to stay calm if he wishes to be of help to his wife during times of back pain. Backache in labor hurts a great deal, and it can be difficult to keep cool when supporting a woman who is hurting. Your presence, words of encouragement, and willingness to participate will be helpful even if she doesn't seem to notice your concern. Above all, remind her often of the final goal of labor, and keep her informed of her progress.

Medication for Back Pain. Many women find that back pain in labor is difficult to manage with noninvasive pain relief measures. In deciding whether or not you will benefit from pain relief medication during this time, keep the following in mind:

- Analgesic drugs given for pain relief during the first stage of labor are not anesthetics. That means they don't take away the pain. Rather, they act on the brain and encourage a feeling of apathy and nonconcern. The pain may stay intense, but you care less about it. Regional, or epidural, anesthesia used during the first stage of labor blocks pain perception by creating numbness along the nerves where it is administered. (See Appendix C for a discussion on the pros and cons of epidural anesthesia.)
- Analgesics can be counterproductive to women who want to stay alert during labor.

The tendency to doze off between contractions may make it difficult to use pain relief measures for the entire duration of a contraction.

- Analgesia may enable a very anxious or tense mother to relax, which can encourage labor to progress. Aggressive emotional support, however, can often have the same effect.

SECOND STAGE: GIVING BIRTH THROUGH ACTIVE PARTICIPATION

The Mother's Experience

In the second stage of labor, your cervix will have completed dilation, and your uterus will contract forcibly at the top (fundus) to press your child through the birth canal. The contractions will have changed in strength, length, and interval time.

Your efforts now change from release to expulsion, and from light breathing to concentrated pushing. Your position should allow as much comfort as possible while enabling you to work with gravity. You may feel a great urge to bear down with contractions. If so, listen to your body; it will help you know what kind of effort to make. If you don't feel like pushing, you may need more active labor support for direction.

As the baby moves down the birth canal, you may feel tremendous pressure on the pelvic floor. As the baby's head distends the pelvic floor, you may feel pressure on the rectum and a stinging sensation around the vaginal outlet. You will need to push into the sensation you feel, even if it is painful. In fact, you probably will feel that you've never worked as hard in your life before!

Husband's/Labor Companion's Role

Help the mother into an effective, comfortable position. Direct her actively in her breathing efforts through praise, encouragement, and reassurance. Watch for the baby, and inform the mother of anything you see happening.

Place your hand on her lower abdomen, just below her navel, telling her to "bulge out" this area into your hand as she presses down with her upper abdominal muscles. Support her physically during her pushing efforts. Remind her to release into the pressure, and ease any fears she might have concerning perineal tearing or having an involuntary bowel movement.

You especially need to encourage her to relax between contractions and follow her doctor's recommendations. Wiping her brow with a cool washcloth can help. Minimize distractions, keeping the room as dim and quiet as possible.

Health-Care Provider's Role

The nurse or midwife will continue the actions described for the active phase of labor, as well as check for progress of the baby as descent through the pelvis takes place. Then the physician or midwife will assist the mother during the baby's birth by supporting the perineum, making an incision if needed to prevent damage to this area. He or she will also be available to perform emergency treatment if needed.

Second Stage Positions

The mother's positions in the second stage of labor should be as follows:

Semi-sitting. Back of bed up, legs relaxed (open with supports), pelvis tilted forward, back of pelvis flat on bed.

Side-lying. Lie on side, curled forward with labor partner holding legs up. (This position is best if your baby is posterior.)

Kneeling. Keep bed upright and legs wide apart, resting against the bed between contractions. Hold self up by placing arms on knees during contractions.

Squatting. Support position with legs wide apart and bed upright.

Standing. Lean buttocks against edge of bed or table with physical assistance; used until baby "crowns."

Second Stage Efforts

Remember the angle of the baby's descent; push down . . . up . . . out. Also, actively release the pelvic floor upon feeling pressure, pushing into the sensation.

Relax the lower abdominal muscles, bulging the lower abdomen out. Contract upper abdominal muscles, using them as levers on top of the uterus.

Keep your eyes open, watching for the baby. And stop pushing upon feeling a burning sensation at the vaginal opening or upon doctor's orders.

Breathing

Use the following breathing techniques, testing to see what is most effective for you:

- Pushing with breath held briefly at bottom of throat. As the contraction begins, take a deep greeting breath. Take a medium breath for the second breath; hold it at the back of the throat and keep breath blocked for three to five seconds. Be sure to contract upper abdominal muscles to maximize your effort, keeping them taut between breaths.
- Light breathing for final expulsion. When the baby's head reaches the perineum, it is imperative that you push only when someone tells you to. Rather than breathing to enhance the work of the uterus, you must breathe to detract from the uterine effort. Just follow greeting breaths with light breathing or puffs of air (blow-blow breathing, see page 107). This allows your baby to be born less forcefully and helps you to prevent injury to your perineal area.

BLOCKED BREATHING FOR PUSHING

Inhalation

Exhalation shaded area symbolizes a contraction

A. Contraction begins.
B. Greeting breath.
C. Inhale medium-sized breath, blocked at base of throat by using the "glottis" muscle. Hold breath for no longer than 8-10 seconds while using abdominal muscles to push.
D. After 3-5 seconds, exhale breath quickly. Inhale and block next breath for 3-5 seconds. The mother does not release her abdominal muscles during this exchange of air, but continues to push throughout the contraction.
E. Contraction ends.
F. Completion breath and thanksgiving.
G. Resume normal breathing rate.

FORCED EXPIRATION FOR PUSHING

Inhalation

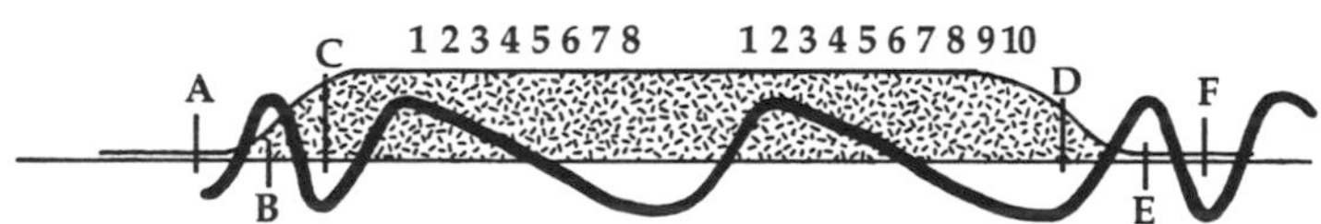

Exhalation shaded area symbolizes a contraction

A. Contraction begins.
B. Greeting breath.
C. Quickly inhale medium-sized breath; then slowly but forcibly exhale for 8-10 seconds. The breath should be somewhat blocked at the back of the throat, but the glottis muscle is partially open to allow air to pass slowly out of the lungs. Be prepared—this gets noisy, but birthing sounds are a sure sign of progress in birth!
D. Contraction.
E. Completion breath and thanksgiving.
F. Resume normal breathing rate.

THIRD STAGE: THE BIRTH OF THE PLACENTA

The Mother's Experience

During the third stage of labor, you will feel cramplike contractions of the uterus as it works to shed the placenta. Expect a certain amount of blood loss (approximately eight ounces total) as the placenta detaches and the uterus grows smaller in size.

Normally within five to fifteen minutes after the birth, you'll feel the placenta slide into your vagina, and you will push it out with your health-care provider's help. Occasionally chills and involuntary shaking due to hormonal and physiological changes will occur at this time.

If conditions permit, you can hold and nurse your baby immediately after giving birth. Don't be surprised if you feel relieved, exhilarated, and exhausted all at once.

You may receive an injection of the synthetic form of the hormone oxytocin, called Pitocin, through your IV or in your upper arm. Oxytocin causes contractions of the uterus and diminishes the flow of blood from the placental site. This hormone also is produced when the baby nurses at the breast.

Your baby will be checked and given an Apgar score based on his color, reflexes, breathing, heart rate, and muscle tone. This score is determined at one, five, and ten minutes of age. The five categories can receive zero to two points each, with ten being a perfect score. Initial scores of seven or above are considered normal. A score of six or below indicates that your baby requires medical assistance.

Husband's/Labor Companion's Role

Now is your time to participate in the first moments of the baby's life outside the womb through touch, picture taking, celebrating, and praising the mother for her effort on her baby's behalf. Help the mother hold her baby as soon as possible, and enjoy this time together.

When the mother is experiencing the expulsion of the placenta, help her maintain her breathing rhythms.

Health-Care Provider's Role

The nurse will administer oxytocin (Pitocin) upon request of the midwife or physician during this stage of labor. She also will assist with the delivery of the placenta if necessary, give the baby Apgar scores, and otherwise evaluate the baby's adjustment to extra-uterine life, encourage the mother to relax and bond with her child, and provide warm blankets as needed.

The physician or midwife will assist the mother in delivery of the placenta, monitor blood loss and the state of the uterus following the birth, and provide medical assistance to the baby if necessary.

Relief Measures

- Maintain as upright a position as possible.
- Relax your pelvic floor to facilitate the birth of placenta.
- Use light or counted breathing if cramps are felt.
- Focus your attention on the baby.
- Cooperate with your physician's or midwife's efforts to assist you with the placenta.
- Use prayer, praise, and Scripture to thank God for his help.
- Nurse your baby, if possible, to encourage your uterus to contract as well as for you to marvel at your newborn child.

FOURTH STAGE: A TWO-HOUR TRANSITION PERIOD

The Mother's Experience

During this two-hour stage, you will continue to feel cramps or "after pains" while the uterus contracts. Your blood pressure and pulse will be checked frequently to determine how your body is adjusting after your baby's birth.

Your episiotomy, or any tears, will be repaired with sutures, and you probably will be given a local anesthetic (if it wasn't administered during late second stage). You will be moved—or you may walk—to a labor or recovery room (if you had your baby in a delivery room), and you may find you are quite hungry and thirsty.

The fundus of your uterus will be checked and massaged if necessary. Also, your blood flow will be monitored.

Your emotions will be varied, and you may or may not feel like making phone calls or receiving visitors. Interact with your baby and nurse as you desire (if your baby is doing well).

Husband's/Labor Companion's Role

During the fundal massage, remind the mother to use light or counted breathing. Be sensitive to her reactions to the birth and to her continued need for companionship and support. Encourage her to interact with the baby.

Health-Care Provider's Role

The nurses will assist the physician or midwife with the repair of the episiotomy, provide appropriate care for the baby, evaluate the mother's and baby's progress, monitor the physical status of the mother, perform fundal massage, adjust medications as needed, bring the mother food and beverages as desired, and inform the physician or midwife as to the mother' progress.

The midwife or physician will examine the cervix, vagina, and perineum and make repairs as needed. She also will monitor the mother's condition (usually based on the nurse's reports) and perform procedures or prescribe medications as needed.

Relief Measures

- Rest and relax.
- Use patterned breathing for cramps and fundal massage.
- Get a clean gown and socks.
- Shower.
- Consume food and beverages as desired.
- Have uninterrupted closeness with the baby, if possible.
- Use an ice bag for swollen perineum.

Self-Check Quiz for Labor

Take this quiz after you have read chapters 5 through 8 and have practiced the techniques you have learned. For the greatest benefit, use the quiz as a "rehearsal" for labor during late pregnancy.

Prelabor and Early Labor

- What signs are associated with prelabor?
- How are Braxton-Hicks (prelabor) contractions different from labor contractions?
- How will you know labor is beginning?
- You awaken at 4 A.M. and use the toilet. On the tissue you notice a bloody vaginal discharge. How might you respond?
- How do you think you'll feel when your labor begins?
- You begin having menstrual-like contractions in the late afternoon. What will you do?
- What types of foods and beverages might be ideal (easily digestible) for prelabor and very early labor? What activities safely stimulate labor?
- As labor begins, what will you expect your labor partner's role to be? What kinds of comfort measures might be useful?
- At what point will you begin breathing patterns? Which type will you use?

Things to Do

- Practice breathing patterns for early labor.
- Rehearse early labor contractions with relaxation, breathing, and attention-focusing.
- Review hospital admission procedures from your tour.

Active Labor

- How may the quality of your labor change between cervical dilation of four and six centimeters?
- What feelings and reactions are typical for this phase of labor?
- How will you know when to change breathing patterns and which ones to use?

- What procedures may be done at this time? According to your health-care provider, what medications may be offered?
- What can you do for dry lips and mouth? Cold feet? Backache?
- How can your labor companion help you to relax, especially between contractions?
- You have been in labor for twelve hours and are dilated three centimeters. Your doctor decides to stimulate your labor. What might he do?
- Your membranes rupture spontaneously. What can you expect to happen, and how might you respond?
- Your back has hurt since the beginning of labor, and you feel the contractions mostly in the lower back area. What can be done?
- Your fingers and lips feel tingly. What's happening, and what can be done?
- Your labor is moving very rapidly, and the contractions are very intense. How can you cope, and what can your labor companion do to help?

Things to Do

- Practice breathing patterns for active labor.
- Review positions and pain relief measures for basic labor.
- Practice contractions in which you become tense and breathe erratically. Have your labor companion coach you in alleviating tension and anxiety.

Transition

- You are irritable and tired, and your legs are shaky. What's happening? How might you cope? What other symptoms are common in this period of labor, and what comfort measures might be used?
- What can your labor companion say and do to help during transition?
- You have an urge to push but are not fully dilated. What can you do to alleviate this?

Things to Do

- Practice breathing patterns and relief measures for transition.

Pushing and Birth

- How might your mood change during pushing? What will happened to the quality of your contractions?
- What physical sensations are associated with the second stage of labor?
- You will be asked not to push but just to give a series of small pushes. Why?

Things to Do

- Practice pushing.
- Practice breathing for crowning and birth.
- Try several positions and breathing techniques.

OVERVIEW OF PHYSICAL ADJUSTMENTS AFTER BIRTH (POSTPARTUM)

Uterus

During pregnancy the amount of muscle fibers and blood carried in the uterus increases as it expands. After the placenta separates from the lining of the uterus (during the third stage of labor), contraction of the muscle fibers must take place to close off the open blood vessels where the placenta was attached. This causes the uterus to reduce in size drastically and to sink into the pelvic cavity.

These contractions or "after pains," which continue as the uterus breaks down and reabsorbs unneeded muscle cells, are most intense while breastfeeding or if Pitocin is given. They occur with greater intensity after each successive child. Conscious release and breathing techniques may bring comfort. Pain medication, such as Tylenol 3 or Darvon, may be taken if cramping is severe.

Just prior to your baby's birth, your uterus is under your ribs and weighs about two pounds. After the placenta is expulsed, your uterus is below the navel and is about the size of a large grapefruit. It stays this size for about forty-eight hours. By the third day, your uterus begins to decrease in size and weight until it reaches its normal size, about six weeks after the birth.

Lochia

This bloody discharge begins to flow after the third stage. It is made up of blood and debris (such as shed muscle cells) from the uterus. Most of this discharge comes from the place where the placenta was attached. This site usually takes between six and seven weeks to heal completely. The discharge color changes from bright red during the first few days to a reddish-brown and then turns yellow-white around the eight or tenth day, becoming watery before ceasing. Sanitary napkins are preferable to vaginal tampons since they allow the discharge to flow more freely and pose less risk of infection.

The amount, rate, and duration of the flow of lochia varies between women and between subsequent pregnancies. At first, because of the accumulation of lochia while lying flat, the flow may become heavier as you stand after resting. The red lochia may persist for longer than a week, or it may occur only off and on. If the flow lasts more than twenty-one days or becomes heavy enough to soak a sanitary napkin in an hour, call your physician.

If the flow tapers off and then gets heavier, you may be doing too much too soon. Try resting more and taking it easy with activities such as housecleaning and lifting. Another way to deal with a bout of heavier bleeding is, if breastfeeding, to put the baby to the breast—if he will cooperate.

If you pass blood clots, it needn't be cause for alarm. As long as a clot is not followed by persistent, bright red bleeding and if you don't pass clots for a period longer than six hours, the clot usually is just blood that has coagulated. However, if either of the two conditions mentioned occur, call your physician.

If the lochia develops a foul odor, is accompanied by vaginal itching (not associated with the healing of the episiotomy), and/or has a green or frothy appearance, get in touch with your doctor. These may be indications of an infection that needs treatment.

Finally, do not douche without your doctor's consent. External cleansing of the perineal area normally is sufficient.

Breasts and Nipples

Your breasts undergo several changes during pregnancy in anticipation of lactation. There is an increase in blood and lymph fluid to that area, and the amount of glandular tissue increases. Small bumps develop in the areola (pigmented area around the nipples), which secrete a fatty substance that helps moisturize and protect nipples from infection.

After your baby is born, the breasts stay the same size for the first few days. The process of lactation, however, is triggered at the time the placenta separates from the uterine lining. During this period, before milk is produced, your baby receives a concentrated liquid called colostrum. This is made in the breasts during the latter part of pregnancy. It is high in antibodies, a laxative, and helps to break up mucus in the baby's digestive tract. There is no substitute on the market for this remarkable substance.

The breasts usually undergo engorgement, or marked swelling, as the milk "comes in" on the second to fourth day. For women who choose to bottle-feed, engorgement may be a problem even though a lactation suppressant probably will be administered. If this happens, most likely engorgement will last twenty-four to forty-eight hours.

Usually the milk supply will diminish if the baby is not nursing. Liquid intake may be reduced to aid in this process, although it's important to drink some fluids throughout the day. Ice packs may be put on the breasts for ten to fifteen minutes every few hours, and the breasts may be bound firmly with a towel.

Nipple care is covered in chapter 3 and should be followed if you wish to help your nipples adapt to nursing. Cleansing of the nipples with warm water can be done and is especially helpful during the first few days as secretions of colostrum dry and collect on the nipple.

Abdominal Wall

Similar to a corset, if the abdominal wall is stretched for a prolonged period of time, it tends to lose its resiliency. After your baby's birth, your abdominal muscles will feel quite loose and will not complete the process of returning to their normal state for about six weeks.

If it has lost its tone, the abdominal wall may remain less firm than you might want even after that time. The section on basic pregnancy fitness exercises in chapter 3 gives several easy toning exercises for this area. These exercises can be started soon after giving birth, if desired. They may be followed up by a more strenuous program with your health-care provider's consent after your six-week checkup.

When you go to the hospital, be sure to take a pair of loose-fitting (or maternity) slacks to wear when you go home. It may take you awhile to fit into your regular clothes, though this is not always the case. Try to remember that your body has several weeks (up to two months) of recuperating to do, and it's best not to expect too much too soon.

Vagina, Genitalia, and Related Structures

The vagina is a muscle membrane that, due to hormones, softens during pregnancy in preparation for giving birth. It stretches considerably during a vaginal birth, and it remains slack until it reduces in size during your recovery. Pelvic floor exercises hasten healing of this area and help you regain muscle tone after giving birth. See the section on the pelvic floor (chapter 3) for discussion of the significance of these exercises.

The lips around the vagina, the *labia minora* and *labia majora,* also stretch considerably during a vaginal birth. Occasionally they have surface lacerations due to the stretching, which may sting during urination. Try to lean on the toilet seat so that the flow of urine is directed away from the burning. The lips may stay somewhat flabby after the birth.

Other structures that undergo changes are the oviducts (fallopian tubes), ovaries, and the suspensory ligaments that support them. After being stretched during pregnancy, they will resume their normal position in the pelvic cavity in the weeks following the birth. Likewise, the cervix is soft and flabby right after birth. By the end of the first week, its opening narrows, and the cervix firms up.

In general, by the sixth week after your baby is born, much healing has taken place, and you've nearly completed the cycle of parturition, or giving birth to your child.

Weight Loss

The average amount of weight lost immediately after giving birth is twelve pounds, though this varies from woman to woman. The twelve pounds include a seven-pound baby, a one- to two-pound placenta, one to two pounds of amniotic fluid, and two pounds of body fluid and blood. Additional weight may be lost by the end of six weeks when the uterus resumes its usual size and body fluids return to normal.

The main variables seem to be the amount of fluid retained during pregnancy due to high sodium concentrations and the amount of fatty tissue stored by the body. If needed, talk with your doctor about a moderate weight-reduction plan at your postpartum checkup.

Energy Level

You may find that you become tired easily during the weeks while your body is returning to its pre-pregnant condition. Fluctuations in hormone levels, the stress of healing, and being up with the baby are a few of the factors leading to fatigue in new mothers.

During the first few weeks, it's important to try to sleep when the baby's sleeping, keeping in mind that your body is working at healing itself. If you cooperate with this process by getting good nourishment, plenty of liquids, and sufficient rest, then you probably will encounter fewer roadblocks on your way to recovery.

Other Things to Consider

Hemorrhoids. Some women are affected by hemorrhoids, the enlarged blood vessels that may protrude as the anus distends during the pushing stage of labor. If you have them, you must avoid straining while having a bowel movement, since that can aggravate the condition.

The pain and itching of hemorrhoids can be helped by soaking in a sitz bath; applying special ointment; pressing them back into the rectum with a clean, lubricated fingertip followed by up to ten minutes of contracting the anal sphincter; and/or applying an anesthetic cream or gauze pad (such as Tucks), which is premoistened with soothing liquid or witch hazel.

You probably will experience a decrease in this problem within two weeks following the birth. If not, make sure your physician examines you at your postnatal checkup.

Constipation. You may not have a bowel movement until the second or third day after giving birth. The intestines seem to be less effective in moving substances, and you may have been thoroughly "cleaned out" by an enema prior to the birth.

Drink lots of liquids to make the first bowel movement easier. Raisins, prunes, bran, and other laxative foods can be eaten to enhance the process. If you're afraid of putting pressure on the healing perineum, wash your hands thoroughly and place a clean gauze pad on the perineum for support as you have your bowel movement. Stool softeners are readily available as an additional remedy.

Hair Loss. Due to hormone levels during pregnancy, many women gain extra body hair. This diminishes during the first few months after giving birth. Hair loss from the scalp is common; it usually takes place from four to six months after the birth and should not last more than two weeks.

Review of Normal Problems and Helps

PROBLEM	**HELP**
Fatigue	Good food, rest—especially when baby rests
Chills after birth	Warm blanket
Backache	Slow breathing, pelvic rock, massage, heat
Body aches	Warm shower, heating pad
Mood swings	Talk about how you feel and accept your feelings
After pains	Relief techniques, pain medication
Change in color of lochia back to red	Take it easy
Sore perineum, itching	Ointment, sitz baths, pain medication, gauze pads soaked in witch hazel
Numbness or bruises in area where IV was placed	Warm, wet compresses
Abdominal wall flabbiness	Curl-ups, tightening, pelvic rock, leg sliding
Engorgement, leaking breasts, sore nipples	Prop towel or cotton pad under breasts, air dry, change position often

Postpartum Symptoms: Notify Your Doctor

- Temperature over 101° F.
- Chills
- Bad-smelling vaginal discharge
- Severe headache
- Faintness, dizziness
- Vaginal bleeding soaking more than one pad per hour over a couple of hours
- Heavy gush of red blood from vagina after flow has tapered off or changed color
- Passage of several clots accompanied by heavy bleeding
- Severe back, abdominal, chest, or leg pain
- Burning with and increased frequency of urination
- Reddened area in breast that feels sore and hot (especially when accompanied by fever and flulike symptoms)
- Any other symptom your doctor tells you to report

GRAPHIC LABOR CHART

(This chart may be copied and used during your labor as a general guide. Feel free to adapt it to your own birthing pattern.)

STAGE	ONE		
PHASE	Early	Active	Transition
WORK DONE	Cervical effacement and dilation. Baby moved deeper into pelvis		
CONTRACTIONS A) DURATION	15–30 seconds 5+ seconds	30–60 seconds 20+ seconds	60–120 seconds 40+ seconds
Intensity and Peak			
B) LENGTH APART	20+ min. to 5 min.	5 min. to 2 min.	2 min. to 30 seconds
DILATION (cm)	1 2 3 4	5 6 7	8 9 10
APPROXIMATE DURATION	40–50% (4–8+ hrs.)	30% (2–6+ hrs.)	10% (30 min.–1½ hrs.)
POSSIBLE BREATHING PATTERNS			
Description of Pattern	Slow Light	3:1 2:1	1:1 Blow-blow
RELIEF MEASURES	Release, relax, and rest Back massage for relaxation Nourishing liquids Use most comfortable position Begin deep breathing if anxious or tense	Urinate often Ice chips, lollipop Counterpressure, passive pelvic rock, and low back rubs (active and transition phases)	Perspective: Last part is hardest but shortest Adapt breathing to contractions Eliminate fear; accept what is happening
(REMEMBER: Position is important!)	Get professional help if needed Warm shower Cuddle with labor partner	Dim lights Change breathing as contractions intensify Warm compresses Praise and encouragement Medication if desired	Get professional help whenever it's needed Remember: Your baby is almost here! Socks for cold feet Blow out to relieve urge to push

STAGE		ONE	
PHASE	Early	Active	Transition
WHAT'S HAPPENING (You may experience a variety, but not all of these symptoms.)	Loss of mucus plug likely Soft b.m.'s Low backache Crampy feeling in lower abdomen Effacement of cervix Membranes may break	Baby moving deeper into pelvis Contractions progressively longer Digestion slows down Nausea, vomiting Backache	Leg shaking Irritability; mood change Decreased desire to talk Nausea, digestive disturbance Hot or cold flashes Rectal and back pressure Early urge to push
EMOTIONAL RESPONSE	Excited Anxious Unsure it's the "real thing" until examination	Greater concentration on use of comfort measures Concern, determination Increased dependence on labor partner and health-care providers	Introspective, withdrawn May feel discouraged, panicky, fed-up Stress reaction: anger, crying, etc.
SPIRITUAL RESPONSE	Praise Thanksgiving Perspective Prayer and Scripture throughout entire labor	Control of thought patterns Avoid fear and anxiety by setting your mind on "things above" Contemplate word pictures from Scripture	Total dependence on the Lord's strength Call upon the name of Jesus Ask for the Lord's help
STAGE	TWO	THREE	FOUR
WORK DONE	Birth	Expulsion of placenta and membranes	Involution of uterus begins
CONTRACTIONS A) DURATION	45–90 seconds 30+ seconds	45–90 seconds	30+ seconds
Intensity and Peak			
B) LENGTH APART	1–2 min.		sporadic
DILATION (cm)	Complete	Cervix closes after birth as uterus contracts	
APPROXIMATE DURATION	10–20% (10 min. to 2+ hours)	5–20 min.	45–60 min.

STAGE	TWO	THREE	FOUR
BREATHING PATTERN			
Description of Pattern	Forced expiration / Breath block	Crowning—Blow out or slow pant	After birth—Slow
COMFORT MEASURES	Push down, up, and out Eyes open. Look for baby! Release perineum and lower abdominals Utilize upper abdominals Rock pelvis back to lift baby forward Release and pant for crowning Local anesthetic for episiotomy	Hold your baby and and enjoy the fruit of your labor Give slow push for placenta Focus attention on baby for repair of episiotomy and use slow or pant-blow breathing, if needed Nurse baby if he/she wants to suck	Warm blankets Juice, food—birthday cake! Hold and nurse baby Slow breathing for massage and contractions Urinate Ice bag for episiotomy may help Pads for lochia (vaginal discharge after birth)
WHAT'S HAPPENING (You may experience a variety, but not all of these symptoms.)	Pressure in vagina and on perineum Back pressure Rectal pressure Strength of urge to push varies Baby moves onto soft tissue and is born! Deep guttural sounds result from pushing	Expulsion of placenta and membranes Repair of episiotomy Baby given Apgar scores; initial exam May hold baby for first time Separation of placenta signals onset of lactation	Recovery room Vital signs checked Uterus checked and massaged if necessary Blood flow is checked Breastfeeding is beneficial to both mother and baby at this time
EMOTIONAL RESPONSE	Complete involvement with work being done Rest periods; withdrawn, sleepy, attempting to conserve energy Disbelief that cause of pressure is baby's head	Awe, exhilaration, relief, gratitude Concern for baby's wellbeing Irritable about repair of episiotomy, post-birth	Many different feelings arise; both parents are emotionally sensitive Accept the way you feel, even if it isn't all positive
SPIRITUAL RESPONSE	Draw on the Lord's strength Be thankful for the new life about to be born	Praise Thanksgiving Give the glory to God	Pray for your new baby Rest in the Lord

First and Second Stage Activities: Your Record

Use this form to take notes in class or to keep notes from this book.

First Stage

Early Phase (1-3 cm)

Quality of contractions

Physical manifestations

Comfort measures and stimulation of labor

Companion's role

Signs indicating medical attention is needed

Active Phase (4-6 cm)

Quality of contractions

Physical manifestations

Routine procedures/possible alternatives

Sources of discomfort/comfort measures

Companion's role

Nurse's or midwife's role

Transition Phase (7-10 cm)

Quality of contractions

Physical manifestations

Sources of discomfort/comfort measures

Companion's role

Nurse's or midwife's role

Second Stage (pushing)

Quality of contractions

Physical manifestations

Sources of discomfort/comfort measures

Options for birth

Companion's role

Nurse's role

Doctor's or midwife's role

Positions attempted during practice

1.

2.

3.

How they felt

Breathing: Which feels best? Are you confident in your body's ability to tell you what to do?

Other considerations

Pushing is good for your baby if this stage isn't overly long. The contractions that occur while your baby passes through the birth canal squeeze fluid and mucus from your baby's breathing passages and stimulate the surface of your baby's skin.

PSALM POWER

Be sure to add your own favorites to the following list of powerful psalms to be used during pregnancy, birth, parenting—and the rest of your life.

Psalm 4—deliverance
Psalm 16—refuge
Psalm 18—salvation
Psalm 20—protection, help, support
Psalm 23—Shepherd, sustenance, shelter, safety
Psalm 27—Savior, safety
Psalm 32—forgiveness, protection, deliverance
Psalm 51—repentance, restoration
Psalm 61—shelter
Psalm 62—rest, refuge
Psalm 63—help
Psalm 67—blessing
Psalm 84—blessing, shelter, strength
Psalm 91—covering
Psalm 101—help
Psalm 117—faithfulness, love
Psalm 121—protection, provision
Psalm 139—searching, knowing
Psalm 142—safety, deliverance, refuge
Psalm 145—compassion

SCRIPTURAL REFLECTIONS AND PROMISES

For I am the Lord, your God, who takes hold of your right hand and says to you, Do not fear; I will help you.

ISAIAH 41:13

Therefore let everyone who is godly pray to you while you may be found; surely when the mighty waters rise, they will not reach him. You are my hiding place; you will protect me from trouble and surround me with songs of deliverance.

PSALM 32:6-7

In him and through faith in him we may approach God with freedom and confidence.

EPHESIANS 3:12

Answer me when I call to you, O my righteous God. Give me relief from my distress; be merciful unto me and hear my prayer.

PSALM 4:1

But those who hope in the Lord will renew their strength. They will soar on wings like eagles; they will run and not grow weary, they will walk and not be faint.

ISAIAH 40:31

Because you are my help, I sing in the shadow of your wings. My soul clings to you; your right hand upholds me.

PSALM 63:7-8

So do not fear, for I am with you; do not be dismayed, for I am your God. I will strengthen you and help you; I will uphold you with my righteous right hand.

ISAIAH 41:10

TEN

HANDLING THE UNEXPECTED

So do not fear, for I am with you; do not be dismayed, for I am your God. I will strengthen you and help you; I will uphold you with my righteous right hand.

ISAIAH 41:10

During childbearing many things can come up unexpectedly, from having a girl (when you really wanted a boy), to going three weeks past your due date (when the doctor said you'd be three weeks early), to more serious complications involving the baby or you. With the many factors interacting to make each labor and birth unique, it just isn't possible to predict with 100 percent accuracy what will take place. Unexpected things have a way of happening to all of us.

Medical complications of any kind during pregnancy or childbirth can be both physically and emotionally trying. Whenever possible, try to avoid comparing yourself to women you know who have had uncomplicated pregnancies and births. Remember, Jesus is with you every step of the way, and he will give you everything you need to meet the particular challenges you face. Reread the parts in chapters 2 and 3 that present ways to strengthen your heart, mind, and family relationships by drawing closer to the Lord.

SPECIFIC SITUATIONS

The following situations, though far from common, can occur during birth. I hope you will find the suggestions here helpful and informative and that you will use them as a part of your birth preparation. This way, should you find yourself experiencing any of these situations, you will be able to better understand and cope with them.

Many of these conditions are reasons for having a baby by cesarean (see chapter 11); all warrant medical or professional care. For a more thorough discussion of these conditions, talk with your health-care provider.

Premature Labor

The premature infant is one born before the thirty-eighth week of pregnancy. In more than 50 percent of premature births, no specific cause of prematurity is identified. A low-birth-weight infant may be any gestational age, but weighs less than five and a half pounds at birth. Babies in these two categories may have similar problems in adjusting to life outside the womb.

Babies born before *term* (thirty-nine to forty-two weeks) generally have greater difficulty handling the stress of labor, an immature digestive tract, poor self-regulation of body temperature, and poor absorption of oxygen due to a less developed respiratory tract.

Fortunately there are many neonatal intensive care units (NICUs) in regional centers throughout the country. These units are equipped to provide an environment for preterm infants who need oxygen, temperature-controlled surroundings, and special feedings to help them survive. Also, medical technological advances in recent years have increased preterm infants' chances of survival. Two of the newest branches of medicine, neonatology and perinatology, have developed to promote the survival of high-risk babies.

You will be more likely than other women to experience premature labor if you have any of the following risk factors associated with prematurity and low-birth weight:

- malnutrition
- cigarette smoking
- alcohol and drug abuse
- high blood pressure (maternal hypertension)
- diabetes
- multiple gestation (more than one baby in the womb)
- teenage pregnancy
- placental insufficiency

If your labor begins prematurely, your health-care provider will likely hospitalize you to track your contractions and the baby's heart rate closely. You will also be prescribed bed rest and adequate fluid intake; medication may be given to help quiet your uterus. If the contractions slow down sufficiently, you will be discharged from the hospital and continue your treatment at home. Restriction of sexual activity, including nipple stimulation, will be advised. When you reach thirty-six to thirty-seven weeks' gestation, your treatment will likely be discontinued so your pregnancy can take its natural course.

If the membranes rupture spontaneously, the possibility of infection may necessitate hospital admission and close medical supervision. Your physician will weigh permitting labor to take place or performing a cesarean to avoid infection against the risks of prematurity. Concern about the risk of such an infection starts twenty-four hours after the membranes break.

In premature labor, *electronic fetal monitoring* (EFM) permits a continuous readout of the baby's heart rate. If labor contractions seem to affect the baby's well-being adversely, a cesarean birth will be advisable. Analgesics or anesthetics during labor or the cesarean birth will need to be selected in light of your baby's needs.

Should the treatment to stop premature labor be unsuccessful, your baby will probably need to be admitted to an NICU where you'll be encouraged to spend time with your newborn. (This may require your baby's transfer to a different hospital, depending on the level of care required.) You can provide the necessary factor of tender love and care in the midst of a stressful, sterile environment of IVs, blipping monitors, and concerned medical teams. Also, in many cases your breast milk may be used to feed your baby, rendering benefits unattainable from any other source.

We don't come out of the womb devaluing love.

JOHN TOWNSEND

I once asked the head nurse of the NICU at the hospital where I worked what helpful advice I could share in this book with expectant parents who might be faced with having a baby early. Mary, a Christian, responded, "Tell them to put their trust in the Lord. That's the single most important piece of advice I can offer." I agree!

Post-term Labor

When a baby is overdue (born more than two weeks past the due date), he may be *postmature*. Between 6 and 12 percent of babies carried longer than forty-two weeks are served by an "aging" placenta, one that is beginning to shut down. When placental function is impaired, the danger to the baby is increased.

A postmature infant may be larger than average, making vaginal birth more difficult. Your health-care provider will likely use a fetal monitor at this point to observe the infant's response to motion and/or simulated labor to help determine which procedure would be best. To facilitate the birth, your labor may be induced artificially through intravenous administration of Pitocin if your baby is considerably overdue; if labor would be too stressful for you or your baby, a cesarean birth will be recommended.

Difficulties with the Placenta

The placenta is a temporary gland that develops from the initial cluster of cells that join together at the time of fertilization. This gland secretes the hormones that maintain the pregnancy after the early weeks of gestation. Your baby's nutritional and excretory needs are met through a complete exchange of substances that takes place through the placenta, which is normally attached to the lining of the uterus until the third stage of labor.

Usually the placenta is attached to the upper portion of the uterus on the front (anterior) or back (posterior) uterine wall. Sometimes, however, it adheres to the lower part of the uterus, covering the cervix. When it is attached between the baby and the cervix, it is called a *placenta previa.* This condition may be suspected if you experience vaginal bleeding during your pregnancy and can be confirmed via diagnostic ultrasound. Placenta previa is a serious condition that may necessitate bed rest during your pregnancy, the avoidance of sexual intercourse, and even hospitalization. This condition occurs in about one out of 300 pregnancies.

The safest method of delivery for the baby when the placenta is covering much of the cervix is a cesarean section. The reason is that the baby's source of oxygen will be restricted if the placenta begins to detach prior to your baby's birth as your cervix dilates during labor.

Another placental condition, where the placenta begins to separate from the uterus before the baby is born and breathing on his own, is referred to as an *abruption of the placenta*, or *abruptio placentae.* Symptoms of placental separation include vaginal bleeding and sharp abdominal pains. Immediate delivery by cesarean is normally advisable. This condition can be caused by malnutrition, shortness of the umbilical cord, elevated blood pressure, overly long (*tetanic*) labor contractions, or grand multiparity (a woman who has had more than five babies). Placental separation occurs in about one percent of all labors, with varying degrees of severity in the abruption.

PREGNANCY WARNING SIGNS REQUIRING MEDICAL ATTENTION

Warning Signs	**Possible Causes**
Cramping; persistent uterine contractions (intermittent abdominal tightening), especially if accompanied by low backache and/or diarrhea, if experienced before 36 weeks' gestation	Miscarriage; preterm labor
Abdominal pain; continuous, painful abdominal firmness	Tubular (ectopic) pregnancy; appendicitis; miscarriage, preterm labor; placental separation (abruptio placenta); tetanic (overlong) contractions
Vaginal bleeding	Miscarriage; preterm labor; placenta previa; placental separation
Sudden rush or leaking of fluid from the vagina (prior to 36 weeks)	Premature rupture of membranes
Fever—body temperature greater than 100° (38° C.) when taken orally	Infection
Conspicuous reduction in baby's activity level	Fetal distress

Painful urination	Urinary tract infection (U.T.I.); sexually transmitted disease
Unusual vaginal discharge or itching; genital sores	Vaginitis caused by bacteria or yeast (*candida albicans*); sexually transmitted disease
Dizziness, light-headedness	Low blood pressure, especially upon lying down (supine hypotension); preeclampsia
Severe, persistent headache	Preeclampsia
Blurred vision	Preeclampsia
Spurt in weight gain (more than 2 pounds in a week or 6 pounds in a month) or sudden swelling of the face, feet, or hands	Preeclampsia
Persistent vomiting	Infection; *hyperemesis gravidarum* (excessive pregnancy-related vomiting)
Painful, reddened area in leg	Inflammation and blood clot(s) in a leg vein (*thrombophlebitis*)

Large Baby, Small Pelvis

When a discrepancy exists between the size of your baby's head and the size of your pelvic passageway, it is termed a *cephalopelvic disproportion*, or CPD. CPD may be diagnosed through the use of ultrasound or by doing an X-ray pelvimetry, in which the distance between the bones in your pelvis is determined through measurement on X-ray films. This diagnosis occasionally is made prior to the onset of labor, but more commonly it's done after some labor has taken place without the baby sufficiently moving down into the pelvis. True CPD is rare.

Upright positioning and walking during labor will encourage the descent of the head when there is adequate space and should be used to promote the progress of labor. These techniques also can help borderline, but not absolute, disproportion.

Difficult Position

When a baby presents his buttocks, feet, shoulders, face, brow, or chin toward his mother's cervix, his birth through the vagina may be difficult or even impossible. For this reason, your health-care provider should check for your baby's position during prenatal visits.

If your health-care provider finds that your baby is in a breech position, she may suggest exercises to encourage the baby's rotation—by elevating your hips for a certain length of time each day. In some cases, health-care providers will attempt to manually "turn" the baby to a headfirst position before the child descends into the pelvis. If the baby does not change position, a cesarean may be required.

You are my refuge and my shield; I have put my hope in your word.

PSALM 119:114

Multiple Pregnancy

Having a multiple pregnancy requires a greater focus on providing yourself with adequate nutrients, appropriate exercise, and plenty of rest. Multiple births are more likely to be accomplished via cesarean section, unless the size and position of twins allows for their safe passage. Triplets and quadruplets often are born prematurely and invariably are delivered by cesarean.

Sharing the uterus means sharing oxygen, nutrients, and space. As a result, babies born together may be of lower birth weight and have a greater tendency to be born preterm. Positioning can be awkward, making passage through the pelvis trickier. Cord problems are not uncommon, and the mother may be more likely to experience high blood pressure and swelling. The risks to both the mother and baby may be reduced substantially through proper prenatal care. The incidence of twins being born among whites in the United States is about one in every ninety-three births; among nonwhites it's one in seventy-eight.

Premature Rupture of Membranes

Most health-care providers recommend that mothers be checked or enter the hospital after the bag of waters breaks. If you're unsure whether the baby is well engaged in the pelvis when this happens, you should lie on your side as much as possible until the baby's position is checked. This is because the cord may descend ahead of the baby when some of the fluid escapes, interfering with the baby's oxygen supply.

When the amniotic sac breaks, it may feel a bit like an internal balloon popping. There is a release of fluid from the vagina and some relief of pressure. It's important to check the color and odor of the fluid, making certain it is clear and fairly odorless.

Occasionally the baby will have had a bowel movement in reaction to stress, and the fluid will have flecks of stool in it or be a dark greenish color. This condition, called *meconium staining*, occurs in about 11 percent of all births. Meconium staining requires the baby's breathing passages to be thoroughly cleaned after birth, usually through a catheter, to prevent him from inhaling any of the irritating fluid into the lungs. Many physicians also recommend that the baby's heart rate be monitored continuously during labor if meconium is present in the amniotic fluid.

Slowly Progressing Labor

Many labors get off to a slow start, and a woman may labor for eight hours or more without any change in the cervix. If you feel your labor needs to begin or to be stimulated, you might try the following:

- Relax your body; don't resist labor. Let your uterus do its work and avoid tensing in response.
- Create a quiet environment with guaranteed total privacy for at least thirty minutes.
- Take a warm bath or shower to encourage relaxation if your membranes, or bag of waters, haven't broken yet.
- Identify and overcome any fears or inhibitions you have about giving birth.
- Walk or sit upright if you're not confined to bed. Walking is a fabulous way to stimulate labor. It gets the baby down against the cervix, exerting greater pressure on it to open up. Sitting upright on your bed or in a chair will help, too.
- Breathe slowly and deeply, as if you were sleeping. Slowing down and deepening your breathing will get extra oxygen to your baby and working muscles.
- Massage your nipples by pulling them out rhythmically and intermittently (one minute on, one minute off) to mimic a baby's sucking, or use an electric breast pump. Recent studies in Israel have demonstrated that nipple stimulation is effective in starting or augmenting labor because the hormone oxytocin is secreted when the nerve endings in the nipples are stimulated. Oxytocin works on two main areas—uterine muscle fibers and cells in the breast that contract to eject milk from the glandular cells where it is stored. The Lord made our bodies so that when a baby nurses in the days after birth, the uterus will contract to close up the wound left by the placenta and thereby reduce bleeding. Nipple stimulation prior to the baby's birth also contracts the uterus and can enhance or induce labor.

Your health-care provider also can do several things to induce labor:

- Administer an enema to promote contractions and the evacuation of the lower intestines. (This may be self-applied at home, but check with your health-care provider first.)
- Artificially rupture the membranes. This commonly used procedure, called *amniotomy*, makes contractions stronger and may make labor more productive.
- Intravenously administer Pitocin. When medically required, and if the above measures are ineffective, uterine contractions may be induced using Pitocin, the synthetic form of oxytocin. If this, too, proves unsuccessful, the baby will be delivered by cesarean. Inductions should be performed only in a hospital setting under obstetrical supervision.

Most health-care providers want the baby, if full term, to be born within twenty-four hours after the membranes have ruptured. There is an increased likelihood of infection for the mother and baby after this period of time.

Maternal Complications

Several health concerns can become aggravated during pregnancy. Your body must adapt in many ways during gestation, and these changes can aggravate health concerns that existed before the pregnancy or even initiate new conditions related to the pregnancy itself. Following are some conditions that may require special care throughout pregnancy and that often make a cesarean birth necessary for the safety of both mother and baby:

- diabetes
- anemia
- vaginal bleeding during pregnancy
- lung, kidney, or heart disease
- genital herpes infection
- narrow pelvis or pelvic infection
- high blood pressure
- incompetent cervix
- previous cesarean birth (vertical incision)
- mother's age being under eighteen or over thirty-five
- malnutrition
- Rh blood incompatibility between maternal and fetal blood
- preeclampsia, eclampsia, and toxemia

Should any of these conditions exist, it is even more important to eat balanced meals and follow the Daily Food Plan in Appendix A. Find a physician you feel comfortable with who can closely monitor your pregnancy. Adequate rest and relaxation will be essential to help your baby grow.

MEETING THE CHALLENGE OF UNEXPECTED EVENTS

Almost every labor has its panicky moments. Here are some ideas for coping if something unexpected happens to you.

While It Is Happening

Stay calm. Present your requests to God, petitioning him in prayer (Phil. 4:6). The Lord is with you and will strengthen you as you cope with your feelings of disappointment, anger, or loss. He truly is the "God of all comfort" (2 Cor. 1:3).

Accept your feelings. Don't be ashamed of the way you feel; the Lord understands. David honestly expressed many of his feelings, and so did Abraham, yet remember how much the Lord loved them. Their faith in God drew them to him for answers to their questions.

Get accurate information. Don't be afraid to ask questions. Be involved in what's going on so that you can better understand how you can help, what can be done, and what the true outlook is.

Pray for those caring for you. Pray that the Lord will guide the hands and thoughts of your health-care providers. Ask him to help them make the best possible decisions and use appropriate treatments for your situation.

Picture Jesus as being "in the same boat" with you. Remember the story of Jesus calming the storm when in the boat with his disciples? Call on his name and trust him to answer you with his calming presence.

Afterward

Don't isolate yourself. Remember: Others have experienced similar situations, so you are not alone. Other parents have lived through what you are experiencing, many of whom are willing to offer support and information. Avoid denying the benefits of allowing others to reach out to you. Ask for a referral from your health-care provider or your church.

Keep your options open. Don't make irreversible decisions. The more critical the situation, the greater the psychological stress—so try to get all the facts before making any ethically complex decisions (e.g., termination of life support systems). Ask your pastor to pray with you if you feel overwhelmed by the circumstances.

Allow time to heal your hurt. Whenever loss is experienced, whether loss of hopes or loss of a life, emotional hurt is produced. Such wounds cannot be healed by doctors. Only God, through time and the help of capable people, can heal in this area.

Don't compare. Your birth or baby may not fit your picture of what is ideal. It's natural to compare, but keep in mind that each situation is unique. Try not to compare your experience with what you may consider normal. Instead, be attentive to what the Lord would have you learn from your situation.

Realize that any loss brings grief. Grieving is a process marked by a variety of emotions including disbelief, denial, sorrow, loneliness, anger, depression, physical manifestations of stress, irritability, frustration, upset in interpersonal communication, restlessness, fantasy, disorganization, and a desire to talk about what is causing the grief.

> *It is of the nature of man to feel pain, to be moved by it, to resist it nevertheless, and to accept consolations, but never to have no need of them.*
>
> JOHN CALVIN

Normal grief is a process that runs its course and eventually leads to restoration of well-being. Complicated grief that becomes prolonged, intensified, or delayed can prevent a person from dealing with life productively. Because of this, the person suffering such a grief may benefit from professional counseling or pastoral care. Read Psalm 77:1-15 and 86:1-7 to discover a picture of the reality of grief and of reliance on the Lord.

Seek pastoral or professional support as needed. Don't hesitate to ask for help. There are times when even the strongest among us needs ministry. If your relationship with the Lord or with those around you has been disrupted, don't let things become even more complicated by refusing to accept professional help. Seek help compatible with your beliefs, and make a sincere effort to follow recommendations you are given.

Try to get adequate rest and avoid substances that aggravate stress. It's impossible to feel clearheaded if the need for sleep and balanced meals is neglected. Avoid excessive caffeine intake, nicotine, and sugary foods that promote nervousness. Instead, drink herbal teas with honey and lemon, or try Postum; buy nutritious, easy-to-fix foods.

Realize that placing blame won't help or change the situation. The chances are good that everyone involved in your situation did his or her best, and no one is at fault. Don't waste your precious energy and thoughts on blame or guilt.

Make peace with the Lord. You may never know why things happened as they did. Accept the fact that God heard your prayers, knew your desires and expectations, and answered them in this way for reasons that only he can understand. Be honest with your feelings, presenting them to him and allowing him to help you work through them. Let him be your help and support, as he has promised.

SCRIPTURAL REFLECTIONS AND PROMISES

> *God is our refuge and strength, an ever-present help in trouble. Therefore we will not fear, though the earth give way and the mountains fall into the heart of the sea, though its waters roar and foam and the mountains quake with their surging. There is a river whose streams make glad the city of God, the holy place where the Most High dwells. God is within her, she will not fall; God will help her at break of day. Nations are in uproar, kingdoms fall; he lifts his voice, the earth melts. The Lord Almighty is with us; the God of Jacob is our fortress.*
>
> PSALM 46:1-7

> *Surely God is my salvation; I will trust and not be afraid. The Lord, the Lord, is my strength and my song; he has become my salvation.*
>
> ISAIAH 12:2

> *The righteous cry out, and the Lord hears them; he delivers them from all their troubles. The Lord is close to the brokenhearted and saves those who are crushed in spirit.*
>
> PSALM 34:17-18

> *Let us then approach the throne of grace with confidence, so that we may receive mercy and find grace to help us in our time of need.*
>
> HEBREWS 4:16

> *We wait in hope for the Lord; he is our help and our shield. In him our hearts rejoice, for we trust in his holy name. May your unfailing love rest upon us, O Lord, even as we put our hope in you.*
>
> PSALM 33:20-22

ELEVEN

ENCOUNTERING CESAREAN BIRTH

"Because he loves me," says the Lord, "I will rescue him; I will protect him, for he acknowledges my name. He will call upon me, and I will answer him; I will be with him in trouble, I will deliver him and honor him."

PSALM 91:14-15

Cesarean section is the term applied to an operation in which a baby is born through incisions made in the abdominal wall and uterus. This method of delivery, also called C-section or cesarean birth, is used when a vaginal birth is considered too difficult or risky for the mother and/or her baby. Though cesarean rates vary with location, almost one in four births are by cesarean section in the United States today—nearly a five-fold increase since 1970.

The rate of cesarean delivery in the United States is among the highest for developed nations. Because increased risks for maternal death and susceptibility to disease are associated with cesarean delivery, a national health objective for the year 2000 is to reduce the overall rate to less than or equal to 15.0 per 100 deliveries (1987 baseline: 24.4 per 100 deliveries) (objective 14.8)—a level last observed in 1978. This report uses data from CDC's National Hospital Discharge Survey (NHDS) to characterize cesarean deliveries during 1993, compares these rates with rates for 1970-1992, and assesses progress toward the national health objective for the year 2000 (*Morbidity and Mortality Weekly Report* [MMWR], April 21, 1995, 44 [15]:303-07).

In recent years numerous maternal health-care providers and organizations have publicly advocated a reduction in current cesarean rates, calling for both parents and professionals to become better educated about ways to safely lower the number of surgical births. Without question, cesarean birth offers a sound medical solution where real danger exists in childbirth. But it has also been estimated that at least one-third of all cesareans are not medically necessary.

It isn't difficult to understand why the rate rose so quickly during the 1970s and 1980s. Cesarean section is a relatively safe surgical procedure a physician can use to quickly resolve a wide variety of labor complications, including prolonged or difficult labor. Yet when an absolute indication for a cesarean birth doesn't exist, there are a number of disadvantages to consider when thinking through this decision: Cesarean birth increases the mother's risk of developing complications from anesthesia, infection, and hemorrhage; lengthens her hospitalization and recovery period; causes more postpartum pain; and is considerably more expensive than vaginal birth.

It makes good sense for expectant parents to do what they can to both prevent *and* prepare for a cesarean birth—to reduce risks that have been demonstrated to contribute to higher cesarean rates and to learn what takes place during surgery and recovery if a cesarean is needed. Either way, your informed participation will enhance your ability to care for yourself and your new baby.

All created things are living in the hand of God. The senses see only the action of the creatures, but faith sees in everything the action of God.

JEAN-PIERRE DE CAUSSADE

INDICATIONS FOR CESAREAN SECTION

Your doctor may recommend you have your baby by cesarean section if any of the following situations exist:

- Fetal malpresentation or malposition. Your baby's position in the uterus makes a vaginal birth difficult or even impossible.
- Cephalopelvic disproportion (CPD). Your baby's head is large, your pelvis is too small, and/or the baby's position prevents passage of the baby's head through your pelvis, preventing a vaginal birth from taking place.
- Fetal distress. Abnormal heart rate patterns or other tests of your baby's well-being demonstrate a need for surgical delivery.
- Maternal disease. Diabetes, heart disease, preeclampsia, active genital herpes, amnionitis (infection of the amniotic sac, usually following the premature rupture of membranes), or another condition you are currently experiencing makes a vaginal birth medically inadvisable for you and/or your baby.
- Prolapsed cord. In this uncommon situation, the umbilical cord passes through the cervix before the baby descends, causing the baby's head (or presenting part) to place pressure on the cord and threatening his or her oxygen supply, indicating immediate delivery by cesarean.
- Placenta previa or placental abruption. (See chapter 9.)
- Prolonged labor (also called uterine dystocia, or "failure to progress"). When contractions are of poor quality, the cervix is not dilating, and/or the baby is not descending through your pelvis, cesarean birth may be medically indicated if alternative methods of promoting labor do not help or cannot be used.
- Previous cesarean birth. Your doctor will advise another cesarean if you have had a previous cesarean birth and your current condition warrants repeat surgery.

Ways to Avoid an Unnecessary Cesarean

Before Labor

Select your health-care provider and place of birth carefully.
Invite your husband (and, if possible, an experienced friend or professional labor assistant) to accompany you through labor and birth.
Weigh the benefits and risks of using electronic fetal monitoring, pain relief medications, and other birth interventions.
Become informed about cesarean prevention. (See Resources.)

During Labor

Pray—for patience, wisdom, strength, help, protection.
Employ upright positions for rest and relaxation.
Walk.
Relax and rest as fully as possible between contractions.
Breathe and consciously release your body during contractions.
Use noninvasive pain relief techniques.
Employ electronic fetal monitoring, pain relief medications, and other birth interventions judiciously.
Maintain your perspective.
Welcome your baby's efforts to be born.

FATHER-ATTENDED CESAREAN BIRTH

The news that a cesarean needs to be performed does not necessarily mean that your planning and the father's anticipation of being involved in the baby's birth has been in vain. Many hospitals will allow a father to attend his child's arrival by cesarean under certain conditions. (Understandably, in an emergency situation, many hospitals prefer to have the father wait outside the operating room.)

This decision rests primarily with the anesthesiologist, because the surgery requires regional or general anesthesia, which is administered and monitored by a specialist. The attending obstetrician will perform the surgery; the anesthesiologist will safeguard the response of the mother to the anesthetic and the surgery. The anesthesiologist "rules the roost," so to speak, and must feel comfortable in order to perform his or her job.

The following conditions normally are used as criteria for permitting a father's presence during surgery:

- The father should be prepared for what to expect through prenatal classes, a film or videotape, or by talking directly to the labor nurse, obstetrician, or anesthesiologist.
- He should assess his ability to be involved in a medical situation.
- The mother often is required to be awake during the birth if the father is to be present.
- The father should be of good health and free of infectious disease.

If you, the father, are allowed to stay during the birth, you will be at the head of the table to talk to and touch your wife. At this point, your role is to assure your wife, encouraging her to think of the end result and reminding her to relax by using the level of breathing appropriate to her tension level. Your emotions probably will fluctuate between apprehension and anticipation, so remember that the Lord is with you both. Recall the Scriptures you used to prepare for the birth and pray frequently.

It is becoming standard practice to have a father hold his baby as soon after she is born as possible. The father, mother, and their new child often are able to spend ten to twenty minutes together if all is going well. After this, the father might accompany the baby to the nursery and be included in the baby's care. Once the mother's surgery is over, the family may get back together in the recovery room as conditions permit.

If you can't be present for the birth, you will be shown where to wait for about thirty to ninety minutes. Occasionally fathers are allowed to be in the hall outside the operating room and can hold the baby almost immediately after birth. Otherwise you will be notified when you can see the baby in the nursery. If possible, you will be reunited with your wife in the recovery room. If you and your wife haven't been with the baby yet, you might ask if the three of you could be together.

Preparing for Surgery: The Father

There are many things you as a father can do in preparation for being present during the cesarean birth. Be sure to eat a light, "nongreasy" meal an hour or two before the surgery. This will help you feel less queasy during your wife's surgery.

Remember to focus on your wife and the Lord during the entire procedure, not on the other people in the room. It's easy to become fascinated or nervous because of all the activity. Just keep in mind that you are there to give spiritual and emotional support to your wife and to say hello to your newborn child.

Help your wife relax by praying with her and reminding her that the Lord is near. Maintain body contact with her throughout the time you are there: Hold her hand, stroke her cheek, give her a few kisses, place your hand on her head.

These things will convey your concern and affection and will help alleviate your wife's anxiety during her surgery. Also, share your excitement about the baby's birth with her. She will benefit from knowing how proud you are of her and how you feel about the baby.

Pay attention to any requests the hospital staff may make. Take slow, deep breaths if you begin to feel light-headed or nauseated. Don't watch procedures that make you feel faint—and remember to relax. Ask questions if you don't understand what's happening or are uncertain where you should be.

You may trust the Lord too little, but you can never trust Him too much.

ANONYMOUS

Preparing for Surgery: The Mother

As you go through this experience, remember to relax, concentrating on the Lord and all you have learned in preparation for your child's birth. If you feel afraid or anxious, share your feelings with Jesus, laying your burdens at his feet. Try to pray, continually thanking and praising God for watching over you, remembering that you are not alone.

If your husband is present, listen to what he is saying. Respond to his voice, touch, and his love for you. Touch your baby as soon after birth as possible, sharing that love and joy with this new child you have labored together to bring into the world.

Immediately after the baby's birth you may feel nauseated or uncomfortable. You also may not feel like interacting much until after the anesthetic wears off and you are on a more mild form of pain medication. Don't worry about this. Your first responsibility is to help your body cope with the surgery. Don't try to live up to an imagined ideal of the perfect birth and bonding experience. Just be yourself and follow the Lord's lead.

WHAT TO EXPECT

Preliminaries

If you know ahead of time that you will have a cesarean, you may want to talk with others who have had the same experience. Generally the decision for first-time cesarean births (primary cesareans) is made during labor when the need arises. Once the choice of performing a cesarean is made, the following procedures will take place before the surgery:

- Admission and surgery consent forms are signed.
- Blood and urine samples are taken, and weight and vital signs are taken and recorded.
- Fetal heart tones are monitored.
- Your medical history is taken, and a physical may be done.
- You and your anesthesiologist will discuss the type of medication you will have and its effects. If you have a preference, discuss this to determine whether or not it would be suitable for your situation. Now is the time to bring up any questions. Carefully consider the pros and cons of the anesthesia available to you.

Before the Birth

Just before the surgery a small, narrow tube or catheter is placed through the urethra to the bladder so that urine may be continuously drained, keeping the bladder out of the way of the surgery. Insertion prior to the administration of the anesthetic may be somewhat uncomfortable. Use a focal point, conscious release, and slow breathing. Push out as you feel the tube being inserted.

You may or may not be given preoperative medication to help you relax. If an IV hasn't been started, it will be begun with a solution of sterile water, salt, and basic sugar. The IV will also be used to administer other medications, fluids, and blood when necessary. Arm boards will be attached to the operating table on which to rest your arms. (Sometimes one arm is fastened securely onto the table. If this is done, you may want to request that it be released so you can touch your baby following birth.)

Your blood pressure will be monitored during surgery, so the cuff will be put on your arm. Also two discs will be attached to your chest to record your heartbeat. Your abdomen will be draped with sterile sheets, and a screen will be placed at your shoulders above your breasts to keep you from contaminating the sterile field (this also blocks your view of the operation). A loose-fitting cap will be placed on your head to cover your hair.

You will be given an anesthetic either to numb your body from just above the top of your uterus down or to put you to sleep. You may be given extra oxygen during surgery through a mask placed over your nose and mouth.

General Anesthesia: Loss of Consciousness

Pros

- The mother is asleep and unaware of the surgery.
- Total pain relief.
- Little risk of fetal depression resulting from the anesthetic, if given properly.
- The obstetrician may find the operating room condition more suitable.
- General anesthesia is preferable in certain situations such as in an emergency when the mother's blood pressure is low.

Cons

- The mother is asleep and unaware of the birth.
- The husband is not allowed to be present.
- Drug depression of baby is more common with general anesthesia than regional anesthesia.
- Changes in mother's heart performance occur related to intubation.
- May be difficult with intubation of mother.

Regional Anesthesia: Loss of Sensation from the Torso to the Feet (Mother Remains Conscious)

Pros

- Mother is awake and experiences the birth.
- Little risk of drug depression for baby.
- Risks related to intubation are avoided.
- Less chance of aspiration.
- Partner may be present under certain circumstances.

Cons

- Mother is awake and aware of the surgery.
- Anesthetic sometimes does not take effect as it should, resulting in inadequate block of sensation. More anesthetic may be required.
- Mother's blood pressure may be lowered.
- Chance of postspinal or epidural headache.
- May be situations when regional anesthesia can't be used (emergencies, low blood pressure, etc.).
- Regional anesthetic may affect the mother's breathing.

The Birth Itself

A cesarean section takes forty-five minutes to over an hour to perform. Incisions are made in the skin, abdominal muscles, lining of the pelvic cavity, and the uterus. The incision on the uterus will be about six inches long and will be vertical (classical) or horizontal (*pfannenstiel*). The membranes are ruptured, and the amniotic fluid is suctioned out. Then the baby is lifted from the abdominal cavity, and the umbilical cord is quickly clamped. It takes approximately ten minutes from the beginning of the surgery to reach this point.

The repair of the uterus and the abdominal walls, which takes the most time, is begun by removing the placenta and administering an oxytocin drug to stimulate uterine contractions. (Vaginal discharge and afterbirth contractions are the same as after vaginal birth, so be certain to read the section describing these occurrences on pages 129-130.)

Flexible rooming-in (which may require a private room) will allow you to choose your rest times and the extent of contact with your new baby. Your husband can visit at any time and can help you with the baby and in moving around.

Use ample pillow support over the abdomen or lie on your side to feel relaxed and comfortable when you breastfeed your baby. If the baby seems to be sleeping because of the medication you received, gently stimulate her back and soles of the feet while making certain she isn't so bundled up that it's producing extra drowsiness.

Mood swings in the first few days are common, especially if you feel disappointed about not giving birth vaginally or if your husband was not able to be present during the birth. Share your feelings with your husband and the Lord as you work toward resolving them.

Recovery

The IV is kept going after the surgery and probably will be left in for twenty-four to forty-eight hours to fight infection and provide fluids and energy. The catheter will be removed after about twenty-four hours, too. If you find it difficult to urinate, drink plenty of fluids once you are able and use your pelvic floor release exercise.

Discomfort in the shoulders may be due to the accumulation of blood and air under your diaphragm, irritating the nerves going to your shoulders. Pain medication can be adjusted to your needs, but be sure you are informed as to what you are being given and why. If you're breastfeeding, ask which drugs will be safest for you to use. While drugs may help reduce pain, some may make it hard for you to feel up to being with your baby.

Get up and walk as soon as possible. This will stimulate your processes of digestion and elimination. Support your incision with both hands at first, taking short steps. Try to stand tall, even though you'll feel like swaying and shuffling. You may feel pain and pulling at the incision; extra support will help, and each time it gets easier. Discomfort from the incision will be noticeably less each day and will have decreased significantly by the seventh or tenth day. Any involuntary movements of your abdominal muscles may hurt. If you anticipate a cough, sneeze, or laugh, support the incision with your hand.

Gas pains signal the return of digestive function, and until then you won't be allowed to eat solid foods. You will be on a liquid diet until gas is passed. Try lying on your side with the underside leg bent and the leg on top straight or in the Sims'-lateral position to get rid of gas. Movement also helps. Avoid carbonated beverages and apple juice.

MAKING RECOVERY EASIER AFTER A CESAREAN BIRTH

In the Hospital

As soon as the blood flow is less heavy, use beltless sanitary pads. Tampons may be used with your doctor's approval.

Get up and walk as soon as allowed. You will find it gets easier each time, and you'll feel better with the improved circulation. A small wedge heel on your slippers will help you to stand and walk more comfortably the first few days.

Crawl into your bed on all fours to avoid using your abdominal muscles. Use slow breathing to help calm yourself, relieve tension, and deal with discomfort. You may find sleeping on your stomach more comfortable during this time.

Select nutritious meals and eat as soon as you are allowed. This gives you more energy and helps you regain your strength. A reducing diet can be started by avoiding foods high in calories and low in nutrients. After six weeks you may lower your calorie intake to help shed unwanted pounds, as long as you have your doctor's approval.

Before leaving the hospital, make sure your doctor discusses your limitations and postbirth care. If your husband can be present, it will help him plan how to help you at home. Ask questions freely so that small concerns don't grow. Have things explained to your satisfaction. Also, acknowledge and accept your feelings. Don't allow others to dismiss your joy, anger, pain, or insights. You feel as you do for a reason.

Keep visitors during the first few days to a minimum. Each day will bring renewed strength, more energy, and a brighter outlook. Visitors are entertaining, but they also can be exhausting.

Because the human body heals faster after childbirth than at any other time, recovery following a cesarean birth is amazingly quick if there are no complications. Postsurgical pain has a reason: If you keep your hurting abdominal muscles inactive, you help them to heal. The discomfort will seem greatest as you doze off and wake up, but take heart: This pain will subside soon. Talk things over with your husband, but realize that he can't meet all your emotional and physical needs. He's tired and adjusting, too. Learn to rely on close friends, a relative, your pastor, and especially on the Lord, as well as your husband.

Trust in him at all times, O people; pour out your hearts to him, for God is our refuge.

PSALM 62:8

Tips for Dad While at the Hospital

You can help your wife after a cesarean birth by keeping her lips moist with ice chips, a cool cloth, and fluids when these are allowed. Help her to sip (but don't use a straw). Other small but important ways to help would be freshening her pillow by turning it over, brushing her hair, giving her a gentle back rub, and adjusting her bed position (sometimes raising her knees helps to relax the pelvic region).

Realize that your wife will be tired at first. Encourage her to rest. If you help her change positions, be careful not to pull on her IV or catheter tubing. Help her use slow breathing by placing your hands on either side of her chest along the ribs and having her breathe expansively into your hands several times. Rotate her feet at the ankles to improve circulation. You might also consider spending the night if your wife is in a private room and your presence seems helpful.

When You Get Home

Forget about the housework. Rest with your feet up as much as possible for at least two weeks. Fatigue is your number-one enemy, so be ruthless about getting rest.

Prepare simple meals before you go into labor and freeze them. There are many put-it-in-all-at-once meals that taste great and involve little time or expertise. Stock up on canned goods and juices. Buy lots of paper plates and cups, and don't worry about messes around the house. Don't neglect to take your prenatal vitamins daily; boosting your protein intake may be helpful as well.

Store a small pillow in the car to place under the seatbelt while your incision is still tender. At night keep a nightlight on in your room. Bring your baby in with you and keep her in a bassinet or cradle nearby, with diapers next to your bed and a pitcher of ice water and a glass at your bedside. Night care of your baby will be much easier this way. If this is disturbing for Dad, maybe he can sleep in another room temporarily.

Finally, remember to pamper yourself, making sure you have at least ten minutes completely to yourself every day. Don't feel guilty about the time you spend unwinding and relaxing—we *all* need some quiet time alone every day, especially when getting used to the new demands of parenthood.

BODY CONDITIONING EXERCISES AFTER CESAREAN BIRTH

(Be certain to talk to your health-care provider before doing any of these exercises.)

The First Three to Seven Days

Breathing to Clear Lungs of Mucus. If a general anesthetic was used, your lungs may collect some mucus due to the slowing of your breathing rate. Expand your chest with two breaths as follows: Breathe in, filling your abdomen up with air; then breathe out, flattening the abdomen. Next place your hands under your armpits and breathe in, expanding the chest wall sideways.

Foot Movements. To increase circulation, the following exercise should be done several times a day (discontinue if you are up and walking throughout the day). Hold legs out straight or bent at knees over a pillow. First, bend and stretch your feet at the ankles for sixty seconds. Then rotate your ankles in circles for one additional minute.

Leg Bracing. To increase circulation in your legs and prepare for walking, put your legs out straight with your ankles crossed. Tighten all the muscles in your legs, press your knees down, and squeeze your buttocks together. Hold for two to three seconds, and then relax.

Bend and Straighten Knees. To prepare for walking, lie on your back with one leg bent at the knee and the other leg straight. Slide the heel of your bent leg down the bed and then back to its starting position. Repeat with the other leg. This can be varied by bending and straightening your legs alternately, working them at the same time.

Abdominal Tightening. Relieve discomfort of trapped air (gas pains) and stimulate sluggish intestinal activity by lying on your back side with your knees bent. Flatten the lower back by contracting abdominal and buttock muscles. Contract the muscles on a breath out and then relax on a breath in.

After Ten to Fourteen Days

Tailor Sit. Relieve back strain by sitting with your legs bent, knees falling outward. Keep your back slightly rounded, allowing the muscles in your back to relax. (See chapter 4 for more exercises.)

It's my hope that the information in this chapter will help guide you through what can be a very difficult and trying situation. Use this material as a supplement to the medical and pastoral care you receive. And, in all situations, always remember that the presence and protection of the Lord are with you; he is more than able to sustain you through tough times.

SCRIPTURAL REFLECTIONS AND PROMISES

> *He who dwells in the shelter of the Most High will rest in the shadow of the Almighty. I will say of the Lord, "He is my refuge and my fortress, my God, in whom I trust." Surely he will save you from the fowler's snare and from the deadly pestilence. He will cover you with his feathers, and under his wings you will find refuge; his faithfulness will be your shield and rampart. If you make the Most High your dwelling—even the Lord, who is my refuge—then no harm will befall you, no disaster will come near your tent. For he will command his angels concerning you to guard you in all your ways; they will lift you up in their hands, so that you will not strike your foot against a stone.*
>
> PSALM 91:1-4, 9-12

> *By day the Lord directs his love, at night his song is with me—a prayer to the God of my life.*
>
> PSALM 42:8

> *Give ear to my words, O Lord, consider my sighing. Listen to my cry for help, my King and my God, for to you I pray. In the morning, O Lord, you hear my voice; in the morning I lay my requests before you and wait in expectation.*
>
> PSALM 5:1-3

TWELVE

Teaching Your Baby About Love

And he said: "I tell you the truth, unless you change and become like little children, you will never enter the kingdom of heaven. And whoever welcomes a little child like this in my name welcomes me."

MATTHEW 18:3,5

Where did you come from, baby dear?
Out of the everywhere into here.
Where did you get your eyes so blue?
Out of the sky as I came through.
What makes the light in them sparkle and spin?
Some of the starry spikes left in.
Where did you get that little tear?
I found it waiting when I got here.
What makes your forehead so smooth and high?
A soft hand stroked it as I went by.
What makes your cheek like a warm white rose?
I saw something better than anyone knows.
Whence that three-cornered smile of bliss?
Three angels gave me at once a kiss.
Where did you get this pearly ear?
God spoke, and it came out to hear.
Where did you get those arms and hands?
Love made itself into hooks and bands.
Feet, whence did you come, you darling things?
From the same box as the cherubs' wings.
How did they all just come to be you?
God thought about me, and so I grew.
But how did you come to us, you dear?
God thought about you, and so I am here.

GEORGE MACDONALD

My initial glimpse of our first child stirred up many emotions in my heart. I was overcome with a sense of awe that two small cells had become our baby. At the same time, I felt the incredible weight of responsibility for her new life falling right between my shoulders. I was amazed at how much a part of her I was while at the same moment realizing that she was a person I had never met before.

I marveled at the smoothness of her skin as I stroked her back, still covered with its protective creamy coating called vernix. I wanted to wrap her up and snuggle her close, knowing that the world she had just entered was full of danger and sin as well as life and joy. I shed tears of concern while grinning with happiness. Birth is a bittersweet experience, I found—an amazing moment when heaven and earth collide in a profusion of possibilities, hopes, and expectations.

How could I teach Joanna about Jesus? Would she come to trust him as her own Lord and Savior someday? Would she question me as I had questioned my own mother? Who would she become? What did life have in store for her? There was no way to answer most of these questions. Only time would reveal what the patterns and rhythms of life would bring to my daughter.

Jesus' mother, Mary, was probably aware of these same concerns as she held her baby boy and nurtured him during the early years of his life. In Luke we read: "Mary treasured up all these things and pondered them in her heart" (Luke 2:19). Mary had no way of knowing what lay ahead. She had to trust the Lord day by day, and we must do the same.

When your baby is born, you will discover what it means to trust the Lord in a new way. Your love for your new daughter or son will teach you to rely more deeply on the Lord day by day. Opening your heart to love this brand-new person will involve risk-taking, personal growth, and an abiding faith in the sovereignty of God the Father.

> *The greatest happiness of life is the conviction that we are loved—loved for ourselves, or rather, loved in spite of ourselves.*
>
> VICTOR HUGO

WELCOMING YOUR BABY

Your baby can learn about Jesus from the first moment of life. By loving and accepting your child, you will demonstrate in a tangible way what the Lord has done for you. You can affirm your baby right away through touch, warmth, words, eye contact, and milk. In saying, "I'm thankful you're here!" and "I will take care of you," you tell yourself as well as your infant you accept him and will meet his needs as well as you can. As you do so, your baby will listen to the tone of your words, feel the timbre of your voice, and will recognize you immediately. He has heard you for many months, since the sense of hearing normally develops prenatally.

The sooner you touch and talk to your baby after birth, the better. The reason for this is that the Lord has designed healthy newborn babies to be quietly alert for two to three hours after birth. If a mother is not heavily medicated and the baby is doing well, these hours can provide a very special opportunity to get acquainted "face to face." Many women find that they experience a surge of energy after an uncomplicated birth and are anxious to begin mothering their baby as soon as possible.

You may want to touch your baby as he emerges from your body, still warm and slippery with vernix and amniotic fluid. While this does not appeal to all women, some mothers are exhilarated by the first sight and touch, regardless of how moist the baby is. You may request that the baby be wrapped loosely in a blanket for holding if you are uncertain about keeping a sure grip otherwise. The routine initial care of the baby can be performed entirely "in arms" if you desire. Although this is now a common practice in many birth centers and hospitals, it's still a good idea to discuss it with your physician or midwife in advance.

As you greet your baby for the first time, remember that he already knows your voice and can see the shape of your face; your baby's mouth is the most sensitive place on his body, and his sense of touch signals your presence; he sees you best from a distance of about twelve inches—the distance between him in your arms at chest height and your face; and you can "talk" to your baby with your eyes, your hands, and your milk as well as by your voice.

I am completely convinced of this wonderful gift: *God made babies to be lovable!* Although they can be exasperating at times, babies thrive on a mother's milk and the tender loving care expressed through cuddling, rocking, singing, bathing, stroking, and keeping the baby nearby. A baby's needs and wants seem to be inseparable until later in the first year of life. The Lord expects us to respond to our baby's needs for food, protection, warmth, and physical affection throughout every day and night. (Why else would he have designed them to nurse at least every two to three hours?)

Babies who receive an inadequate amount of physical affection can become victims of a syndrome described as *failure to thrive*. Earlier in this century, it was discovered that institutionalized infants could actually die of a disease called "marasmus," caused by not being held. The practice of keeping babies in cribs, infant seats, and playpens for hours on end so as not to "spoil" them is not based on a factual view of the needs of infants. Rather it is the result of following the theoretical teaching, advice, and writings of secular behavioral psychologists from the late 1800s onward, who popularized the fear of spoiling. *Be wary of any author, psychologist, or health-care professional who offers a one-size-fits-all approach to solving the highly personal challenges of mothering, regardless of how "biblical" their teaching may sound.*

You will need to find a balance between meeting your baby's needs while meeting your own needs and those of other family members. Finding this balance takes time as you listen to your heart—and your baby. Still, it's possible to keep your baby close by, hold your baby often, and have everyone happier as a result. Why? Because satisfied babies cry less, and their mothers find it easier to relax when they receive God's built-in mothering rewards.

KEEPING YOUR BABY CLOSE

Unless there is a medical reason for your baby to be out of your sight, it really makes sense to keep your baby near you. This encourages the continuing development of the bond between the two of you that began while the baby was still inside your womb.

The process of attachment, or bonding, is not as automatic as it might seem. If the baby is the "wrong" sex (not what you were hoping for), ill, fussy, overly active, or generally not what you expected, the bond can be strained. *Togetherness fosters attachment, and attachment fosters a mother's ability to take care of her baby.* The father's presence is included here as well, even though breastfeeding is God's gift to the mother alone.

Rooming-in is available at most hospitals for the purpose of encouraging families to be together during the first few days after birth. Some couples opt to go home after four to twenty-four hours because they feel they can relax, adjust, and recover better in familiar surroundings. The usual postpartum stay is one to two days for a vaginal birth and three to four days for a cesarean birth. Private rooms provide the greatest degree of privacy and flexibility. If we continue the wedding analogy introduced earlier, this time compares to the honeymoon period. I prefer to think of it as the "babymoon."

Your baby will be weighed, measured, and thoroughly checked after birth. A prophylactic eye treatment against gonococcus is usually required (by state law) to be administered within two hours of the baby's birth. Silver nitrate was used for this purpose until recently. Now you can request that an antibiotic be used instead, since the application of silver nitrate irritates the mucous membrane of the eye and may temporarily interfere with the baby's ability to interact with you visually.

All of these procedures may be done at your bedside or with you watching in the nursery if you choose to arrange it. (To have the baby suddenly disappear to the nursery is not unlike having the groom vanish after the ceremony while the reception is taking place!)

The babymoon begins when the parents are alone with their baby for the first time with no nurses, physicians, or grandparents present—just the family. There is a real need for uninterrupted privacy then. Post a Do Not Disturb sign on the door and turn the phone off. This is a time of discovery that shouldn't be interrupted, even by well-wishers and advisors.

Your baby probably will have a strong desire to suck and nurse during the first few hours and then will fall into a deep sleep. The alternating patterns of activity and sleep vary from baby to baby. It's really quite wonderful to hold your sleeping baby against your chest. You'll find that you can gaze at him for hours, but you'll need sleep too. (Chapter 13 presents ways to obtain the nutrients and rest you will need during the fifth stage of labor.)

The idea that keeping the baby near tires the mother out is such an odd notion. I have found that mothers and babies sleep much better when they are in close proximity. This is because they have been "as one" for nine months. Being close is reassuring, comforting, and soothing. Remember how you first felt about your mate? While you were falling in love, your engrossment in his life was profound. The more you were together, the closer you felt.

Likewise, the babymoon is a time to devote to learning to love your baby. It's a time to embrace what it means to be a mother or a father and learn the rhythm of your baby's personality and temperament. It's a time to take a total break from everyday worries and duties. Your relationship as a parent to this child-person will be built on these early weeks together.

Life is not a holiday, but an education. And the one eternal lesson for us all is how better we can love.

HENRY DRUMMOND

EASING THE TRANSITION FROM THE WOMB TO THE WORLD

While your baby was growing in your uterus, he never experienced hunger, cold temperatures, bright light, or loud noises. Intrauterine life provided the warmth of your inner body, the rhythmical movement of your digestion, breathing, circulation, and bodily activities such as walking. It provided the constant sounds of your heart beating, blood pumping, lungs breathing, and intestines rumbling. A mixture of nutrients passed directly from your blood through the placenta and umbilical cord into the baby's circulatory system. Diffused light came through your abdominal wall and muffled sounds from the world outside. In effect, you were mothering your baby perfectly—without any extra effort on your part or having to consciously think about it.

When your baby moves from life inside your womb to existence on the outside, you will ease this transition by thinking about how to continue meeting your baby's needs for warmth, movement, sound, nutrients, and visual stimulation. A bright nursery lit up by fluorescent lights twenty-four hours a day with babies lined up in isolettes must be a rather rude awakening for newborns. The Lord equipped mothers to provide just what their babies need. All we mothers have to do is realize it.

When you cradle a baby in your arms, he still hears your heartbeat and your breathing. When you swaddle him in a blanket, you provide a feeling of security and warmth. When you nurse your baby on demand, you give him the perfect follow-up to nutrients he received inside your womb. And when you respond quickly to his cries for comfort, you teach him that you are dependable. Numerous studies have demonstrated these two important by-products of attachment mothering: Babies who have close physical contact with their mothers are soothed more effectively if responded to quickly and learn to be independent earlier. Makes sense, doesn't it?

Babies like to be held firmly, with a good grip placed on the thigh or buttocks. They prefer the peaceful sound of your heart to lots of "baby talk" while nursing. Babies are fussiest and experience colicky episodes at the end of a long day when Mom and Dad are tired and tense. Relax! Did you do much housework or errand-running or meeting-attending during your honeymoon? While in the hospital or at home during the early weeks, a comfortable rocking chair and clean bed will soon become the places you like the best.

Great works may not always lie in our way, but every moment we may do little ones excellently, that is, with great love.

FRANCIS DE SALES

PERSPECTIVE

Your baby will be growing away from you from the moment of birth. T. Berry Brazelton has said that "the goal of attachment is detachment." This simply means the parent-child relationship begins with the dependence of a child and should aim toward moving the child away from the parents into a productive life of his own. *Your baby needs you to be there responsively in order to learn a basic sense of trust.*

This seems like a big task until we look at the larger picture. Each day will bring new capabilities to your infant, as well as new growth. It's a process that takes only a few years, and then you will have a child who is capable of doing a great deal all by himself. The early period of complete dependence will gradually dissolve into independence. Trust me—it happens!

The art of parenting requires sensitivity to the changing needs and perceptions of children. The way I express my love to my first daughter, who is now a pastor's wife and the mother of two daughters, is somewhat different from how I express it to my youngest son, a senior in high school. The apostle Paul describes the wisdom of developmental parenting well as he compares spiritual maturity to human development: "I gave you milk, not solid food, for you were not yet ready for it" (1 Cor. 3:2).

Your baby will need you to be available to meet his needs in a physical, tangible way. Later on he will challenge you to be available in a much wider sense—intellectually, spiritually, and emotionally. Babyhood is a unique time during which Christ's love can be wonderfully expressed in terms of comfort, warmth, milk, and gentle protection.

It's what you listen to when you're growing up that you always come back to.

AL COHEN

SCRIPTURAL REFLECTIONS AND PROMISES

Every good and perfect gift is from above, coming down from the Father of the heavenly lights, who does not change like shifting shadows.

JAMES 1:17

From heaven the Lord looks down and sees all mankind; from his dwelling place he watches all who live on the earth—he who forms the hearts of all, who considers everything they do.

PSALM 33:13-15

But we proved to be gentle among you, as a nursing mother tenderly cares for her own children.

1 THESSALONIANS 2:7 NASB

I pray that out of his glorious riches he may strengthen you with power through his Spirit in your inner being, so that Christ may dwell in your hearts through faith. And I pray that you, being rooted and established in love, may have power, together with all the saints, to grasp how wide and long and high and deep is the love of Christ, and to know this love that surpasses knowledge—that you may be filled to the measure of all the fullness of God.

EPHESIANS 3:16-19

Know that the Lord is God. It is he who made us, and we are his; we are his people, the sheep of his pasture. Enter his gates with thanksgiving and his courts with praise; give thanks to him and praise his name. For the Lord is good and his love endures forever; his faithfulness continues through all generations.

PSALM 100:3-5

THIRTEEN

SUPPORTING THE NEW MOTHER

Give her the reward she has earned, and let her works bring her praise at the city gate.

PROVERBS 31:31

The fifth stage of labor begins two hours after a baby is born and lasts six weeks—a time of tremendous physiological, anatomical, and emotional adjustment. A woman's hormone levels shift and sway, the uterus sheds extra cells and shrinks in size, and the breasts swell with milk and other body fluids as lactation is established.

The days and weeks immediately following a baby's birth bring many changes. Normal routines are disrupted. It's not a typical time in one's life. Instead, it's a period of transition and moving from one physical and emotional state to another, of assuming new roles and responsibilities, and of learning to accommodate the shifts in schedules, in normal body functions, and in everyday habits.

This forty-two-day period is a unique and demanding time. Activities must be adjusted and prioritized to accommodate the special needs associated with postpartum. The mother especially deserves to receive "the reward she has earned" and will reap real benefits from being given a month-long break from her usual routines and responsibilities.

A FEW WEEKS OF REST

After returning from the hospital, a new mother should refrain from the following activities for two to four weeks (no, I'm not kidding)—laundry, shopping, cooking, cleaning, primary care of older children, and church attendance. I consider this a mandatory recuperation vacation. (See Leviticus for additional scriptural support for a six-week recovery period *sans* housework, sexy nightgowns, etc.)

The mother's first and foremost responsibility is to *rest* and *relax* while she gets to know her new baby. She deserves a complete break from her usual activities while her body adjusts to breastfeeding and a post-pregnant state. This is a time in a woman's life when she needs to be loved, supported, nurtured, and cared for—in short, to be treated like a queen! *A hospital stay of two to five days is* not *a long enough period for a mother to adjust to her baby and her body.*

Now comes the problem: Who will perform these tasks? Since fathers often are exhausted, too, it helps to have relatives and friends pitch in. Casseroles may be brought over and tasks given to those who wonder how to help. Unfortunately our culture often does not offer new mothers the real support and help they need. We mistakenly think that we help a new mom by feeding, dressing, and bathing the baby. Emphatically not! We can help the mother much more by giving her good food, providing her with clean sheets and clothing, and watching over the baby while she gets time to herself in the bathroom. New mothers need assistance, not direction.

"Mothering the mother gives the new parent time to cuddle, care for, and love her own infant," explains Dr. Dana Raphael. "It gives her the chance to watch the baby and build a schedule around that infant which is compatible with her own preferences. It allows the mother to enjoy her matrescence [transition to motherhood] and not find it a burden or a nightmare. Help from others allows this to happen."

TASKS NEW MOTHERS SHOULD AVOID

- cooking
- cleaning
- laundry
- grocery shopping
- errand running
- church attending
- primary care of children under five

God gives us two hands—one to receive with and one to give with. We are not cisterns made for hoarding; we are channels made for sharing.

BILLY GRAHAM

FOR HUSBANDS ONLY

In a sense, *new mothers need mothering*. They do not need visitors (who drain their energy), or criticism (which drains their self-esteem), or outdated advice (which drains their patience). Assisting a new mother means letting go of being the boss and becoming a servant, the biblical model at all times. It means knowing how to tackle undone tasks in a cheerful, quiet, supportive manner. It also means recognizing that the new mother will learn from her mistakes as she gets to know her baby. It means providing a safe place for her to talk about surprising discoveries.

Humility must always be doing its work like a bee making its honey in the hive; without humility all will be lost.

TERESA OF JESUS

In recent years a word has been assigned to the person who assumes the "mothering-the-mother" role: *doula*—the Greek word for "one who serves." The new mother's doula may be her mother, mother-in-law, stepmother, sister, friend, a professional—or her husband. It's a "by-invitation-only" exclusive job to be fulfilled by the person the baby's mom thinks will provide the best care.

Turn back to chapter 8 and read the section "Working Together: The Labor Partner's Role" (p. 96) to see what a woman needs in labor and how labor companions can meet these needs. The fifth stage of labor requires the same kind of support from loving labor companions. It's really no different, even though the contractions have subsided and the work doesn't necessarily seem to be demanding. The fact of the matter is that many processes are taking place that require rest and a quiet environment if a mother is to adapt smoothly. Postpartum depression, or "the baby blues," is due more to fatigue, lack of support, and a sense of abandonment than just hormones.

"At no time in history have new mothers been expected to do so much for so many with so little help," Dr. William and Martha Sears point out. "Cultures around the world have always recognized the importance of mothers and babies nesting-in."

The weeks following a baby's birth create a clear need for family support. New moms, even if they have borne eight children, benefit from time alone with the new baby and time for short rests at intervals throughout the day and night. Frequent snacks (see Appendix A) and beverages should be served as needed. Since a nursing mother needs about 500 extra calories a day, her foods should be nutritious yet appealing. A pitcher of juice or water should be kept available at all times.

Keep phone calls and visitors at a minimum. If someone wants to move in to help with the baby, the new mother should feel completely at ease and comfortable with having that person around constantly. Expectations of the guest should be made explicitly clear before her arrival; she is not coming to teach but to support the mother's own learning and discovery. Such a guest must be willing to adapt to the role of a labor companion and perform household tasks with little direction. It is an honor to be included in the babymoon, not a right.

Consider setting visiting hours for sixty to ninety minutes per evening, or refrain from accepting visitors during the first week at home. Don't feel bashful about restricting phone calls and visits. You didn't when you were first married! The transition period after a baby is born is not the time for extensive socializing.

If Mom needs a break from mothering, suggest a long shower or a walk outside if the weather is pleasant. Volunteer to watch the baby so she can have time to herself to be refreshed. She will need some rest uninterrupted by noise, and she should be encouraged to sleep whenever the baby is sleeping. A back rub at least once a day can be a great help, and she needs to know that she is accepted even though she will be unable to make love for at least a month. Explore ways of soothing one another through touch that is not geared toward sexual arousal. This is a wonderful way to comfort and reassure her.

Your sexual needs as a husband may be met, without having intercourse, when she is rested, available, and willing to be with you. (Remember that Levitical law provided for a time without sexual activity following childbirth, as well as a break from everyday routine.) Until the uterus recovers and the discharge called lochia stops (usually within three to four weeks), a woman's body is not healed sufficiently to resume lovemaking. Your understanding and flexibility in this area will go a long way toward promoting her recovery.

True Christianity is love in action.

DAVID O. MCKAY

Being sensitive and responsive to a new mother's need to be with her baby may help you overcome possible feelings of jealousy. It is important to keep in mind that most of her energy is being consumed by the tasks of the fifth stage of labor (physical recovery, psychological adjustment to the baby, and the onset of lactation). This is a temporary phase, and she will learn to balance all of the needs of the family in time. Just as she seemed preoccupied and unable to respond fully to you during active labor, so will she be distracted now. If you wish, set up a special post-babymoon date and look forward to doing something romantic together, without the baby, for a couple of hours.

If you find yourself becoming critical or starting to complain, try not to direct it toward your wife. Either take it to the Lord in prayer or share your feelings with a fellow Christian you know well. Constructive direction is helpful, while unloving criticism only maims relationships. Be wise about how to communicate your concerns and feelings; be gentle and careful about what you say and how the words are spoken. If your wife is breastfeeding, consider some ways *you* can express love to your newborn other than by bottle-feeding the baby. Last but not least, read some books on parenting for additional support.

Peace and union are the most necessary of all things for men who live in common, and nothing serves so well to establish and maintain them as the forbearing charity whereby we put up with one another's defects.

ROBERT BELLARMINE

Write down several ways a dad can express love to a newborn baby, other than by bottle-feeding the baby.

Write down several current books or articles you've read—or plan to read—on breastfeeding, parenting, and baby care, including those from the recommended reading sections of this book.

GREAT WAYS TO SUPPORT A NEW MOTHER

Here are some things women especially appreciate during the transition period. These suggestions were gleaned from more than 2,000 expectant and new mothers I've taught over the past twenty-five years.

- Buy fresh flowers and put them in a lovely vase by her bed or rocking chair.
- Praise her accomplishment.
- Be a good listener.
- Give her a back rub.
- Bring her an attractive new nightgown or leisure outfit.
- Cook a simple, delicious dinner she likes.
- Offer empathy and understanding.
- Protect her privacy while she naps.
- Tell her you will pay for her to receive a facial, manicure, pedicure, or massage.
- Rent a few of her favorite videos.

- Respect her need for quiet.
- Put together a basket filled with favorite toiletries.
- Serve her breakfast in bed.
- Focus on the positive.
- Prepare her a sitz bath.
- Compliment her on the way she holds the baby.
- Buy magazines she likes.
- Fix her favorite snacks.
- Admire her abilities.
- Make her bed up with fresh linens and extra pillows.
- Provide calming comfort.
- Avoid talking about your own childbearing experiences unless she asks.
- Coordinate brought-in meals.
- Assist with limiting visitors.
- Respect her concerns.

What Not to Do

(Also based on over 2,000 true-life stories)

- Rearrange the house.
- Say she has never looked better.
- Demonstrate the "right" way to parent.
- Invite your friends over to see the baby.
- Discuss politics (if you disagree).
- Tell her you are exhausted.
- Cook meals she does not like.
- Cancel hired help without asking.
- Say that you wouldn't be there unless you loved her.
- Complain about the pet(s).
- Talk often about your work, health, or marital problems.
- Give gifts she cannot enjoy.
- Make her feel inadequate.
- Start planning your next fishing trip.
- Reorganize the kitchen.
- Buy food she will not eat.
- Offer your advice, unless asked for it.
- Take over the household.
- Compare her with yourself.
- Act like an expert (or a martyr).
- Tell her friends they should be more considerate.
- Comment on her—or anyone else's—size, shape, weight gain, or need for exercise.
- Do too much videotaping or picture-taking.
- Tell her to ignore the baby's crying.
- Refer to fat grams and calories in foods.
- Disturb her privacy.

Baker's Dozen of Balanced Snacks

1. Stir together and serve in a small bowl:
   ½ c. vanilla yogurt
   1 small apple, cored and chopped
   4 walnut halves, chopped
   sprinkle of cinnamon
2. Put the following ingredients in a blender with four to six ice cubes and blend until ice is crushed:
   1 6-oz. can frozen orange juice
   1 6-oz. can water
   ⅓ c. nonfat dry milk powder
   ½ tsp. vanilla extract
3. Put the following ingredients in a blender and blend until smooth (about 30 seconds):
   1 c. skim or low-fat milk
   ½ c. unsweetened frozen strawberries, partially thawed
   ½ tsp. sugar
   ½ tsp. vanilla
4. Bran muffin, orange sections, glass of milk
5. Baked potato with a selection of toppings served on the side, glass of milk
6. Make a pizza muffin:
   ½ English muffin
   1 T. pizza sauce
   1-2 oz. shredded mozzarella cheese

Choice of toppings: ham, mushrooms, spinach, pepperoni, green pepper, feta cheese, etc.

Place under broiler until cheese melts, OR microwave on high for 35-40 seconds. Serve with decaffeinated iced tea or lemonade and fruit salad.

7. Toasted bagel topped with cream cheese, ten toasted almonds, fresh pear
8. Four to six whole wheat crackers spread with peanut butter, one-half grapefruit, glass of herbal iced tea
9. Vanilla, lemon, or coffee-flavored yogurt; two graham crackers; Spanish peanuts; iced or hot tea (decaffeinated)
10. Cinnamon-raisin bread spread with lemon curd (or favorite preserves); fresh strawberries, blackberries, or raspberries; glass of milk
11. Chicken strips, seasoned and cooked; two to three cups air-popped popcorn; one cup seedless grapes

12. Carrot and celery sticks, low-fat sour cream dip, hard-boiled egg, glass of sparkling fruit juice
13. One-half cup creamed cottage cheese, two pineapple slices or pear halves, Ry-krisp or melba toast

Grab-and-go Snacks

- Cheese and crackers
- Rice cakes
- Whole grain cereal and milk
- Frozen bagels and English muffins with reduced-fat flavored cream cheese spread
- Fresh fruit
- Cottage cheese
- Low-sodium pretzels
- "Lite" microwave popcorn
- Veggies-in-a-bag: salad mix, carrots, broccoli flowerets, celery hearts, etc.
- Reduced-fat granola bars
- Low-fat, whole grain, high-fiber muffins
- Roasted almonds, cashews, pistachios, or peanuts
- Dried fruit: apricots, apples, raisins
- Instant pudding
- Angel food cake
- Frozen fruit bar

Setting Your Priorities

Once you become involved in caring for your wife and taking over household responsibilities, you may find yourself overdoing it. If so:

- Slow down.
- Take regular breaks.
- Care for yourself, too.

Using the following list and charts as a guide, make the most of your time. Don't allow temporary stresses and demands to sidetrack you from your primary purpose—providing tender loving care to your wife and new baby.

SIMPLE SUGGESTIONS FOR MANAGING YOUR TIME

1. Decide what your priorities are.
2. Make a list of what you want to accomplish.
3. Do your least favorite tasks when your energy level is highest.
4. Keep things simple.
5. Hire/find someone else to do work you can't (or don't want) to do.
6. Give yourself a break.
7. Stay in touch with your support network.

Things I need to do:

Things I'd like to do:

Things I feel I should do, but don't have time to do:

Things I won't do:

DAILY ACTIVITY LIST

Date:

Morning Afternoon Evening

SHOPPING LIST

Pharmacy:

Grocery:

Other:

❧ A WORD TO NEW MOTHERS

The first days at home with a new baby are exhausting. Forget about the clock and the world outside. This is a time to find out who your baby is and to avoid trying to make the experience what you think it should be. Buy disposable diapers and paper plates and cups. Minimize distractions. Lie down and relax with your baby. Dismiss all those things you've heard about how long a baby should sleep and how often a baby needs to eat. Let others take care of you. Just respond lovingly to your baby's cues and be sensitive to your own need for rest and good food.

Enjoy this precious time, those tiny fingers, that delicate skin, the unique smell. Keep your baby close by if you are nursing him, for his presence will stimulate your body to release prolactin and will ensure a successful milk supply. Sleep when he sleeps; eat or drink while he eats. Take one day at a time, not worrying if you're doing it all right. Some mothers make newborn care so complicated and organized they become unable to establish a milk supply or to enjoy the simple pleasure of holding a baby for hours on end. Your pants and blouses may not fit, and you may feel quite different from your usual self, but be patient. It will all come back to you soon enough.

Be kind to yourself and praise the Lord for the life he has entrusted to your care. Thank him for what he has given to you. Try not to complain; it only leads to ingratitude and self-pity. If you are feeling angry, guilty, helpless, lonely, or generally depressed, get help and communicate what is on your mind.

All new mothers need companionship, reassurance, and encouragement. The fifth stage of labor has a way of making us feel vulnerable, like it or not. Being a Christian does not confer a super humanity upon us or exempt us from the effects of inevitable life changes. Instead, we can consider David's words in Psalm 103:1-19, reminding ourselves that God is indeed with us eternally as an example of what being a parent is all about.

❧ SCRIPTURAL REFLECTIONS AND PROMISES

Praise the Lord, O my soul; all my inmost being, praise his holy name. Praise the Lord, O my soul, and forget not all his benefits—who forgives all your sins and heals all your diseases; who redeems your life from the pit and crowns you with love and compassion, who satisfies your desires with good things so that your youth is renewed like the eagle's. The Lord works righteousness and justice for all the oppressed. He made known his ways to Moses, his deeds to the people of Israel: The Lord is compassionate and gracious, slow to anger, abounding in love. . . . He does not treat us as our sins deserve or repay us according to our iniquities. For as high as the heavens are above the earth, so great is his love for those who fear him; as far as the east is from the west, so far has he removed our transgressions from us. As a father has compassion on his children, so the Lord has compassion on those who fear him; for he knows how we are formed, he remembers that we are dust. . . . But from everlasting to everlasting the Lord's love is with those who fear him, and his righteousness with their children's children—with those who keep his covenant and remember to obey his precepts. The Lord has established his throne in heaven, and his kingdom rules over all.

PSALM 103:1-19

FOURTEEN

BREASTFEEDING YOUR BABY

For you will nurse and be satisfied at her comforting
breasts; you will drink deeply and delight
in her overflowing abundance.

ISAIAH 66:11

The analogy of breastfeeding is used in the above verses to describe satisfaction and love—and rightly so. It is in the arms of his mother that a baby first receives warmth, food, and affection. As an infant's hunger vanishes and his need to suck is provided for, he learns what it means to "delight in her overflowing abundance."

The Lord designed maternal breasts to supply just the right nutrients and soothing skin-to-skin contact for the youngest among us. Breastfeeding is a lovely expression of God's provision for nurturing new life.

According to Dr. Dana Raphael, the founder of the Human Lactation Center, the keys to successful breastfeeding are: 1) Knowing the benefits, 2) Understanding the process, 3) Discounting confusing folklore, and 4) Mothering the mother.

If you follow Dr. Raphael's recommendations, breastfeeding can be a satisfying experience for you and your baby. With the right advice, information, and support, nearly all women can breastfeed their babies for as long as they choose. Think for a moment about what you have heard about the advantages of breastfeeding for you and your baby. Given the facts, it is difficult to find anything that isn't beneficial about nursing. But, because we live in a culture where most of us acquire little firsthand knowledge about lactation prior to having our first baby, the choice to breastfeed may be guided by factors unrelated to nursing's distinct advantages.

KNOWING THE BENEFITS

Your prenatal preparation for breastfeeding is only one of the factors that will influence this experience with your baby. Your lifestyle, beliefs, plans for the future, upbringing, family, health-care provider, and feelings about your body will also have an impact. Considering these things ahead of time may enable you to be even more comfortable with your decision after the baby is born.

FACTORS THAT WILL AFFECT YOUR BREASTFEEDING EXPERIENCE

- Personal beliefs
- Knowledge about breastfeeding
- Approach to human sexuality
- Physician/midwife/lactation consultant support
- Lifestyle and work schedule
- Future plans
- Health considerations
- Peer support
- Husband's and family's support
- Education
- Family upbringing

Knowing the benefits of breastfeeding before nursing begins will contribute to your commitment to nursing your baby, especially during the early weeks as you're adjusting to lactation. Keep these benefits in mind as your milk supply is getting established and you're coping with the common discomforts associated with postpartum recovery.

The following benefits are exclusive to breastfeeding—that is, they can't be duplicated by any other infant-feeding method. Breastfeeding provides colostrum—a nutrient-packed substance with no commercial equivalent—immediately after birth to about four days after giving birth. Colostrum contains water, minerals, sugar, proteins, and a high number of antibodies. Even a few days of nursing provides your baby with this transition diet.

Breastfeeding supplies breast milk, a "living fluid" also containing antibodies and organisms to promote health with possibly less illness, until weaning occurs.

Breastfeeding promotes physical closeness and skin-to-skin contact between you and your baby.

Breastfeeding avoids allergy sensitization. Breast milk is God's specially designed diet for human infants, a "species specific" food source for all human infants. As long as your diet is appropriate, your breast milk can't be too thick, too rich, or allergy-provoking.

Breastfeeding enhances your baby's oral and facial development due to stronger sucking.

Breastfeeding discourages digestive problems such as constipation or diarrhea. Organisms in breast milk keep your baby's intestinal tract healthy.

Breastfeeding eliminates the need to prepare and store formula. Breast milk is germ-free and readily available at just the right temperature as long as you're around. Baby's milk is "free," a product of the food you eat. It's also ecological; there's no waste. And no costly energy is used to make, refrigerate, and heat the formula or to prepare the bottles.

Breastfeeding adapts easily to your active lifestyle—no bottle preparation required whenever you bring the baby along.

Breastfeeding helps diminish postpartum bleeding and hastens the return of your uterus to its normal size.

Breastfeeding normally (though not necessarily) delays the return of fertility and menstruation for an average length of twelve to fourteen months *if* your baby nurses frequently, continues night feedings, and avoids pacifiers.

A SUMMARY OF BENEFITS OF BREASTFEEDING

- Species-specific
- "Living" fluid with antibodies and organisms to promote health, possibly less illness
- Allergy-free
- Readily available, no preparation or storage
- Promotes physical closeness and skin-to-skin contact
- Periods often delayed six to twelve months
- Exclusive bond between mother and baby
- Aids physical recovery after birth
- Considerably less expensive

IF BREAST MILK IS SO GOOD FOR BABIES, WHY DON'T MORE WOMEN NURSE?

From the beginning of history until the mid-twentieth century, human milk was almost exclusively used by mothers and wet nurses to feed infants. Modern technology didn't make bottle-feeding possible until the 1920s. (For comparison, remember that the importance of hand washing to prevent infection wasn't discovered until the 1840s and not used widely until twenty to thirty years later.)

Commercially produced formulas, bottles, and sterilizers gained popularity over several decades until bottle-feeding became the method chosen by most women during the fifties and sixties. As a result, breastfeeding came to be viewed as an old-fashioned, unattractive, messy nuisance, while bottle-feeding was considered a modern wonder.

This trend hasn't been unique to the United States. The prevalence of bottle-feeding and early weaning has been noted by experts throughout the world as an accompaniment to industrialization. In less industrialized cultures, breastfeeding has remained essential to the health of children under the age of two years because mothers who live in poorer countries don't have enough money to buy formula. Neither can they pay for the medical care that's often necessary when unsanitary water is used in formula preparation.

Bottle-feeding is only appropriate when proper hygiene is possible and when antibiotics are available. Because breast milk provides both immunities and organisms that protect the baby's gastrointestinal tract against infection, bottle-feeding is a "luxury" only a small percentage of the world's population can afford.

Given the trend away from breastfeeding during the twentieth century, why have so many women returned to the practice of nursing their babies? The primary reasons for this encouraging change seem to be:

(1) numerous research studies performed during the past twenty years emphasizing the physiological and psychological benefits of breastfeeding.

(2) the promotion of breastfeeding by professional organizations such as the American Academy of Pediatrics, through mother-to-mother help made available through groups such as La Leche League, and in childbirth preparation classes.

(3) the "natural-is better-for-you" trend that has reacted to the high costs of technology by stressing the value of healthier and simpler lifestyles.

These and other factors have contributed to a widespread change in popular opinion. Breastfeeding is once again the feeding method used by the majority of American mothers. Complications, however, are not uncommon. Many women discontinue breastfeeding within eight weeks after giving birth. This isn't surprising. The majority of women currently of childbearing age were predominantly bottle-fed. Even if they were breastfed, few were nursed longer than eight weeks. As a result, many American women who nurse their babies receive little knowledgeable support from their moms, extended families, or older women in their churches or neighborhoods—the age-old traditional sources of breastfeeding support in previous eras.

Why do so many decide to wean their babies from the breast so soon? Possibly it's because few women are prepared for what nursing a baby will be like when the time comes. Breastfeeding is viewed as the natural way to feed a baby, so many people believe it's an uncomplicated, easy-to-learn, instinctive process. This is not necessarily so. Breastfeeding must be learned from other women who have breastfed—and in our culture few of us were raised in households where long-term nursing was practiced.

Also, we can't ignore the fact that we live in a country where breasts are seen as sexual objects and erogenous zones rather than primarily viewed as the supply of nutrition for infants. Living in a culture that eroticizes breast exposure admittedly makes it difficult to learn about breastfeeding by watching women nurse their babies without embarrassment. In addition to these cultural factors, many women have unrealistic expectations about what nursing a baby involves and compare it too closely to bottle-feeding—simply put the baby to the nipple, let the baby suck, and the feeding is over when the milk is gone.

Breastfeeding is an entirely different process than bottle-feeding, however, and requires the mother to respond in a flexible way to her baby's signals of hunger and satisfaction. If a mother lacks sound support and accurate information about breastfeeding, she will not understand how it differs from bottle-feeding and may become anxious about the frequency and duration of her baby's feedings. Bottles may become necessary as she limits nursing her baby to strictly scheduled times. Her milk supply then diminishes as the baby's times at the breast become too brief and too infrequent to stimulate an adequate production of milk. With little support from friends and relatives, who question the frequency of feedings and offer to feed the baby to "let her get some rest," the mother may not know that she really needs rest from housework, laundry, cooking, shopping, and outside employment instead!

UNDERSTANDING THE PROCESS

The Letdown Reflex

When you nurse your baby, his sucking will stimulate sensitive nerve endings in your breast, which will send a specific signal to your brain's "regulatory center." When this area (the hypothalamus) receives the right information, it will cause your pituitary gland to secrete two hormones into your bloodstream—oxytocin and prolactin.

The circulation of blood through your body occurs at a rapid rate and will quickly carry these substances to cells in your breast. Within thirty to ninety seconds, the secretion of oxytocin will normally be at a sufficient level to cause milk to be ejected from the glandular cells in your breasts where the milk is produced. Thousands of tiny cells will then contract in unison in what is termed the "letdown reflex," compressing milk out of nearby secretory (gland) cells. The milk then will flow into vessels that will carry it to large collecting ducts and eventually to the milk sinuses. (See "The Letdown Reflex" chart.)

THE LETDOWN REFLEX

30-90 seconds

Start

- Baby sucks at breast
- Nerves stimulated
- Message received by the brain (hypothalamus)
- Message received by posterior pituitary gland
- Gland secretes oxytocin into bloodstream
- Oxytocin reaches muscle cells in breast
- Muscle cells compress gland cells
- Milk flows into sinuses and ducts
- Milk is released from breasts

Finish

If you can picture the trunk of a tree leading to smaller branches, which in turn split into thousands of twigs, then you have an idea of how this system in your breast will function. The trunk is like the sinus; the branches, the larger milk ducts; the twigs, the smaller ducts; and, if the analogy is taken even further, the clusters of leaves, the milk glands.

In order for oxytocin to be secreted efficiently, you will need to get plenty of rest and enjoy your baby. Tension, fear, pain, fatigue, and worry can interfere with the release of oxytocin into your bloodstream. (See "Interference with the Letdown Reflex" chart.) Oxytocin will also cause your uterus to contract as it is resuming a smaller size after your baby's birth. The system through which a baby receives nourishment while promoting the mother's recovery is God-created and is not merely a biological accident.

INTERFERENCE WITH THE LETDOWN REFLEX

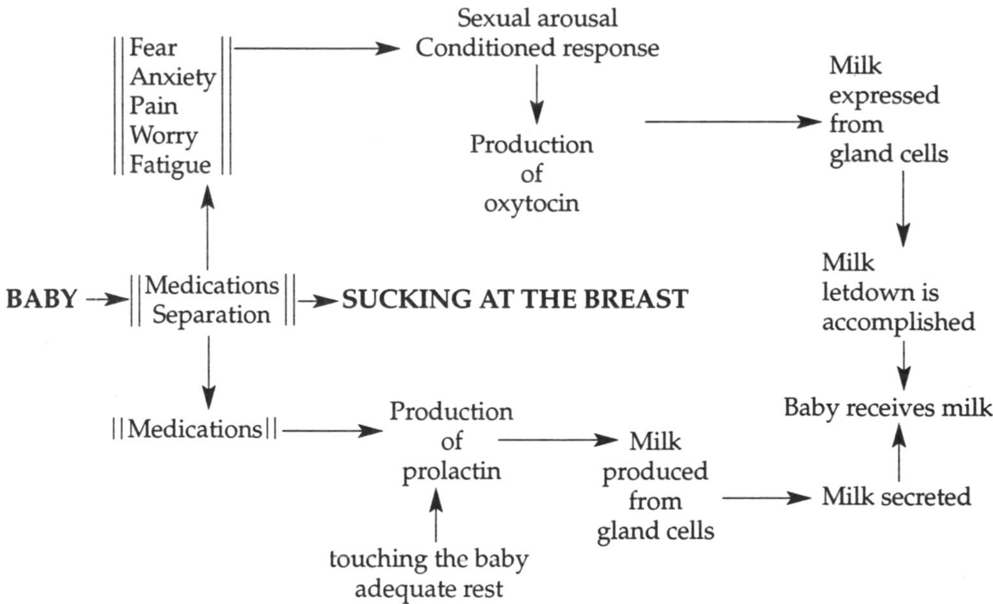

Key:
→ Promotes secretion of hormones and milk
|| Inhibits secretion of hormones and milk

The hormone *prolactin* will cause the gland cells in your breast to actually manufacture the milk from nutrients in your bloodstream. It's a highly selective process and one that will occur without much effort on your part. The sucking of your baby is all you'll need in order for prolactin to be released.

Avoid using any medication without your health-care provider's advice, as some drugs can interfere with the secretion of these hormones. The chart shows what factors can promote and inhibit the process of lactation.

THE PRINCIPLE OF SUPPLY AND DEMAND

The most common mistake made by nursing mothers is trying to schedule feedings by the clock. Your baby will accept your breast when you offer to nurse her if she wants to suck. Don't be afraid to do so, since your milk supply will be abundant if your baby's demands are frequent.

A baby may nurse several times on each breast before she is satisfied. Rely on your baby to be your guide. Otherwise, if you restrict the length of time according to your idea of how much nursing is enough, you may interfere with your milk supply. Supplemental bottles, feeding schedules, and misinformation about the physiology of lactation are the greatest threats to successful breastfeeding.

On the other hand, if you grasp the beauty of the supply and demand system, you'll soon see the Lord's wisdom is behind this process. On some days your baby will nurse more; on others, less. Your supply will reflect your baby's varying requirements if you feel confident in freely responding to her needs. All this takes place without your giving it a second thought.

The general rule of thumb is to nurse ten minutes on the first side and as long as your baby seems to want to nurse on the other side. Then if she's still interested in nursing on the first side, go ahead and switch. (Some experts suggest letting your baby finish nursing on the first side first and then switching to the second breast if she's still interested in nursing.) Most of the milk in your breast will be given to your baby in ten minutes. Since your milk doesn't flow during the entire nursing, much of your baby's feeding is to satisfy her need to suck. Pacifiers and thumb-sucking are possible options worth exploring if you find unlimited nursing isn't possible.

Frequent breastfeeding has a nice advantage—your baby's sucking will inhibit your ovulatory cycle and tend to delay the return of your menstrual periods. This appears to be God's way of protecting your baby's nutrient source and enhancing your body's recovery. (If you do become pregnant while nursing, your milk supply will likely diminish.)

In the majority of cases, a baby doesn't need any other food or liquid besides breast milk for about the first half year of life. After this time, her digestive system will become more mature, and she'll be able to chew and swallow solid foods. Isn't our Creator amazing?

GETTING STARTED

Your first consideration in beginning to breastfeed your baby should concern when and where your first nursing experience will take place. While your comfort and choice at that time may be influenced by many things, it is important that you understand the benefit of breastfeeding immediately following your baby's birth, if the birth was uncomplicated. Here are several reasons why early and frequent feedings at the breast promote successful lactation.

1. The infant's sucking reflex is most intense during the first twenty to thirty minutes after birth. Delaying gratification of this reflex can make it more difficult for the baby to learn the sucking process later.
2. The baby begins immediately to receive the immunities in colostrum (and at peak levels during the first twenty-four hours following birth).
3. The baby's digestive processes will be stimulated by nursing; this has a laxative effect on the baby's bowels.
4. Later breast engorgement can be alleviated somewhat by the early and frequent removal of colostrum from the breast.
5. The baby's sucking stimulates contractions of the uterus, aids the expulsion of the placenta, and helps to control excessive blood loss, all of which benefit the mother after giving birth.
6. The process of milk production is accelerated, and the milk appears sooner when the baby is encouraged to nurse upon delivery and frequently thereafter. This, in turn, diminishes the baby's total weight loss after birth.
7. Attachment or bonding is promoted at a time when both mother and baby are particularly sensitive and ready for this attachment.

Nursing soon after delivery requires your statement of this preference to your health-care provider. If desired, you can wait, see how things go, and decide when the time comes when you prefer to start nursing. The expulsion of the placenta and the repair of the episiotomy may be distracting. However, many mothers have found that having their baby in their arms at this time is truly rewarding. If you wish to begin nursing soon after birth, one of your health-care providers will check the baby for any conditions that would interfere with his ability to breastfeed. After this brief check, your position must be such that nursing will be easy to accomplish.

Your decision about when to begin should be based on what is happening, how you feel, and how the baby is doing. Find out ahead of time whether your health-care provider encourages or discourages breastfeeding immediately after birth. If he or she is against it, perhaps you could discuss this concern during a prenatal visit. The decision is yours, but it also may help to consider the viewpoint of your birth attendant and the situation you encounter upon giving birth.

The First Feeding

When you're ready to begin:

1. Have your labor companion or a nurse help you get into a comfortable position. If you are trembling following the exertion of giving birth, ask for a warm blanket to help soothe you. If thirsty, request a glass of juice or water. A semi-sitting position is good, unless you have had a spinal anesthetic. If you have had an epidural block and/or a cesarean birth, you may begin nursing lying on your left side if you're right-handed (the right side if you're left-handed) with a few pillows behind your back to prop you up.
2. Check your nipple to be sure it is erect. Gently grasp your nipple and pull it slightly outward. This will make it easier for your baby to suck. Compress the areola (the circular area of darker skin surrounding the nipple) between your thumb and forefinger and grasp firmly. Make sure the nipple is shaped to fit comfortably into the baby's mouth.
3. Hold your baby securely in the crook of your arm. Turn your baby toward you so that you are "tummy to tummy," rather than holding him with his body facing up. If your baby tries to put his hand in his mouth before your nipple, wrap a blanket firmly around him in swaddling fashion with the arms tucked inside, or tuck his arm under your arm. With your free hand, grasp your breast, with your thumb on top and two fingers beneath, and then brush the baby's cheek with your nipple. The baby will turn in the direction of this signal and open his mouth in what is known as the rooting reflex.
4. Firmly place your nipple and a large portion of the areola in your baby's mouth while aiming toward his palate (roof of the mouth) behind the upper gums. Hold your nipple there until the baby grasps it. This may take several seconds or even minutes. Some babies do not decide to suck vigorously right away; they prefer to nuzzle, lick, and sniff the skin on your breast. This is all part of your baby's getting to know you. Try again a few minutes later.
5. Don't forget to include Dad. Make sure your husband gets the opportunity to hold and touch your new son or daughter.
6. Allow your baby to suck as long as he seems interested. Break the suction by inserting the forefinger of your free hand into your baby's mouth. Then resume nursing on the opposite side if your baby wishes. Contrary to some opinions, nursing by demand does not increase nipple soreness. There is data to support unlimited

nursing time if the mother and baby are willing. Limiting the time at the breast merely postpones the adaptation of the nipples to lactation. Make sure to follow the guidelines for nipple care in chapter 4. (Remember, encouraging your baby to nurse on demand will stimulate your milk supply and cause the baby to suck less vigorously than when feedings are delayed or limited.)

A Quick Reference Guide for Nursing Your Baby

1. Position Yourself.

Using pillows as necessary, sit up in bed or in a rocking chair with your baby held comfortably by placing your knee, a pillow, or the arm of the chair under the elbow cradling the baby's head. Pillows are a nursing mother's friend; they help prevent back strain and promote relaxation.

2. Position Your Baby.

Whenever possible, undress your baby (leaving the diaper on, of course!) to promote skin contact and keep your baby alert. Cuddle your baby in your arms with his head in the crook of your arm, his bottom in your hand, and his back supported by your forearm. His head should be on an even plane with his body; it is neither bent forward nor arched backward. Also, his head is not turned to the side, but his whole body faces you, "tummy to tummy," with his head directly facing your breast.

3. Manually Express a Few Drops of Colostrum.

Express colostrum or milk to get started. This moistens the nipple and areola and makes the nipple less rigid so that your baby can grasp it more readily.

4. Cup Your Breast with Your Free Hand.

Support your breast by holding it with several fingers underneath and your thumb on top.

5. Encourage Your Baby to Open His Mouth Wide and Latch on Correctly.

Stroke his cheek nearest to your breast to stimulate the rooting reflex. As he turns to face your breast, he'll open his mouth and hunt for the nipple. Tickle his lips with your milk-moistened nipple. When his mouth opens wider, press your shaped, supported nipple and areola into his mouth toward the area behind his upper gums. His tongue should lie underneath your nipple, with his lips relaxed but not quite visible.

Latching on shouldn't hurt. If you don't get enough of the areola into your baby's mouth, the pressure will be directed onto the nipple and feel painful. When this happens, pull his lower jaw downward with your thumb placed on his chin. Break the suction and start again if he doesn't cooperate. Encouraging him to do it right from the start is vital. Many babies have no trouble sucking correctly; others need to be taught. For assessment and assistance, contact a trained lactation consultant, or if you're still in the hospital, ask a knowledgeable nurse to help you.

WHY DO BABIES SUCK SO OFTEN?

The idea of a schedule for a breastfed baby is a misconception. The only schedule your baby knows is determined by his individual needs. Keep in mind that the supply-and-demand principle is the foundation of successful breastfeeding and means that your baby's demand determines the amount of milk that you produce. Clock-watching interferes with the development of a mother's ability to respond to her baby's hunger cues.

The majority of infants learn to nurse in a pattern that best suits their biological and emotional needs. Nursing on demand can be tiring for Mom and a threat to continued nursing if you try to fit your baby into an inflexible feeding pattern. Adapting your sleeping habits and activities to incorporate demand feeding is appropriate. In fact, it's just good common sense.

Understanding the biological design of demand feeding may help you accept your baby's feeding patterns more easily. The following factors influence the frequency of nursing and your breastfeeding relationship:

1. *Your baby sucks as long and as often as his nutritional needs require him to nurse.* While some babies obtain 80 to 90 percent of the milk in the first five minutes of nursing, others are less efficient. Some women have a stronger letdown reflex compared to other women who have several letdowns during a feeding. Your baby's cues are the only "timer" to use.

You may find that your baby prefers to switch sides. There is intelligence at work here. On the first breast, your baby might obtain thinner milk, called foremilk, for the first few minutes. Continued sucking stimulates the letdown reflex and brings a greater abundance of creamier milk. While your baby nurses on one side, the other side leaks foremilk. In switching to the other breast midway through the feeding, your baby receives the more satisfying milk. Who says babies aren't very smart?

2. *The fat content in your milk varies not only within the feeding itself, but with the time of day and throughout the months that you nurse your child.* Babies often nurse more frequently at times of the day when the fat content is lowest, since the fat makes them feel more satisfied. Late afternoon and early evening are the most frequently noticed times for this to occur.
3. *Your baby will digest your milk much more quickly than he would formula, since it is more easily assimilated by the digestive system.* Since he will not feel full as long, he will probably nurse more often than he would if he were bottle-fed.
4. *You will have days when the baby will want to eat more frequently.* At around six weeks and three months, for example, babies go through a growth spurt that increases the amount of milk they need in accordance with their growth pattern. A more detailed consideration of this can be found in the section later in this chapter titled "Questions to Consider."

5. *Many babies enjoy nonnutritive sucking that satisfies emotional rather than physical needs.*
6. *One- or two-minute feedings are not unusual.* These satisfy your baby's thirst rather than his hunger by giving him the more watery, less-filling foremilk. Trust your baby to adjust the frequency and length of his feedings to obtain the more watery foremilk when he is thirsty, get more calories when he is growing, and seek the fattier milk when he is hungry. Because it isn't possible for you to measure or interpret these differences, you will do best when you let your baby be the guide.

Remember, your breast milk differs in fat content and calories during each feeding and throughout the day—a living substance that can't be matched by any formula currently available. Comparing the feeding patterns of a breastfed baby to a bottle-fed baby denies this fundamental fact and can be discouraging. Know that demand feeding and variable calories control obesity and encourage appetite control, thereby promoting a healthy approach to eating habits beyond infancy.

Additional Reasons God Designed Babies to Nurse Frequently

1. *The fifth stage of labor lasts six weeks.* This means that your body needs rest. If your baby is nursing eight to twelve times per day, it's unlikely that you'll be overdoing it. Nursing makes moms sit down and put their feet up.
2. *You need to get to know your newborn.* Extensive nursing allows mothers to spend time cuddling their babies and learning all about this new little person. No matter how many children you have, you'll still need to get to know the unique character of each one. Time at the breast promotes becoming well acquainted with one another through touch, smell, eye contact, and speech.
3. *Your baby needs you.* A newborn baby is totally dependent on others for sustenance. Being together is promoted by a frequent nursing pattern.

We can do no great things; only small things with great love.

MOTHER TERESA

NURSING A SLEEPY BABY

Some babies fall asleep after sucking only a short time. This is discouraging and sometimes can be overcome by:

- Undressing your baby to increase skin-to-skin contact.
- Keeping your baby's attention by talking.
- Manually expressing milk just before nursing to soften your breasts, thus allowing your "little sleepyhead" to get more of the areola into his mouth. Compression of the areola during nursing will enable him to get milk more easily from the ducts underlying this area.
- Tickle, tap, or nibble to awaken him as he starts to lose interest and doze off. It needn't be excessive or desperate; just have fun!

- Use the "bubble and switch" technique. Remove him from the breast if you've done all of the above. Sit him up, allowing the air bubble in his stomach to rise, and then burp him. Often the jostling and thumping of bubbling will wake a baby up, and you can resume nursing on the second breast. Repeat as necessary.
- Relax. Your baby eventually will outgrow this tendency. Small babies, jaundiced babies, and contented babies are more likely to be sleepers than fussy babies, babies who love to suck, and babies who are more alarmed by noises. Avoid being anxious and get some sleep.

COPING WITH FUSSY PERIODS

Contrary to popular opinion, crying is not a sign of health but is largely of reflex origin. *Crying is not a voluntary expression in young infants*. That is, your baby doesn't diabolically plot out how he can get you to pick him up because he is lonely. Neither does he think to himself, as far as anyone knows, "I'm hungry. Let's see now, I think I'll cry to get my way."

Many experienced parents and other child development experts are beginning to question the concepts of "spoiling" and "normal fussiness." These concepts miss the point: *Babies cry in response to pain, loneliness, and hunger.* Some babies seem to be fussier by nature, possessing a temperament that makes them more reactive to their environment and their feelings. Fussy babies are more demanding and more difficult to parent than more placid babies.

Here are a few suggestions that may help you cope if you are the mother of a more expressive child:

- Realize it's not your fault. Babies seem to fuss because of their own orientation to life and not because of your mothering abilities.
- Adjust your expectations. Perhaps you've imagined a fantasy baby based on TV commercials, shows, magazines, stories, etc. Let's face it—no television show has ever shown what life with a new baby is really like. Experienced parents of fussy babies will help you to understand that your baby is more normal than you realize.
- Fussy babies often grow up to be above average, intelligent, creative children. This calls for above-average, intelligent, creative parenting and acceptance of your baby's potential.
- Infants don't cry to annoy, consciously manipulate, or take advantage of their parents. They cry to express a genuine physiological or emotional need. Ignoring the cry equals ignoring the need. Not meeting these needs decreases your baby's ability to trust you and increases dependency (spoiling). Meeting your baby's physiological and emotional needs promotes trust and independence.
- Responding to your baby's crying in the first weeks of life may make your baby less likely to cry uncontrollably later. According to research on personality and childhood behavior, the development of trust and a basic sense of security early in life seem to be an important factor in the development of your baby's personality.
- Arrange for frequent contact that is interrupted as little as possible from the moment of

birth. Feeding on demand, skin-to-skin contact, and cloth infant carriers promote maternal-infant bonding. Given this contact, fussiness is kept to a minimum.

- Use stress management and relaxation techniques when you're tense and tired.
- Figure out when your baby's fussiest period of the day is likely to be and plan for it. Use his happiest periods for play and learning activities. During his grouchy times (often between 4:00 and 8:00 P.M.) promote peace and quiet with Crock-Pot meals, decreased activity, less noise, and a back rub for Mom.
- Your fussy baby will likely make you and the entire family fussy. Marital tension often rises. Talk together and spend moments being loving rather than fussing once the baby stops being crabby. And don't forget to pamper *yourself*.
- Make sure there is no physical cause of the fussiness. A thorough examination by your baby's physician is important as a means of ruling out this factor. Colic is different from mere fussiness and needs to be dealt with more specifically. If your baby's given a clean bill of health, consider allergens in your milk, cigarette smoke, hair sprays, and the like as possible irritants.
- If there are no physical reasons (and there often aren't), fussiness may be alleviated by:

  Praying for your baby out loud, using a soothing voice
  Motion and physical contact
  Baby massage
  Bathing with a parent in the "big bath"
  Music, mechanical sounds (dryer, car, dishwasher, vacuum, etc.)
- Seek help from those who will listen, empathize, and offer you genuine help. Avoid people who will offer quick advice ("Let him cry!"). What you need is support, not advice.

  You will benefit from hearing:

  "It's okay to have these feelings."

  "Your love is what he needs most."

  "He's not taking advantage of you."

"It's normal to resent your baby sometimes; what really matters is that you love him far more than you resent him."

"Your baby is changing daily; you'll feel less tied down soon."

Take each day one at a time. Pray often. Remember, it's not your fault. And enjoy the cuddling, snuggling, and close times that far outweigh the intense periods of fussiness.

TIPS FOR TREATING A COLICKY BABY

- Feed and burp your baby in an upright position.
- Burp early and frequently.
- Feed your baby in a quiet, dimly lit room. Make sure that you relax, too!
- If using a bottle, enlarge the nipple hole. If breastfeeding and you have a strong let-down, allow the initial spray to drain onto a cloth diaper or towel.
- Keep your baby in an upright position with gentle motion for half an hour after nursing.
- Try a different position for burping. Carry your baby in the "football-hold" position—

holding him horizontally in front of you, with your hand supporting his abdomen, facing him away from you.
- Hold your baby in a relaxed and secure fashion. A baby carrier that can be worn in the front may be useful.
- Clear his nasal passages; mouth breathing may increase air swallowing.
- Avoid sudden noises that may startle him.
- Consider the possibility of allergies (substances in your diet passed into the milk). Examples: iron supplements, dairy products, caffeine-containing beverages, citrus fruits and juices.
- Seek help from support groups—that is, other people who really are capable of empathizing, not criticizing or scrutinizing.
- Don't forget: Colic usually disappears when the baby is between three and six months old. Pray that it will be over even sooner. Amen.

QUESTIONS TO CONSIDER

The following helpful ideas are based on information contained in a classic La Leche League International reprint. If you think your milk production is low or inadequate, if you're not sure that your baby is getting enough milk, ask yourself these questions:

Have I used both breasts for at least ten minutes at each feeding? The best pattern for ensuring an adequate supply is ten minutes on the first side and then as long as your baby wishes to nurse on the other side. Make sure to begin nursing on the side you left off on at the next feeding. Occasionally babies get too much milk if you use both breasts. You'll be able to recognize if this is happening because your baby will spit up large amounts of milk after nursing on both sides. This means you have an ample supply and perhaps should nurse your baby on one side for a longer period of time.

Am I nursing my baby for as long as he is interested and content to nurse? If you forget about that clock and let your baby be your guide, you will be a happier nursing team and make more milk as well.

Am I feeding him when he is hungry? Often babies will nurse for only a short period of time and then must eat more frequently. Nurse according to your baby's cues. Also, remember that one feeding does not mean just the allotted time at each breast. *A feeding is however long it takes your baby to finish eating and be satisfied.*

Are there at least six soaking-wet diapers in a twenty-four-hour period? A baby who has at least this many wet diapers is receiving an adequate amount from the breast.

How much liquid am I drinking? Most nursing moms desire two to four quarts of liquid per day, with a substantial portion of this being water. Any beverage that contains caffeine should be avoided, since caffeine enters the milk and will interfere with both your sleep and your baby's. Never force fluids; drink to satisfy thirst. Just be sure to drink the necessary amount of two to four quarts.

Is my diet balanced, and am I eating regularly? The quality of your milk is partly a reflection of the quality of your diet. Six small meals per day are better and more satisfying than three large meals. Brewer's yeast reportedly causes the milk supply to increase but may make you and your baby "gassy."

Do I understand the principles of supply and demand and the letdown reflex? The amount of milk you produce is directly related to the amount of milk that is removed from your breasts. The amount of milk your baby gets is related to your ability to relax and establish the letdown reflex. The production of milk requires your baby's suckling, the giving of milk, and your peace of mind. Any supplements, rigid schedules, or upsets will interfere with your body's ability to nurse your baby.

Am I worried about my milk supply? Many women in our culture become concerned about their milk supply. They also tend to be much less aware of the things that contribute to successful breastfeeding than they are to what facilitates successful bottle-feeding! The two methods are very different in terms of how they work. Once you understand the principles of successful nursing—*relax*. Think positively about making milk and sharing yourself with your baby in this unique way. Avoid giving credence to the comments of well-meaning friends and relatives who aren't familiar with lactation. Worrying too much can affect the release of oxytocin and the process of letting-down your milk.

Have I started solids too soon? In most cases, babies aren't going to need any solid food until about the middle of the first year of life (five to seven months). If you are following the ideas you've learned and are applying the principles to your experience, your milk will be the ideal food for your baby to receive in most situations. If you must begin solids earlier, be sure to nurse your baby before offering solids so that your milk supply is maintained.

Do I compare my baby with babies who are bottle-fed? Making comparisons can lead to apprehension and confusion. A baby who is breastfed: 1) digests breast milk much more rapidly, 2) excretes it more easily, with less waste, 3) must work harder by sucking more vigorously to obtain milk, and 4) should be fed on demand since there is no way to determine how much your baby is getting. Sleeping and nursing patterns may reflect this, just as they do with babies who are not receiving breast milk.

At six weeks old is my baby going longer between feedings? If so, this may reduce your milk supply. Although some longer spans of time between nursings for newborns are fine, remember that frequent nursing stimulates your breasts to make more milk. Encourage your infant to nurse at least once every four hours, with possibly one longer stretch in a twenty-four-hour period (every five to six hours).

Is my baby acting hungry all the time and not satisfied with the usual number of feedings per day? "Nursing binges" are common at times when your baby must stimulate a greater production of milk. During a growth spurt, particularly around six weeks and three months, your baby will nurse more frequently for twenty-four to forty-eight hours. This will be followed by a reduction in the frequency of nursing once your baby is satisfied that your milk supply has increased enough to meet his needs. Some other situations when "frequency days" may be expected—during an illness (yours or your baby's), following a hectic couple of days (when you may have nursed less often), while traveling (because your baby picks up your tension or your letdown reflex is not up to par), on weekends if you're working and separated during the week.

DISCOUNTING THE FOLKLORE

When you make the decision to breastfeed, you may find yourself becoming the target of all sorts of comments and advice. Many of the things you hear will be based on what was thought about breastfeeding many years ago. *Discount any breastfeeding advice if it is based on belief rather than fact*. Also discount the advice if it's an idea left over from someone else's unsuccessful nursing experience, received from any books published prior to 1970, or aimed at proving the person right or easing her concern for you rather than at providing you with *genuine* support and *accurate* information

The most helpful source of information, other than books, is a certified lactation consultant (CLC) or another woman who enjoyed nursing her baby and who breastfed for at least eight months. Your health-care provider can also be an excellent source of information if he or she values breastfeeding as a special relationship that involves you and the baby, instead of simply as a means to get nutrients into your child.

The following statements are commonly made by people who don't understand breastfeeding. If you hear any of them—and believe me, you will—realize that you don't have to defend yourself or prove that what you're doing is correct. Misinformation about breastfeeding is the norm rather than the exception, and you can politely refuse to be affected by it.

- "Are you sure your milk is rich enough?" (See pages 197-199.)
- "He couldn't possibly be getting enough. You just nursed him twenty minutes ago." (See pages 203-204.)
- "You'll spoil him if you nurse him every time he acts hungry." (See page 209.)
- "You'll be lucky if you have enough milk; I didn't." (See pages 203-204.)
- "I'd be able to help you more if I could feed the baby for you." (See pages 200-201.)

There are many reasons why people make comments like these to nursing mothers—disappointment at personal failure with breastfeeding, feelings of exclusion, a desire to have you mother your baby in the way that seems "right" to the person speaking, or concern for your baby's health. In Proverbs 15:1, we find that "a gentle answer turns away wrath." Through understanding why someone would make critical or hurtful remarks, you may find it easier to answer the advice you receive.

When you're faced with comments that reflect a lack of understanding about breastfeeding, keep in mind Proverbs 15:23: "A man finds joy in giving an apt reply—and how good is a timely word!" You'll find that an "apt reply" or a "timely word" will clear the air and prevent later misunderstandings in most situations. Be kind and gentle; demonstrate your commitment to your relationship with the Lord as well as your commitment to breastfeeding your baby.

EXPRESSION AND STORAGE OF BREAST MILK

While you're breastfeeding, you may have times when you either need or want to be apart from your baby. Sometimes it's possible to time your separations so that you don't miss a feeding. This is ideal, because your breasts will not become uncomfortably full if you nurse your baby every two to three hours. Also, it's important to remember that regular, frequent nursing stimulates your milk supply and ensures that your baby is getting enough milk.

If you find it's necessary that the baby miss one or more feedings, you can plan ahead and express breast milk to be used in your absence. The advantages of supplementing with breast milk rather than formula are that your baby will have fewer digestive upsets, continued protection against infections, and no risk of an allergic reaction. Breast milk is the best source of nourishment for your baby

You may express your milk by hand or with a breast pump. The best time of day to obtain milk is when your milk supply is highest, usually in the morning. Don't be discouraged if you express less than one ounce at first. It takes awhile to become adept at expressing milk and for the letdown reflex to respond to the stimulus of manual expression or use of a breast pump.

To establish a letdown reflex (without which little milk is expressed) in response to expression, relax. Avoid expressing when you are under pressure to obtain milk. Plan in advance, practice in a calm setting (in the tub or while taking a shower), and realize that you won't get much at first. You're learning another new skill, just as you learned to breastfeed. At first it can seem awkward, but before long it will seem quite natural.

Today there are many excellent commercial breast pumps available through lactation consultants, medical supply stores, and maternity shops. They can be purchased or leased. If you'll be returning to work and plan on expressing milk several times a day, an electric model with a double-pump setup would be a worthwhile investment, because it works very quickly and tends to provide a higher milk yield than hand expression. Follow the directions from the manufacturer and give yourself time to learn how to get the best results.

Hand expression involves no equipment and can work well once you learn the technique. Place your thumb above the nipple, with several fingers beneath. Press your breast against your chest wall for greater pressure and then press inward with your fingers. This is done in a fairly quick movement and repeated rhythmically—press and squeeze, press and squeeze, etc. Sooner or later the milk sprays out of several openings in the nipple, slowly accumulating in a very clean bowl, cup, or plastic bottle. Rotate your hand so that you obtain milk from all the ducts underlying the areola. You will be able to tell if you are doing this correctly when you see milk spraying out of different openings when you change positions.

If you find this procedure difficult, you can apply warm compresses and massage your breasts prior to expressing, in the same way that you were shown for prenatal preparation. This will encourage the ducts to open and your milk to letdown.

You can express one breast or both breasts at a time, using one or two bags or jars. This is not appealing to some women and can only be done successfully if you're comfortable touching your breasts in this way.

Freeze the milk even if you are able to obtain only one or two ounces. The next time you express, chill the milk thoroughly and add it to the frozen milk until you have four ounces. Freeze four-ounce quantities to avoid waste. Never thaw the milk at room temperature—only in the refrigerator or under slightly cool running water—and do not warm it beyond skin temperature (feels neither warm nor cool when dropped on your wrist). Once the milk is thawed, it must be used within twenty-four hours. Once you've warmed it, discard any remaining milk.

Breast milk may be stored up to forty-eight hours in the refrigerator, two months in your freezer, or one year in a deep freeze. If you plan ahead and are careful about preparing and storing the bottles, breast milk supplements can be an excellent way for someone else to feed your baby while you're away.

BREASTFEEDING AND WORKING

Your decision to return to work or attend school after your baby is born doesn't have to mean that you must wean your baby, but it will take special effort and planning on your part to make the necessary arrangements to continue breastfeeding.

Do the advantages of nursing outweigh the disadvantages? Let's consider some advantages of nursing and working:

- Breastfeeding offers an exclusive bond between you and your child.
- There are numerous physiological benefits related to breast milk.
- You and your baby might feel reassured by the physical intimacy related to nursing.

Some of the challenges of nursing and working include:

- Special arrangements must be made, taking extra time and energy.
- Initially you may need to spend time at work pumping your breasts in the washroom.

- The baby's caretaker(s) has to have a supportive attitude, necessitating more communication between the two of you. Look for someone familiar with the advantages and processes of breastfeeding, open to your plans to work out this arrangement, and willing to cooperate.

Your milk supply does not need to be reduced due to your times away from your baby. If you can postpone returning to work until after your baby is three months old, your milk supply will have been firmly established through frequent contact with your baby.

If you do decide to return to work before your baby is three months old, your milk supply may become diminished if you don't get enough rest, neglect to eat nutritional foods and drink plenty of liquids, and are tense or worried. You can help resolve these problems by napping on weekends, going to bed earlier, taking a nap after work, nursing while you rest, and getting extra help with household tasks.

You may find it important to work out sharing of household tasks (cooking, cleaning, laundry, shopping, child care, yard maintenance, etc.) with your husband. Some studies suggest that working women who share a household with a working mate are often saddled with an inordinate amount of the household tasks and child care. You may be able to avoid this situation by talking about it with your spouse ahead of time and also on an ongoing basis.

Keep in mind that even without returning to work, most mothers are busy with five jobs requiring a good deal of their time and energy—self-care, care of the household, mothering, supporting relationships, and milk production (if nursing). Commitments made beyond these responsibilities take away from the time and energy available for their management. All of the parts are affected by the whole. Management of these parts requires prioritizing and organization. Very often working mothers are left with little time for themselves and for friends outside of the home. With careful planning this needn't always be the case.

How can you keep up milk production within this framework that is affected by time needed for the other parts of your life? Several options are available.

Complete Breastfeeding

Keeping your baby on breast milk can be accomplished in the following ways:

Work at home. Do you have any skills you could use in the home for pay? Typing, art or music lessons, and research for a professor are examples of such work. This allows you time with your baby without child-care expense.

Establish a caretaker near your workplace. If you can arrange for a caretaker who lives within a few miles of your workplace, you can arrange to be with your baby during the day. This allows you more contact with your child and alleviates the necessity of expressing milk.

Work on a flexible work schedule or find a part-time job. Broken shifts, short segments of work spaced at your convenience, and jobs that take up less than twenty hours per week will give you more contact with your child by cutting down on the number of hours you'll need to be away in one stretch.

Work full time, leaving your baby with the caretaker for the full period of time. This arrangement provides the least amount of contact with your baby during the day and requires the use of expression and storage of milk. You may find that your baby requires more attention from you after longer separation. (Usually partial bottle-feeding is the only way to deal with this situation. Once your baby is on solid foods, he will require fewer bottles during the day. Keep in mind, though, that he might nurse just as often when with you—for emotional support.)

Formula-Feeding and Breastfeeding

You can still give your baby the benefits of your milk even when you can't be with your baby during work hours. Before returning to work (two to three weeks ahead), begin expressing your milk. (Reread the section in this chapter entitled "Expression and Storage of Breast Milk.")

If you are able to and wish to express milk at work, you will benefit from having access to a refrigerator. The milk can be expressed directly into nurser bags or a clean jar and kept chilled and then frozen at home. Many women take a small ice chest to work for this purpose.

If expressing milk becomes too difficult, you may wish to have your baby's caretaker give bottles of formula while you are away. You can keep your milk supply stimulated by nursing your baby often when you're together. You may need to express some milk at work at first, but eventually your breasts will not be as full during long separations. Be sure the caretaker does not feed the baby close to when you'll be picking him up. Nurse your baby soon after your arrival, and nurse your baby before leaving in the morning so that your breasts will be empty at the beginning of your time away.

Other Things to Think About

When you are working, your baby may sleep more during the day and nurse more frequently during the evening. Even babies who were sleeping long periods at night may begin to nurse at night again. This need not be a problem if you sleep with your baby, either in your bed or on a bed in the baby's room, or if you transfer your baby to her own bed after she goes to sleep next to you. Extra snuggling from Mom is often what is being asked for, and mothering at night can be a positive experience for both of you, especially if you consider the night hours a replacement for the hours you are away during the day.

Each baby reacts differently to having Mom work outside the home. Please do each other a favor and evaluate it a step at a time, weighing the advantages and disadvantages, and the total effect the separation has on your family.

Attending school can be similar to working but in many circumstances is a more flexible situation. Often there is child care available either on or near campus, so that nursing between classes becomes a possibility. Expressing milk between classes also works well if your schedule is well planned. A small baby often is permitted to come along to class if he is content nursing or if kept in a cloth carrier, but always check this out with your instructor! Remember that you will need one hand free for note-taking.

It goes without saying that the father who can cook, shop, clean, and provide encouragement is invaluable. A supportive husband can make life easier for the family by simplifying the running of the household through his participation. If your husband can drive you to the sitter, it will also give you more time to nurse while he is driving. (This is illegal in some states.)

Traveling can be easy with a breastfed baby, but if you must be away from your baby for a day or more, you need not abruptly wean your baby. Purchase plastic breast shields to collect the milk that leaks and discard the extra milk. The greatest relief of engorgement can be obtained by using an electric breast pump (rent one and take it along) and an oxytocic nasal spray. This will help ensure near complete emptying of your breasts. Upon your return, your baby may detect your diminished milk supply and will have missed you, so you can count on him nursing frequently and for long periods for a few days.

Some babies seem fine during their mother's absence, but others become disoriented and confused. If you realize that you are taking a chance as you leave your baby, then you will be better able to cope with the outcome. A few babies actually refuse the breast if the mother has been gone for an extended period, but you might be able to pick up where you left off if you display patience and perseverance in encouraging your baby to resume nursing.

Don't forget: People's lifestyles differ. There are many ways to approach any desired outcome. Seek encouragement. Spend uninterrupted time with your baby. And don't forget that all of this extra effort is for the very best of reasons—your baby.

Rest, relax, and enjoy the time you spend feeding your child. Before you know it, your child will be weaned and more independent. The early months of your baby's life are precious indeed. It will be only a matter of time until your son or daughter is anxious to toddle away from you instead of into your tender embrace. The hours you invest rocking and holding your baby will be an experience that you'll never, ever regret.

Give what you have. To someone it may be better than you dare think.

HENRY WADSWORTH LONGFELLOW

SCRIPTURAL REFLECTIONS AND PROMISES

In quietness and in confidence shall be your strength.

ISAIAH 30:15 KJV

O Lord, our Lord, how majestic is your name in all the earth! You have set your glory above the heavens. From the lips of children and infants you have ordained praise because of your enemies, to silence the foe and the avenger.

PSALM 8:1-2

There is a time for everything, and a season for every activity under heaven.

ECCLESIASTES 3:1

The Lord is my shepherd, I shall not be in want. He makes me lie down in green pastures, he leads me beside quiet waters, he restores my soul.

PSALM 23:1-3

And whatever you do, whether in word or deed, do it all in the name of the Lord Jesus, giving thanks to God the Father through him.

COLOSSIANS 3:17

FIFTEEN

Promoting Peace in Your Family

May the words of my mouth and the meditation of my heart be pleasing in your sight, O Lord, my Rock and my Redeemer.

PSALM 19:14

Words and actions, saying and doing—a marriage is made or broken on the basis of such things, and a family tree may blossom or wither according to the level of compassion, wisdom, and nurture.

Jesus was born into a family as a firstborn son. He experienced a family relationship and yet was without sin in the midst of imperfect family members. By the time he entered his brief period of ministry outside of his community, he had had the opportunity to learn about human relationships firsthand. Because of God's willingness to send his own Son to be one of us, we can fully trust his Word to speak to us where we are.

Although God understands that there are no perfect people and no perfect relationships, he instructs us to follow Christ's example. Jesus forgave, and so he expects us to forgive; he served, and so he expects us to serve. Jesus would not have said, "Go and do likewise," if he hadn't expected us to benefit from his instruction. We grow in wisdom when we learn to adjust our expectations to fit what's real in terms of who God knows us to be.

Do you remember the key line in the movie *Love Story?* It declared that "love means never having to say you're sorry." But this idealistic phrase doesn't fit who we really are. The relationships we share with other family members as sons and daughters, brothers and sisters, husbands and wives, and parents and children test us. Within the framework of the family our selfishness gets ground away by the friction of opposing needs, outlooks, desires, and personalities.

Learning to say we're sorry and to extend forgiveness to one another promotes peace in a Christian home. No one is excluded. We all fall short every day. Yet we can continually discover the value of compassion if we seek to follow what the Bible tells us about how we are to behave toward one another. God's Word speaks to who we are and to what he created us to be.

The way we cope with disagreements, disappointments, and communication conflicts deeply influences family relationships. No matter how hard we try, we can't love perfectly. Even so, we can promote peace in our families when we:

- Acknowledge our imperfections and are gracious about noticing them in others.
- Learn and practice the art of making appropriate apologies—saying we're sorry.
- Accept conflict and bruised feelings as inevitable parts of family life.
- Ease conflict through improved communication.
- Find ways to express our anger appropriately and fairly.
- Refuse to nurture feelings of self-pity, resentment, emotional dependency, and dissatisfaction.
- Become faithful in forgiving others.

Lord, make me an instrument of Thy peace.

FRANCIS OF ASSISI

BABIES BRING CHANGES—AND CONFLICTS

The appearance of a new baby in the family produces conflict and tension as well as joy and a sense of accomplishment. Roles must change. There's more work to do, more money to be earned—and spent. Schedules are readjusted to accommodate the baby's needs for cuddling, food, and sleep. Decisions must be made and certain liberties restricted.

Children demand attention, space, protection, and guidance—among other things. The advent of parenthood brings about an explosion of responsibility. Learning to balance the baby's needs with personal and marital needs doesn't occur overnight. There are no cookbook answers to spell out a recipe for Adjusting to Parenthood. It takes time for a couple to develop a sense of balance and a state of equilibrium after becoming parents.

Think of a family you know whose members are emotionally well balanced and seem to have successfully adapted to one another. Such a family knows how to play together as well as work, worship, and live together.

Healthy families aren't born with the arrival of a baby; they're carefully constructed by the individuals who are committed to creating them. As a mother and father, you each will bring your own separate histories to your children, as well as the history you've shared as a couple. Your child's history and experiences will be closely woven with yours at first, but as the years go by, she will experience more on her own. These shared histories, and their resulting points of view, create a rich texture of ideas and perceptions that blend each life together to make a family.

As the days go by, each person will continually be challenged to see beyond his or her own point of view in order to understand where another family member is coming from. The apostle Paul understood that relationships in the Lord simply can't be built on a bedrock of egoism. If we limit ourselves to basing our relationships on our own histories and our own viewpoints, how can we possibly "maintain the same love," as Paul advises believers to do in his letter to the Philippians, or become "united in spirit, intent on one purpose"?

In Philippians 2:1-4, Paul provides a powerful antidote: "Each of you regard one another as more important than himself"(NASB). Without this foundation, marriages can't fulfill us as men and women, and families dissolve into mere shadows of what the Lord intended them to be.

OUR CREATED CAPACITY FOR ONENESS

In her book *Lifelines: The Ten Commandments for Today*, Edith Schaeffer wrote:

> *God created people, male and female, with a capacity for oneness with each other, a fruitful physical oneness that would bring forth another generation of people. God created people with a capacity for oneness in working together, communicating verbally, exchanging ideas, doing creative works, eating together, and walking and talking with God in the cool of the evening. People were made in his image that they might have a three-way oneness—intellectually, spiritually, and physically—on a horizontal level.*
>
> *People were made so that they could have a oneness with God spiritually, to love him, worship him, have communication with him, and to be able to seek his counsel and advice and help day by day. These two onenesses have been set forth to us in his Word, the Bible, and have to do with our knowing who we are and what will fulfill us. It is not a question of right and wrong; it is a question of what is. To act contrary to what is is to constantly bump one's head against a wall. We all do it in a variety of ways—and we all have bruises from the variety of walls we have hit!*

So what can we do about all those bumps and bruises then? First, we can accept the immutable fact that we're not going to be perfect marriage partners—or parents. We can do our best and then trust God to cover the rest.

Second, we can say we're sorry and ask the Lord to enable us to change, even though many changes will take place gradually. We can avoid some conflicts, and we can find ways to express anger fairly when situations arise faster than we can prevent them.

Third, we can learn to empathize with each another. To learn how to empathize more effectively, try:

Arranging for a time to be alone (or in a separate room), when it isn't likely that you'll be interrupted.

Setting aside what's currently on your mind. Noises, worries, physical discomfort, and other distractions interfere with your listening ability.

Thinking about what it's like to actually be your mate, not just thinking how *you* might feel in his or her circumstances.

Listening and watching for your spouse to identify his or her thoughts and emotions. How does she appear to be feeling? What is the sound and rhythm of his speech? Is she tense or relaxed?

Naming your mate's emotions silently, as accurately as you can. The emotions expressed may be subtle or blatant, obvious or hidden. What are you seeing, hearing, and sensing that confirms what the feelings are?

Reflecting back your spouse's feelings. After identifying what you think the feeling is, let your mate know what you are picking up. Say something to the effect: "It seems to me you're feeling . . ." or "I hear you saying . . ." or "It sounds as if you are . . ."

Focusing your response on the person instead of on the content of what's being said. Recognize and affirm your mate for who he is, instead of who you want him to be.

Curbing defensive listening behaviors. If you find yourself doing any of these things while you're listening, it will detract from your ability to actively hear and respond to your spouse:

- Explaining.
- Asking questions to satisfy your curiosity.
- Criticizing.
- Competing—talking about your own experiences.
- Daydreaming.
- Complaining.
- Sugarcoating—denying the other person's feelings by putting an optimistic spin on your responses.
- Advising without being asked for your opinion.
- Tuning out—assuming you know what the other is going to say before he says it or that you've already heard it before.
- Completing her sentences.
- Judging.
- Distancing—acting as if you already know how he feels.
- Allowing yourself to be distracted as an escape from uncomfortable emotions.
- Feeling frustrated or impatient.
- Interrupting.
- Projecting—thinking of what you might feel in her position.

DAY BY DAY

As we draw closer to the Lord and follow him day by day, we can better learn how to behave toward others. His Word sets forth guidelines we can use to inform and direct our actions.

The style or manner in which we live out our interpretation of Scripture varies from family to family. Yet the qualities that result from walking with the Lord are shared among all believers—honesty, humility, kindness, patience, gentleness, self-control, joy, peace, generosity, hospitality, and love are the spiritual fruit of our faith. Each can be expressed in an endless variety of ways.

The daily demands of family life involve dividing up household tasks, learning to communicate effectively with one another, preparing meals, earning money, caring for children, and making decisions about how to spend time, money, and energy.

While each family is unique, our Creator has provided a pattern for family life that gives us a framework to fill in with our individual talents and perspectives. Each day of family life involves many chances for disagreement. Who will change this diaper? Do this load of dishes? Take out this bag of garbage? Are there male and female tasks? Should I work outside the home? What physician should we take the baby to? The choices—and potential opportunities for conflict—are wide-ranging.

The way that we cope with disappointments, disagreements, and everyday "disasters" directly influences our family relationships. The really big issues of our faith often are not as problematic as the little annoyances that can distract us from our calling as wives and husbands, mothers and fathers.

The way questions are asked and answered, such as, "How could you let this toast burn?" can either disrupt or promote family peace. We need to be careful that our questions and actions don't become vehicles for expressing anger and hurtful put-downs to get a point across.

Potential Sources of Conflict During Early Parenting

- Outlook on parenting and child-rearing—values, goals, and expectations
- Housekeeping style
- Relaxation and recreation: Who gets breaks, why, and for how long?
- Money
- Where to spend the holidays
- Grandparents' role and level of involvement
- Career and day-care plans
- "Spoiling"—how much to hold the baby
- Breastfeeding vs. bottle-feeding; scheduled vs. demand feeding
- Bedtime and sleeping location—flexible or strictly scheduled; early or late; family bed or crib
- Pacifiers; thumb-sucking
- Weaning
- Toilet training
- Toys—type and amount
- Entertainment in the home—TV, movies, videos, electronic games, etc.
- Child discipline

ESTABLISHING VERBAL BOUNDARIES

Picture an action that conveys caring—a courteous gesture, the warmth of a gentle embrace, a cool cloth placed on a feverish brow, the sweetness of a genuine smile, a kind word spoken to provide reassurance, an offer to help.

Compare these behaviors to what can happen when wills clash and tempers flare up: Words are spoken that pierce the heart, eyes flash with harsh judgment, a hand shoves to push away, stony silence is the response to real need, a back is turned to prove a point—declarations that "I'm not with you."

We possess the ability to hurt and to heal, to tear down or build up those we claim to love. The ways we choose to express our inner thoughts and feelings matter. Our words are powerful reflections of what's going on inside our minds and hearts. Our actions can bring peace and serenity or strife and disturbance to the home front.

Criticism within families is a prime source of fuming, feuding, and fighting. We expect criticism from colleagues and casual friends, but we have a much greater emotional investment in our most intimate relationships. Our family members and closest friends are supposed to love and accept us unconditionally. Yet no one can love us perfectly.

How can we constructively communicate our expectations and in-bounds criticism concerning family relationships? If we took as much care in communicating with one another as we do with people we respect at church and work, it would significantly reduce family tension. Consider the following points:

Understanding our mates as they actually are—not who we want them to be—builds mutual trust and respect. Out-of-bounds criticism can destroy both.

In-bounds criticism is an acceptable way to communicate your desire for behavior changes. It takes into account both party's expectations, is given at the appropriate time, and contains a constructive, instead of destructive, message.

Out-of-bounds criticism is always destructive. It's never acceptable or appropriate to belittle, bash, or berate someone else. Whether the off-limits criticism is offered in public or in private, it's still hurtful to the receiver of the message—and to your relationship. If you grew up with a verbally abusive parent, you're already well acquainted with the long-lasting effects of toxic words.

Before you criticize, stop and think carefully about what you intend to say and why you want to say it. Ask yourself:

- Is this for my mate's benefit or mine?
- What will he or she gain from what I'm saying?
- Will he or she accept my criticism?
- Is the change I expect from him or her reasonable?
- Can he or she make the change I expect?

If your spouse won't benefit from your criticism, isn't capable of changing, or can't accept what you have to say, it's time to rethink your position and approach. If you still believe that your viewpoint is valid and valuable, you'll need to state clearly what the purpose of your criticism is and what the desired outcome or action will be.

CRITICAL BOUNDARIES: THREE THINGS TO REMEMBER

Think ahead. Before you speak, ask yourself: "What do I want or expect from this person?" If you know the answer to this question and understand what the desired behavior is, you may prefer to express your opinion in a different way.

Explain your expectations. Take time to explain clearly what you expect. Avoid subtle hints and silent messages. Say what you expect up front before misunderstandings arise.

Consider asking. It is easy to assume that others know what we are concerned about. Instead of telling your child what you want, try asking first.

CONFRONTING CONFLICT CONSTRUCTIVELY

Family conflicts will arise no matter how much we respect and value one another. At such times good communication and sensitive listening go a long way to produce family peace and mutual understanding.

"Contrary to popular belief, conflict is not necessarily bad. In fact, conflict can be a powerful tool for strengthening relationships and solving problems," explain Dr. Frank Minirth, Dr. Paul Meier, and Stephen Arterburn in *The Complete Life Encyclopedia.*

"When two people or two groups enter into an experience of conflict, many positive results can emerge—if the people involved in the conflict understand how to manage conflict in a caring and constructive way." To achieve this goal, the authors recommend using these guidelines:

- Learn to separate major issues from minor issues.
- When conflicts arise, confront them as soon as possible.
- Stick to the subject at hand.
- In times of conflict, avoid generalizing; be specific.
- Avoid personal insults and character assassination.
- Express real feelings; avoid intellectualizing.
- Demonstrate unconditional love and affirmation but avoid patronizing.
- Demonstrate empathy and reflective listening.
- Affirm publicly; confront privately.
- Confront to heal, not to win.

"In any conflict, the only real winners are the ones who learn how to manage that conflict to bring about a positive, constructive resolution," conclude the

Minirth-Meier counseling team. "When we approach conflict with courage, honesty, and love for the other person, conflict is no longer the enemy of relationships. It becomes our ally."

QUICK TIPS FOR CONFRONTING MARITAL AND FAMILY CONFLICT

- Once the disagreement comes to light, it needs to be discussed as soon as possible.
- The person with whom the conflict originated may need to be heard first while the other one listens.
- If you are angry or upset, you're likely to find it difficult (if not impossible) to listen with love or sensitivity. Take time to reduce your stress level before the discussion; tell your spouse that you'll listen once you've had a chance to calm down.
- During your conversation, use "I" (versus "You") messages.
- Let your mate know you accept the way he or she feels—it doesn't mean you've given in, negated your own feelings, or agree with his or her point of view.
- You may find that using one or a combination of the "Four C" strategies will work for you:

  Compromise—you both yield, moving toward common ground.

  Coexistence—you agree to disagree.

  Concession—one of you, though not always the same one, submits to the other.

  Conciliation—you commit yourselves to working together to make your views compatible.

Conducting a Family Meeting

Choose the right time and the right place. When possible, meet in a prearranged location in a pleasant, stress-free setting—a quiet restaurant, a stroll in the park, etc.

Don't issue orders. Adults are typically not open to being dominated or told what to do. You'll be better off aiming for a two-way conversation.

Steer clear of falling into an advice-giving pattern in the heat of a disagreement. Avoid blaming and bossing. Approach one another with sincere respect instead.

Avoid sentences that begin with "You." Share your opinions and feelings as "I" statements: "I think what's worrying you most is . . ." "I'll admit it bothers me when . . ." "I understand that you are . . ." "I see your point of view about . . ."

Communicate your feelings and preferences. Taking into account that *how* you express yourself helps or hinders your spouse's ability to listen to what you say, deliver your message so that it is more likely to be received.

Be what you wish others to become.

JO PETTY

PRACTICING DISCERNMENT

As your family grows up, I hope you'll find that the walls you run into eventually come tumbling down when you call upon the Lord for help.

We serve an almighty, living God who has given us many promises upon which to base our faith and hope. What we say and do matter. We can directly affect the lives of others and, in so doing, demonstrate the truth of God's Word and the reality upon which it is based.

Jesus has supplied us with a clearly marked map that shows us how to get where we want to go. If we choose to follow him, we're on the side of life and freedom. The next time you're tempted to think small, try envisioning the larger picture instead.

We need wisdom and discernment to determine what really matters in respect to eternity—it helps to do what the Lord requires of us when we keep in mind why we're here, where we're headed, and who we are as God's precious children.

The Lord loves each of us as sons and daughters. May we keep learning every day of our lives to reflect better what we've received from him within our own families while we're here.

SCRIPTURAL REFLECTIONS AND PROMISES

> *A new command I give you: Love one another. As I have loved you, so you must love one another. By this all men will know that you are my disciples, if you love one another.*
>
> JOHN 13:34-35

> *Let love and faithfulness never leave you; bind them around your neck, write them on the tablet of your heart.*
>
> PROVERBS 3:3

> *Love must be sincere. Hate what is evil; cling to what is good. Be devoted to one another in brotherly love. Honor one another above yourselves. Never be lacking in zeal, but keep your spiritual fervor, serving the Lord. Be joyful in hope, patient in affliction, faithful in prayer.*
>
> ROMANS 12:9-12

> *The law of the Lord is perfect, reviving the soul. The statutes of the Lord are trustworthy, making wise the simple. The precepts of the Lord are right, giving joy to the heart. The commands of the Lord are radiant, giving light to the eyes. The fear of the Lord is pure, enduring forever. The ordinances of the Lord are sure and altogether righteous. They are more precious than gold, than much pure gold; they are sweeter than honey, than honey from the comb. By them is your servant warned; in keeping them there is great reward.*
>
> PSALM 19:7-11

Finally, all of you, live in harmony with one another; be sympathetic, love as brothers, be compassionate and humble. Do not repay evil with evil or insult with insult, but with blessing, because to this you were called so that you may inherit a blessing.

1 PETER 3:8-9

Peace be to this house.

LUKE 10:5 KJV

APPENDIX A

FAMILY NUTRITION GUIDE

Do you feel that your diet is healthful? You can find out if it is by keeping a record of what you and your family eat for three days. You may then use the dietary guidelines and daily food guide included here to evaluate what was eaten and to determine the quality of your diet.

SUGGESTIONS FOR HEALTHY EATING HABITS

1. Eat a variety of foods. Try to keep in mind that no single food contains all the nutrients in the amounts you need. Eat a variety of basic foods at each meal, using the daily food guide. (See page 235 for recommended daily food amounts.)
2. Maintain a healthy weight. While pregnant, do not go on a reducing diet. You may, however, increase physical activity through a program approved by your health-care provider; eat less fat and fatty foods; eat less sugar and sweets; omit the use of alcohol.

   If you are within your normal weight range, eat and exercise to maintain your weight. Be sure you understand the growth curve of your developing baby, and accept the additional weight associated with your pregnancy. If you are 15 or 20 percent underweight when you become pregnant, increase your caloric intake beyond that recommended here and revise your exercise habits.
3. Avoid too much fat, saturated fat, and cholesterol. Moderation seems to be the key here. Choose lean meat, fish, poultry without skin, dry beans, and peas as your protein sources. (While you are pregnant, eggs are an excellent source of protein that you don't need to restrict as much, since you are producing high amounts of estrogen.) Limit your intake of butter, cream, hydrogenated margarine, and coconut oil, as well as foods produced from these products (most commercial bakery products). Trim excess fat from meats; skim the fat off stews and gravy. Broil, bake, boil, or grill your meats rather than frying them.

Cholesterol is one of the sterols (a lipid) manufactured in the body for a variety of purposes. It also is found in animal fats. Saturated fats are generally of animal origin and are solid at room temperature (exceptions are palm and coconut oils).

SATURATED/POLYUNSATURATED FAT CONTENT*

Type of Fat/Oil (g)	Calories in 1 T.	Total Fat Content (g)	Saturated Fat (g)	Polyun-saturated Fat (g)
Vegetable Fats				
Margarine, regular	100	12	2	3
Margarine, soft	100	12	2	4
Vegetable shortening	120	14	2	5
Whipped topping	15	1	1	trace
Vegetable oils				
Coconut	120	14	12	trace
Corn	120	14	2	8
Cottonseed	120	14	4	7
Olive	120	14	2	2
Palm	120	14	8	2
Peanut	120	14	2	5
Safflower	120	14	1	10
Soybean	120	14	2	8
Salad Dressing				
French, low-cal	15	1	trace	trace
French, regular	65	6	1	3
Italian	85	9	2	5
Mayonnaise, light	65	6	1	3
Mayonnaise	100	11	2	6
Animal Fats				
Beef tallow	115	13	6	1
Butter	100	12	7	trace
Chicken	115	13	4	2
Half-and-half cream	20	2	1	trace
Heavy cream	80	6	4	trace
Lard	115	13	5	1
Sour cream	25	3	2	1

*Developed by Harriet Kohn, nutritionist

MOCK SOUR CREAM

2 T. skim milk or ⅓ c. buttermilk
1 T. lemon juice
1 c. low-fat cottage cheese
Mix all ingredients in blender or food processor until smooth.
Yield: 1¼ c.

Mock Cream Cheese

1 c. low-fat cottage cheese
4 T. margarine
1 T. skim milk
Mix all ingredients in blender or food processor until smooth.
Yield: 1¼ c.

Substitutes for Saturated Fats

If the recipe calls for:	*Use:*
1 c. butter	1 c. margarine*
1 c. evaporated whole milk	1 c. evaporated skim milk
1 egg (for thickening)	1 T. flour
1 c. sour cream	1 c. plain yogurt or mock sour cream (see recipe)
1 oz. baking chocolate	3 T. cocoa powder plus 2 tsp. oil
1 T. cream cheese	1 T. mock cream cheese (see recipe)

*Better yet, use a spread with no hydrogenated fat.

High consumption of saturated fats may raise blood cholesterol. Polyunsaturated fats are generally of vegetable origin and are liquid at room temperature. An increase in polyunsaturated fats over saturated fats tends to lower blood cholesterol. Monounsaturated fats have no effect on blood cholesterol. Two examples of monounsaturated fats are peanut and olive oils.

4. Eat foods with adequate starch and fiber. As you reduce your intake of caloric fats, you should increase your intake of calories from starches, called complex carbohydrates, in order to supply energy. Select foods that are also good sources of fiber, such as whole grain breads and cereals, fruits and vegetables, beans, peas, and nuts.
5. Avoid too much sugar. Exposure to sugar on a frequent basis promotes dental decay and may lead to the development of obesity, diabetes, high cholesterol and hypoglycemia. New studies also suggest that eating too much sugar may raise the risk of heart disease and compromise the immune system. In addition, sugars are relatively high in calories compared to the nutrients they contain, making them low in "nutrient density." Many foods contain "hidden" sugar, so read the labels. Select fruits that are fresh or canned without sugar.
6. Limit your use of sodium—a factor associated with high blood pressure. It is estimated that about 20 percent of all Americans react unfavorably to sodium. At this time, there is no test to determine who is sodium-sensitive and who isn't. Table salt consists of about 40 percent sodium, so it is prudent to avoid adding salt at the table. Also, use little salt in cooking and limit your intake of salty foods.

HIDDEN SUGAR IN COMMON FOODS

Food	Serving Size	Tsp. of Sugar Per Serving
Chocolate bar	1 average	15
Chocolate cake	1/12 cake (2 layers with icing)	7
Marshmallow	1 average	1½
Angel food cake	1/12 cake	6
Plain doughnut	3" diameter	4
Brownie	2" x 2" x ¾"	3
Ice cream	½ cup	5–6
Sherbet	½ cup	6–8
Apple pie	1/6 medium pie	12
Cherry pie	1/6 medium pie	14
Pumpkin pie	1/6 medium pie	10
Ginger ale	12 oz.	7
Sweetened soda pop	12 oz.	10

A SALT-FREE SEASONING ALTERNATIVE

2 T. onion powder
1 T. garlic powder
½ T. basil
1 T. paprika
2 T. parsley flakes

Combine spices together and blend well. You can use different proportions of ingredients depending on personal preference.

7. Drink alcohol only in moderation. Alcohol is very high in calories and low in nutrients. When pregnant, it is wise not to drink at all due to alcohol's link to birth defects. More than two drinks daily when you are not pregnant is inadvisable.
8. Limit caffeine intake during pregnancy and lactation. Caffeine is a mild stimulant. According to the FDA, it can cause insomnia, nervousness, irritability, anxiety, and disturbances in heart rate and circulation. While moderate amounts of caffeine can improve endurance, a U.S. Army study showed that the most beneficial amount was about two milligrams per pound of body weight. With an intake beyond this, the advantages of caffeine were nearly eliminated. A 150-pound person would need about twelve ounces of coffee to consume two milligrams per pound.

(Note: the first seven guidelines are based on those provided by the U.S. Department of Agriculture and the U.S. Department of Health.)

SOME FOODS AND DRUGS THAT CONTAIN CAFFEINE

Foods and Drugs	**Milligrams of Caffeine Per Serving**
Coffee, 1 c.	250 mg.
Mountain Dew, 12 oz.	83 mg.
Cola, 12 oz.	65 mg.
Excedrin, 1 tablet	64 mg.
Tea, 1 c.	46 mg.
Midol, 1 tablet	32 mg.
Chocolate bar	25 mg.
Hot cocoa	10 mg.
Decaffeinated coffee	3 mg.

DAILY FOOD GUIDE

Food can serve a variety of purposes—to satisfy hunger, to solace one in a time of pain or stress, to bring people together socially—but a woman who is pregnant or breastfeeding needs to eat! The nutritional requirements of pregnancy and lactation can draw down one's energy reserves quickly, and the baby who must rely on the mother for growth is affected by what she eats. Eating well is a vital component of a healthful lifestyle for both mothers and their children.

Keep in mind that in order for a meal or snack to produce satiety (the feeling of the absence of hunger), the meal should include:

- fiber (or bulk)
- carbohydrates
- protein
- fat (not so surprisingly)

The following list of foods can be considered a "raw ingredients" chart. By combining these items creatively, you will find that midmorning, midafternoon, and before-bed snacks, in addition to your meals, will keep your energy up without tipping the scales. Be sure to pay attention to the portion sizes and stock up on foods that appeal to both your appetite and your waistline.

Fruits. (All roughly equal ten grams of carbohydrates and forty-five calories.) Fruits contribute vitamins, minerals, fiber, and carbohydrates to the diet. Eat the washed skins of many fruits to increase your intake of fiber. Nearly all fruits are low in fat, and none contain cholesterol. The body can make better use of the iron from food when it is eaten with a source of vitamin C at each meal.

Apple, 1 small
Apple juice, ⅓ c.
Applesauce (unsweetened) ½ c.
~+Apricot halves, dried, 4
+Apricots, fresh, 2 medium
Banana, ½ small
Berries (unsweetened)
- *Blackberries, ½ c.
- Blueberries, ½ c.
- *Raspberries, ½ c.
- *Strawberries, ¾ c.

Cherries, 10 large
Cider, ⅓ c.
~^Dates, 2
~^Figs, dried, 1
*Grapefruit, ½
*Grapefruit juice, ½ c.
Grapes, 12
Grape juice, ¼ c.
*Mango, ½ medium
Melon
- +*Cantaloupe, ½ small
- *Honeydew, ⅛ medium
- +Watermelon, 1 c.

+*Nectarine, 1 small
*Orange, 1 small
*Orange juice, ½ c.
*Papaya, ½ c. cubed
+Peach, 1 medium
Pear, 1 medium
Pineapple, ½ c.
Pineapple juice, ⅓ c.
Plums, 2 medium
~^Prunes, 2 medium
~^Prune juice, ¼ c.
~^Raisins, 2 T.
*Tangerine, 1 medium

(*Vitamin C source) (+Vitamin A source) (~Iron source) (^Calcium source)

Vegetables. (One-half cup contains about fifty-six grams of carbohydrates, two grams of protein, and twenty-five calories.) Vegetables contribute vitamins, minerals, and fiber to the diet. Some vegetables are also a significant source of carbohydrates, classified as a bread exchange. Vegetables are very low in fat, and none contain cholesterol.

*Asparagus
Bean sprouts
Beets
~*Broccoli
*Brussels sprouts
*Cabbage
Cauliflower
Celery
Eggplant
Green pepper
Okra
Onions
Greens
- +*Beet
- Chard
- ~+Collards
- Dandelion
- ~+*Kale
- ~Mustard
- +*Spinach
- +*Turnip

Mushrooms
*Tomatoes and juice
V-8 juice

Sauerkraut
String beans
Zucchini

The following vegetables contain fifteen calories or less per serving:

Chicory
Chinese cabbage
Cucumber
Endive
Escarole
Lettuce
Parsley
Pickles, dill
Radishes
+Watercress

(*Vitamin C source) (+Vitamin A source) (~Iron source) (^Calcium source)

Breads and Cereals. (One serving contains about fifteen grams of carbohydrates, two grams of protein, and seventy calories.) Whole grain and enriched breads and cereals are important sources of B vitamins, iron, protein, and carbohydrates. Whole-grain products also contribute magnesium, folacin, and fiber to the diet.

Bread, 1 slice:
- White (including French and Italian)
- Whole wheat
- Rye
- Pumpernickel
- Raisin
- Bagel, small, ½

Crackers
- Arrowroot, 3
- Graham, 2 squares
- Matzo (4 x 6 in.), ½
- Oyster, 20
- Pretzel Thins (sticks), 25
- Ry-krisp, 3
- Saltines, 6
- Soda (2½ in. square), 4

English muffin, ½
Plain bread roll, 1
Hot dog bun, ½
Hamburger bun, ½
Dried bread crumbs, 3 T.
~Tortilla, 6 in.

(*Vitamin C source) (+Vitamin A source) (~Iron source) (^Calcium source)

Muffins, bran or corn, equal 1 bread and 1 fat (about 105 cal.)
Cereal
Bran flakes, ½ c.
Ready-to-eat cereal, unsweetened, ¾ c.
Puffed cereal (unfrosted), 1 c.
Cooked cereal, ½ c.
Cooked pasta, ½ c. (spaghetti, macaroni, noodles)
Popcorn, unbuttered, 3 c.
Cornmeal, dry, 2 T.
Flour, 2½ T.
Wheat germ, ¼ c.

Meats, Cheese, and Nuts. (One ounce of any of these equals about seven grams of protein, three to five grams of fat, and fifty-five to seventy-five calories.)

Protein. This group is high in protein, phosphorus, vitamins B_6, B_{12}, and other vitamins and minerals. B_{12} is only found in foods of animal origins. Some of these foods are higher in certain nutrients: red meats and oysters—zinc; liver and eggs—vitamin A; dry beans, peas, and nuts—magnesium. Meats, fish, and poultry are all good sources of hemeiron, a type of iron well absorbed and utilized by the body.

Poultry cooked without skin, 1 oz.
Fish, fresh, frozen, or canned, 1 oz.
Low-fat cottage cheese, ¼ c.
Mozzarella or Farmer's cheese, 1 oz.
Parmesan cheese, 3 T.
Egg, 1
Peanut butter, 1 T.

Milk and Dairy Products. (One serving of milk equals about twelve grams of carbohydrates, eight grams of protein, a trace of fat, and eighty calories.) Milk and most dairy products are high in calcium. They also contribute riboflavin, protein, and vitamins A, B_1, B_6, and B_{12}. Some dairy products are fortified with vitamin D. Choose low-fat or skim milk if you wish to reduce calories and cholesterol in your diet.

Skim or nonfat, reconstituted, 1 c.
Powdered, ⅓ c.
Yogurt, from skim milk, unsweetened, 1 c.
Buttermilk, from skim milk, 1 c.
Low-fat milk or yogurt—add 1 fat serving to each for accurate calorie count
Ice milk, ⅓ cup

Fats. (One serving equals about five grams of fat and forty calories.)

Avocado, 4 in. diameter, 1/8
Bacon, crisp, 1 slice
Butter or margarine, 1 tsp.
Cream, light, 2 T.
Cream, heavy, 1 T.
Sour cream, 2 T.
Cream cheese, 1 T.
French dressing, 1 T.

U.S. Recommended Daily Allowances (U.S. RDA)

Vitamins, Minerals, and Protein	Unit of Measurement	Children 4 or More Years Old and Adults	Infants Up to One Year	Children 1–4 Years of Age	Pregnant or Lactating Women
Vitamin A	Int'l Unit (I.U.)	5,000	1,500	2,500	8,000
Vitamin D	I.U.	400	400	400	400
Vitamin E	I.U.	30	5.0	10	30
Vitamin C	Milligrams	60	35	40	60
Folic Acid	Milligrams	0.4	0.1	0.2	0.8
Thiamin	Milligrams	1.5	0.5	0.7	1.7
Riboflavin	Milligrams	1.7	0.6	0.8	2.0
Niacin	Milligrams	20	8.0	9.0	20
Vitamin B_6	Milligrams	2.0	0.4	0.7	2.5
Vitamin B_{12}	Micrograms	6.0	2.0	3.0	8.0
Biotin	Milligrams	0.3	0.5	0.15	0.3
Pantothenic Acid	Milligrams	10	3.0	5.0	10
Calcium	Grams	1.0	0.6	0.8	1.3
Phosphorus	Grams	1.0	0.5	0.8	1.3
Iodine	Micrograms	150	45	70	150
Iron	Milligrams	18	15	10	18
Magnesium	Milligrams	400	70	200	450
Copper	Milligrams	2.0	0.6	1.0	2.0
Zinc	Milligrams	15	5.0	8.0	25
Protein	Grams	45	18	20	+30

Calories of Popular Fast Foods

McDonald's:

Egg McMuffin	352
Hot cakes with butter and syrup	472
Hash browns	130
Cheeseburger	306
Quarter-pounder	418
Quarter-pounder with cheese	518
Big Mac	541

Filet-O-Fish	402
French fries (small)	211
Vanilla shake	323
Sundaes:	
Carmel	282
Hot fudge	290
Strawberry	229
Pineapple	230

Taco Bell:

Taco	159
Tostada	206
Bean burrito	345
Beefy tostada	291
Burrito Supreme	387
Pintos 'n' cheese	231
Enchirito	391

Wendy's:

Hamburgers:	
Single	360
Single, everything	472
Double	669
Triple	853
Single with cheese	577
Double with cheese	797
Triple with cheese	1,036
Chili, small	210
Chili, large	310
Frosty, regular	391
Grilled chicken	310
Breaded chicken	440
Baked potato, plain	310
Chicken nuggets, 5	230

Pizza Hut:

Thin and crispy (2 slices):	
Cheese	340
Pepperoni	370
Super-style cheese	410
Super-style pepperoni	430
Standard pork sausage/mushroom	380

Supreme	400
Super Supreme	520
Thick and chewy (2 slices):	
Cheese	390
Pepperoni	450
Super-style pepperoni	490
Standard pork sausage/mushroom	439
Super-style pork sausage/mushroom	500

Burger King:

Hamburger	293
Hamburger with cheese	347
Double-meat hamburger	413
Double-meat hamburger with cheese	519
Whopper Jr.	369
Whopper Jr. with cheese	424
Whopper Jr. double-meat	488
Whopper Jr. double-meat with cheese	543
Whopper	631
Whopper with cheese	740
Whopper double-meat	843
Whopper double-meat with cheese	951
Apple pie	250
Onion rings:	
Regular	266
Large	331
Chocolate shake	337
Vanilla shake	336
French fries:	
Regular	209
Large	359

Kentucky Fried Chicken:

Original recipe chicken:	
Wing	136
Drumstick	117
Breast	199
Thigh	257
Extra crispy chicken:	
Wing	201
Drumstick	155
Breast	286

Thigh	343
Original recipe dinner:	
All white meat	604
White and dark meat	661
All dark meat	643
Extra crispy dinner:	
All white meat	755
White and dark meat	828
All dark meat	765

NOTE: All dinners include two chicken pieces, roll, mashed potato/gravy, coleslaw. White meat includes wing and breast. Dark meat includes drumstick and thigh.

Roll (without butter)	61
Coleslaw	122
Kentucky Crisp Fries	156

Long John Silver's Seafood Shoppes:

Fish with batter:	
2 pieces	409
3 pieces	613
Clam strips (5 oz.)	465
Fries	275
Hush puppies (3)	153

Arby's:

Roast beef	350
Beef 'n' cheese	450
Super roast beef	620
Junior roast beef	220
Ham 'n' cheese	380
Turkey	410
Turkey deluxe	510
Club	560

APPENDIX B

CARDIOVASCULAR FITNESS

Cardiovascular or aerobic fitness is brought about through large muscle activity that is done rhythmically and continuously for a period of twenty to thirty minutes every other day. The heart and lungs must work to bring blood and oxygen to the working muscles, which results in an increase in breathing and pulse rates. Initially, the heart rate will be quite high. As the cardiovascular system adapts to the stress of exercise, the heart and lungs become more efficient, so that after six weeks of aerobic exercise, the heart rate is lower and the breathing calmer. Check with your health-care provider before beginning any exercise program, especially while you are pregnant.

There are many benefits to cardiovascular exercise. (See benefits chart.) Since this type of exercise spares blood sugar, the blood sugar level is maintained and the person is not hungry following exercise. Also, the energy level is increased by avoiding blood sugar fluctuations, which helps relieve tension, alleviate depression, and increase feelings of well-being.

OBSERVED BENEFITS OF AN EFFECTIVE EXERCISE PROGRAM

1. Increased mental alertness.
2. Improved memory.
3. Ability to study effectively and efficiently.
4. Ability to cope effectively with problems of stress.
5. Ability to communicate effectively.
6. Self-discipline leading to a healthier lifestyle.
7. Increased ability to affirm others.
8. Goals clarified to achieve greater spiritual development.
9. Increase in overall level of energy.
10. Decrease in the severity, duration, and frequency of illnesses.
11. Affirmation by others.
12. Ability to recognize feelings and to express them constructively.
13. Positive outlook on life.
14. Sense of well-being.
15. Self-confidence.
16. Sense of accomplishment.
17. Nutritional awareness.
18. Ability to use the relaxation response effectively.
19. Decreased or eliminated periods of anxiety or depression.
20. Improved coordination.

When muscle tissue is developed during aerobic exercise, fatty deposits are used as energy, thereby exchanging "fatty weight" for lean weight. The body becomes firmer, leaner, and healthier.

Cardiovascular fitness also results in increased stamina so that your body can perform under stress without undue fatigue. Stimulation of the heart and lungs makes them stronger, enabling them to work more efficiently throughout the day and making them less prone to illness. The stress of childbirth will not be as hard on your body if you have participated in a cardiovascular fitness program during pregnancy.

DETERMINING TARGET HEART RATE (T.H.R.) AND RANGE

1. Subtract your age from the number 220 (220-20=200).
2. Find 70 percent (.70 x 200=140) and 85 percent (.85 x 200 = 170) of the result. These two numbers make up your T.H.R. range.
3. You should stay between the 70 percent and the 85 percent range, called your target zone, for twenty to thirty minutes to achieve the full benefits of aerobic exercise. Stay at the lower end of your range or below while you are pregnant.

MAINTAINING PULSE RATE IN TARGET ZONE

Your workout consists of three equally important and distinct parts:

1. *The Warm-up Period*. Warm-up consists of five to ten minutes of less strenuous exercise, which should include stretching movements. This part provides for a gradual buildup in heart rate so that your cardiovascular system is not suddenly taxed, and injuries and soreness are prevented.
2. *The Stimulus Period*. Next comes exercise that is rhythmical and continuous for a twenty- to thirty-minute period, designed to keep your heart rate in your target zone. Periodic self-monitoring of your pulse is advisable. Do this by placing your first and second finger upon the large artery on one side of your neck and counting the number of beats over a six-second period. Multiply this number by ten to obtain your heart rate per minute (16 beats for 6 seconds x 10 = 160).
3. *The Cool-down Period*. For five to ten minutes at the end of your workout, you simply lessen the intensity of activity to allow your heart rate to dip to 120 beats per minute or below. If you suddenly stop exercising, you might inadvertently trap all the blood within the muscles that have been working. This may result in poor circulation to your brain, heart, or intestines, causing dizziness, extra heart beats, and nausea.

It's best to choose one type of exercise (see training pattern diagram) and stay with it for at least six weeks to become trained in that particular activity. Begin slowly and work up to your target zone over the six-week period, exercising three or four times weekly. After two or three weeks, you should notice improved physical fitness; after five or six weeks, the improvement should be significant. Your body will be more efficient; you may sleep more soundly and feel less tired. (During late pregnancy and for six weeks after giving birth, avoid exercise that involves bouncing, hopping, and jumping.)

As your fitness level improves, you'll need to exercise with vigor if you wish to make further progress. Always be sure to keep your heart rate in the 70-85 percent range. Evaluate your program monthly, updating it as needed.

CARDIOVASCULAR FITNESS TRAINING PATTERN

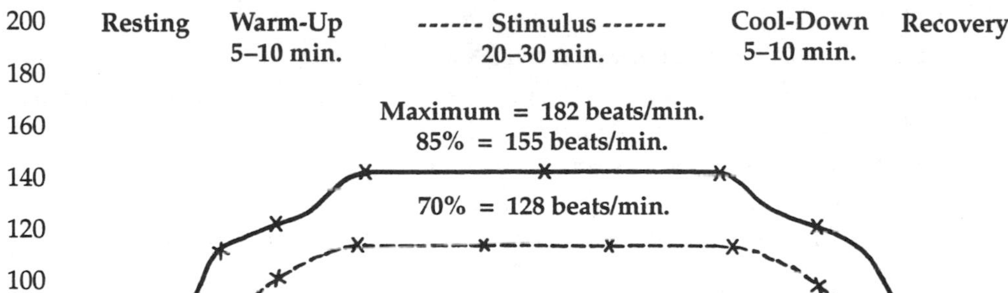

X = take pulse
— = nonpregnant
---- = pregnant
Examples of aerobic activity to build up to:
Cycling: 11-13 miles per hour (mph.)
*Walking: 5 mph.
Jogging: 5 mph.
Aerobic dancing
Rope skipping: Work up to 70-80 steps per minute, alternating feet.
Stair climbing: 10 steps—work up to 8 round trips per minute, using banister. May be done for 11 minutes 5 times per week.
*Swimming: 600 yards in 13 minutes.
*Ideal forms of aerobic exercise during pregnancy.

WARNINGS

Exercising in hot weather or at higher altitudes may increase your heart rate very quickly. Under such conditions, be especially careful to monitor your heart rate frequently. Drink extra fluids on warm days. Also, you may find that the "average" values for determining your target heart rate are too high for you. Evaluate and adjust your program if any of the following occur within a twenty-four-hour period following your workout:

1. *Nausea and/or vomiting*. Too little oxygen to digestive tract caused by too vigorous a workout or too quick a cool down. Exercise less vigorously; cool down gradually and for a longer period.
2. *Extreme breathlessness* lasting longer than ten minutes after workout. Exercise is too taxing for your heart and lungs. Keep your heart rate at the lower end of your target zone. If symptoms continue, keep heart rate even lower. While exercising, you should be able to talk.
3. *Prolonged fatigue* lasting longer than twenty-four hours. Exercise is too strenuous. Keep your heart rate at lower end of target zone or below, increasing level gradually.
4. *Side stitch*. Caused by too little oxygen. Take deep breaths, exhaling slowly. Lean forward to press pelvic organs up against your diaphragm.
5. *Charley horse or muscle cramps*. May be due to muscles unaccustomed to the activity reacting to strenuous exercise. Take a warm bath to eliminate waste products that build up on muscles and exercise less vigorously the next time.
6. *Pain in calf muscles* that only occurs during periods of heavy exercise. Can be caused by exercising on hard surfaces, unconditioned muscles, or poor circulation to the legs. Use thick, solid shoes and heavy socks. Cool down slowly. Cramps should disappear after a couple of sessions. If not, then circulation is more likely to be the cause of this problem. Consider switching to another form of exercise, such as swimming rather than jogging.
7. *Shin splints*. This pain on the front and/or sides of your calves is caused by inflammation of connecting tissue or by muscle tears. Work out on softer surfaces; wear thicker, more solid shoes; or change to an activity that puts less demand on your lower legs.
8. *Inability to sleep* (which did not exist before you began working out). You are probably exercising too vigorously. Stay at lower end of target range or just below. Gradually work toward remaining in the target zone.
9. *Flare-up of gout or arthritic condition* in joints (knees, ankles, hips, or toes). This pain is usually due to trauma in regions that are already vulnerable. You can apply remedies that may have helped in the past. Rest and delay returning to your program until the condition subsides and wear adequate shoes. Begin at the lower end of your target range when you return to your program.
10. *Dizziness, lack of coordination, confusion, light-headedness, cold sweats, pallor, glassy stare, blueness, or fainting*. Your workout is too vigorous, resulting in a lack of oxy-

gen to the brain. Rather than cool down, lie flat with your legs elevated, or put your head between your knees while sitting until the problem passes. Talk to your doctor before resuming your activity.

11. *Abnormal heart action*. Sudden burst of rapid heart beats, persistent rapid beats five to ten minutes after exercising, irregular pulse, jumpy or fluttery pulse, or sudden slow pulse may or may not be dangerous and should be checked by your physician.
12. *Pain or pressure in the center of your chest, arm, or throat* due to exercise. If you experience this pain either during or after exercise, you should see your doctor before resuming your program.

SELF-CHECK QUIZ

Ask yourself these questions periodically:

1. Am I including adequate warm-up and cool-down periods?
2. Do I exercise on at least three nonconsecutive days per week?
3. Do I spend at least twenty minutes in my heart rate target zone?
4. Do I avoid all warning symptoms?
5. Am I adjusting the rate and patterns of my exercise program to fit the special needs of pregnancy and postpartum?

APPENDIX C

SUMMARY OF OBSTETRIC PROCEDURES AND MEDICATIONS

It's wise to review common obstetrical procedures and drugs as you prepare for childbirth. This will insure your ability to give your physician or health-care provider informed consent.

Informed consent—a legal-medical concept—implies that you have been provided with understandable information that will help you to decide whether or not to allow a health-care provider to perform a specific procedure.

The following procedures and drugs are currently used throughout the United States. Each has its own indications for use, its benefits, and its risks. If you have any concerns or questions, your health-care provider should be able to discuss them with you and give you additional information.

DIAGNOSTIC PROCEDURES

Amniocentesis

This procedure involves the withdrawal of amniotic fluid from the uterus to gather any of the following information before the baby's birth:

Age of the fetus, detected from the examination of discarded skin cells in the fluid.

Sex of the fetus, determined from the presence of the sex chromosomes in discarded skin cells.

Fetal lung maturity, indicated by the ratio of the substances called lecithin and sphingomyelin present in the fluid. This ratio is a direct indication of fetal age and is especially important when planning an elective cesarean section.

Absence or presence of a number of genetic syndromes, detected by counting chromosomes in discarded skin cells.

Disorders resulting from abnormal or missing enzymes, discovered by examining the chromosome makeup.

Bilirubin content, important in determining whether an Rh-positive baby within an Rh-negative mother needs a blood transfusion while still in the uterus, or if labor should be induced because of danger to the fetus.

Adequacy of the baby's oxygen supply, determined by measuring the gas content of the amniotic fluid.

Some benefits. Amniocentesis provides parents who are at risk of having a child with genetic abnormalities with means of determining whether certain abnormalities exist. However, abortion, or "pregnancy termination," is often offered as a solution in the event of abnormalities. The National Institutes of Health book *Antenatal Diagnosis* points this out clearly: "It is critical to note the pivotal 'permissive role' played by the liberalization of abortion statutes in the late 1960s, which facilitated greatly the growth and utilization of amniocentesis and prenatal diagnosis services as a meaningful reproductive alternative" (U.S. Department of Health, Education, and Welfare, Bethesda, MD, April 1979).

Another benefit of amniocentesis is its role in determining the lung maturity of the fetus if medical reasons exist that require the baby to be born when gestational age is uncertain.

Possible risks. Theoretical possibility of risks to the mother include intrauterine bleeding and infection within the amniotic fluid. (This risk is about 1 percent.) Risk of injury to the fetus from the needle or from a resulting miscarriage is also around 1 percent. The culture of fetal cells or analysis of the fluid may not be successful, and, in the case of undiagnosed twins, the results pertain to only one of the pair. Many Christian parents who would not choose to abort after an amniocentesis may be exposing the pregnancy to unnecessary risks.

Ultrasound Scan (Sonogram, Ultrasonography)

Ultrasound is the use of sound waves beyond the range of hearing to display anatomical outlines. It provides diagnosis of early pregnancy; assessment of fetal growth and age; localization of the placenta; identification of multiple gestation; diagnosis of fetal death or confirmation of fetal life, attitude, and presentation; guidance for amniocentesis; detection of certain fetal abnormalities; fetal breathing effort and measurement of fetal heart tones (Doppler ultrasound).

Some benefits. Aids in the diagnosis of the above conditions and guides medical treatment and management of pregnancy and birth.

Possible risks. Ultrasound diagnosis seems relatively safe, but this may be due to the fact that its long-term biological effects have yet to be adequately studied. The National Institutes of Health have recommended that ultrasound be used only when medically indicated.

Urine Estriol Collection and Measurement

Estriol is a form of the hormone estrogen, which is produced in high levels during late pregnancy. Estriol is excreted in the urine, which can be collected for a twenty-four-hour period and measured for estriol levels.

The production of estriol is an indicator of placental function and fetal well-being. Some common indications for urinary estriol monitoring include diabetes, high blood pressure (chronic or induced by pregnancy), poor previous obstetric history, postmaturity, eclampsia, and toxemia.

Some benefits. Provides information on the condition of the fetus and placenta and allows for direct obstetrical management when complications of pregnancy arise.

Possible risks. None are known, other than possible errors that could occur in the testing procedures.

Oxytocin Challenge Test (OCT)

This test provides a way to assess how the mother and fetus would react to labor by conducting a "trial run." Labor is simulated through the administration of an intravenous drip of oxytocin, the hormone that contracts the uterus during birth. Uterine contractions and fetal heart rate patterns are recorded on an electronic fetal monitor (see following discussion). The fetal heart rate is studied as it responds to the contractions of the uterus. A negative test may indicate that the fetus would be adversely affected by the stress of actual labor, helping to determine whether a vaginal or cesarean birth is in the best interest of the baby.

Common indications for administering the OCT include high blood pressure, diabetes, toxemia, low urinary estriol levels, possible postmaturity, and suspected intrauterine growth retardation.

Some benefits. OCT provides a controlled setting for determining whether the fetus and/or the mother might respond adversely to actual labor.

The mother can use her trial labor, if it was medically indicated, to practice her skills for coping with labor. (This, however, is not a reason in itself to attempt actual uterine stimulation.)

Possible risks. Slight possibility of a false positive OCT. Also, there is a theoretical possibility that the strength and length of induced contractions, with resulting shorter rest periods, create stress that the OCT records when actual labor may not create the same degree of stress.

Nonstress Testing (NST)

The basis for the NST to evaluate fetal well-being is the assumption that the healthy fetus produces characteristic fetal heart rate (FHR) patterns. One type of NST measures the FHR by using the external electronic fetal heart monitor without additional stimulation of the uterus or fetus. This provides a readout of the FHR over a period of time, which can be examined for unusual changes.

Another type of NST uses an auditory stimulus to arouse the fetus. Fetal activity is provoked with sound waves (2,000 cycles per second of pure tone), which are amplified and conducted by a small speaker attached to the mother's lower abdomen.

Some benefits. Use of either of the NSTs may eliminate the need for an OCT, which is more expensive and takes more time. Also, use of the NST can provide valuable information to guide medical management of the pregnancy, especially when the OCT is inadvisable.

Possible risks. Additional studies are needed to confirm the reliability of the second method of nonstress testing.

Daily Fetal Movement Count (DFMC)

Some investigations have reported a significant decrease in fetal movement before an episode of fetal distress. The DFMC can be studied in various ways. Fetal movements may be counted by oneself or others for a twelve-hour period or during intervals throughout the day.

Some benefits. DFMC is inexpensive, available outside of a clinical area, and easy for a woman to do herself.

Possible risks. Further studies are needed to confirm the value of this test in specific situations, and a mother may become overly anxious about the absence of fetal movements, which normally decrease in late pregnancy.

Maternal Blood Studies

A number of conditions pertaining to the well-being of the fetus can be detected by studying a variety of enzymes, hormones, and antibodies present in the mother's blood. There is no apparent risk associated with the procedures used in obtaining blood for these studies.

Electronic Fetal Heart Monitoring (EFM)

Continuous fetal heart monitoring before and or during labor provides information on the condition of the fetus by tracing fetal heart patterns electronically. There are two modes of EFM. The external mode uses external transducers (leads), which are strapped onto the mother's abdominal wall. These measure the fetal heart rate (FHR) and the uterine activity. The internal mode uses a wire electrode that is inserted into the scalp of the fetus just under the skin, which measures the FHR, and a catheter placed in the cervix or uterus measures intrauterine pressure.

In the case of the external mode, ultrasound or high frequency sound waves are emitted from the transducer, which measures the FHR. As the sound waves strike the moving surface of the fetal heart a signal is directed back to the transducer. The FHR is then printed out on a strip chart, and a wave pattern is made visible on a screen (oscilloscope).

With the internal mode, an actual electrocardiogram of the baby is monitored. This is not subject to the many interferences that may limit the use of the external monitor.

Some benefits. Provides a continuously recorded display of the fetal heart rate. Variations between heartbeats can be seen and interpreted, and the quantity and quality of uterine activity is measured.

Possible risks. Accurate diagnosis of the fetal heart tracings requires skilled personnel. The skills of medical personnel in attendance are not always highly developed. Also, there may be a tendency on the part of some health-care providers to over-diagnose when fetal distress is present. Normal fetal distress will be difficult to distinguish from fetal distress that is due to the poor condition of the fetus.

It is not fully known how normal labor is affected by physical restraint of the laboring woman and by her emotional responses to laboring while connected to a mechanical device.

Also, the use of the internal monitor can increase the risk of intrauterine infection.

Fetal Blood Sampling (FBS)

This measurement of the blood pH (acidity) when fetal distress is suspected, as depicted on the electronic fetal heart monitor, is not used alone in determining the condition of the fetus. In fact, this procedure is not routinely used, since many factors can influence the blood pH of the fetus. Also, the procedure can be uncomfortable for the mother, as she must lie on her back for several contractions while the sample is being taken.

Some benefits. When the EFM detects fetal distress, this test can provide further evidence that distress exists.

Possible risks. The maternal blood pH can influence the fetal blood pH. Laboratory errors in determining the pH level can occur. The pH can be a reflection of the stage of labor and the influence of the stress of intrauterine pressure. The sample can become contaminated with room air or amniotic fluid. The cause of the drop in pH may have been short-term in nature.

OBSTETRICAL PROCEDURES IN LABOR

Enema

Although this procedure certainly isn't confined to obstetrical use, it is sometimes part of the obstetrical management of labor.

Some benefits. Empties the lower bowel so the baby will have more room and avoids the possibility of an involuntary bowel movement during the expulsion of the baby. Also helps to stimulate uterine activity.

Possible risks. Enemas may cause additional discomfort and anxiety for the mother.

If you have already had several bowel movements in labor, an enema may cause some dehydration and can upset the electrolyte balance in your blood.

Routine Administration of Intravenous Fluids (IV)

An IV of glucose (basic sugar) and sterile water may be routinely administered to a woman soon after admission to the hospital. Tubing is inserted into a vein, often at the back of the hand, to feed the liquid into the mother's circulatory system.

Some benefits. An IV provides energy and fluids when food and liquid by mouth are not given. Other medications can be added readily to the fluid. An IV started early in labor may avoid additional discomfort when labor is more strenuous. Some physicians feel that an IV is justified in case an emergency arises, at which time it might be difficult to properly start an IV. (Note: It is possible to have a partial IV inserted, called a "Heparin lock," to "keep a vein open," but not be attached to IV tubes until necessary.)

Possible risks. An IV can be difficult to insert, and repeated attempts at insertion are irritating. Being hooked up to an IV influences mobility and can contribute to a feeling of illness rather than of wellness. Some women are very anxious about needles; maternal anxiety can disrupt uterine activity in labor.

Partial Shaving of the Mother's Pubic Hair

This procedure also may be routine following admission to the hospital. It is not necessary since there is no clinical evidence to show that shaving reduces the chance of infection. If you arrange it ahead of time, you can carefully clip the excess pubic hair from around the area of your vagina prior to going to the hospital if you wish. Any hair that remains is thoroughly washed with an antiseptic solution before the baby's birth.

Some benefits. To facilitate the repair of the episiotomy and to help with hygiene after the birth takes place.

Possible risks. Shaving the pubic hair may actually increase the possibility of infection in some cases.

Amniotomy (Artificial Rupture of the Amniotic Sac)

During the first stage of labor, some physicians artificially rupture the membranes (amniotic sac) if these have not broken earlier. This is done by inserting a sterile plastic blunt-ended instrument called an amnihook into the vagina and through the opening of the cervix. The membranes are then torn with the amnihook, and fluid escapes from the uterus through the vagina. This procedure itself is normally painless. However, the uterus may become very irritable during the contractions that follow this procedure, creating a need for more strenuous application of pain relief measures.

Some benefits. This procedure often changes the quality of uterine contractions, making them more intense. This can be of benefit when labor is progressing slowly. Amniotomy may be done to enhance the quality of the contractions if labor is to be started artificially. Also, if the internal EFM is to be used, the membranes must be ruptured.

Amniotomy may be performed to check for meconium staining, an indication of fetal distress.

Possible risks. Once the membranes are broken, there is a greater possibility of infection. The longer they have been broken, the greater the incidence of infection. Studies have shown that the amniotic fluid within intact membranes helps to evenly distribute the amount of pressure that the uterus applies to the baby's head. Consequently, the baby's head is more vulnerable once the membranes have broken. Further studies need to be done to evaluate what effects this procedure has on the fetus. Rupturing the membranes can cause compression of the umbilical cord, which affects the fetal oxygen supply.

Stimulation and Induction of Labor Through Pitocin-Drip

Pitocin is the trade name given to a synthetic form of oxytocin, the hormone that causes uterine contractions in labor and during breastfeeding. Often the drip is metered through an infusion pump that measures the number of drips a mother receives per minute. Uterine contractions that are weak can be stimulated by Pitocin. The uterus also can be provoked to contract through the administration of this drug.

Some benefits. If diagnostic tests reveal that a mature baby is overdue by three weeks or more, an induction can avoid complications associated with postmaturity of the baby and placenta.

If a medical problem exists for the mother, it is often important to begin labor before the problem becomes more hazardous to both the mother and the baby. If the membranes have ruptured spontaneously, and labor doesn't begin within an optimal length of time, induction of labor can decrease the possibility of infection. (However, avoidance of vaginal exams can also help to decrease the risk of infection, and Pitocin can be used to stimulate contractions that are weak and are not opening the cervix.)

Possible risks. Contractions can be longer and closer together under the influence of Pitocin. This can increase the risk of reducing the baby's oxygen supply. Because the contractions are often more intense, a mother may be more likely to request pain relief medication, with resulting risks to the baby. Also, some studies have shown a slightly higher risk of jaundice in newborns after Pitocin was given to the mother.

Pitocin can overstimulate the uterus if the dose is too high. This, in extreme cases, increases the risk of premature separation of the placenta, asphyxiation of the fetus, or uterine rupture.

Miscalculation of the baby's due date can lead to premature delivery of an infant, with a greater possibility of the baby having more medical problems than a full-term newborn.

Episiotomy

An episiotomy is a surgical procedure a doctor or midwife may use to enlarge the vaginal outlet. It involves making an incision in the perineum, which is made up of body tissue located between the vagina and the rectum. A local anesthetic is typically administered to numb the area. The incision is sutured after the baby and placenta have been delivered.

Some benefits. If the perineum is inelastic or hasn't had time to stretch and distend gradually, an episiotomy will prevent uneven tearing of tissue. When a quick delivery is necessary due to fetal distress, an episiotomy can hasten the birth. Also, it is widely believed that the use of episiotomy helps to prevent relaxation of pelvic floor muscles, since the baby's head may be stretching the muscles for a long a period of time during the second stage of labor. If the baby's head is disproportionately large in comparison to the vaginal opening, an episiotomy will help to avoid accidental damage to the perineum.

Possible risks. Discomfort associated with the repair and healing of the episiotomy site can impair the comfort and ability of the mother to a care for her newborn baby. Blood loss and infection are possible complications of this procedure.

All drugs used for anesthesia are potentially toxic. If injected into a blood vessel or given in too high a concentration, the medication will adversely affect the mother. (This is unlikely to happen if the anesthetic is administered by a competent health-care professional.)

Dorsal/Lithotomy Position

In this position, a woman lies flat on her back with her legs propped up above her body in stirrups. The position is used for several operative procedures other than childbirth. The dorsal/lithotomy position was adopted when women received general anesthesia during the second stage of childbirth and were asleep for the birth of their babies. Since all voluntary effort to enhance the baby's birth is impossible if a laboring woman is unconscious, her body had to be positioned to allow the physician to assume the active role in the baby's delivery. Forceps were commonly used to take the baby out of the mother's body.

If the mother is conscious and able to assume an active role in birthing her baby, she should use a position that allows her to utilize gravity and helps her to avoid the many negative effects of the dorsal/lithotomy position.

Some benefits. Gives the attending physician or midwife a clear view of the birth. Facilitates the use of forceps or vacuum extraction of the baby and the episiotomy procedure. If an epidural anesthetic has been administered and the legs cannot be voluntarily controlled, stirrups must be used.

Possible risks. Negatively affects the mother's urinary output, circulation, breathing, level of oxygen in the bloodstream, and alignment of bones in the pelvis. This position has been demonstrated to increase the length of labor and decrease the strength of uterine contractions. Also, there is a greater need to perform an episiotomy if the mother is flat on her back, since the baby is pressing down onto the lower part of the perineum and upon the rectum.

The mother cannot see what is happening and assumes a passive role in birthing her child. She cannot brace herself and use much voluntary effort to push during the second stage. There is an increased possibility that the placenta will be retained during the third stage of labor rather than spontaneously detaching from the uterine wall.

This position is not conducive to early breastfeeding and does not allow the mother to hold her baby comfortably after the birth has taken place.

Low Forceps/Vacuum Extraction

Obstetrical forceps are metal tongs used to rotate or deliver a baby if the mother is unable to birth the baby herself or when the baby's condition requires a speedy delivery. Vacuum extraction is often used instead of forceps and for the same reasons as forceps. Vacuum extraction involves applying suction through a disc placed upon the baby's head to bring the baby out of the mother's pelvis.

Some benefits. If fetal distress is present (fetal heart rate below 100 or over 160), obstetrical assistance can bring about a quicker delivery for the baby. Also, when the mother is exhausted or unable to push because she has had a regional anesthetic, either of these procedures may be used to deliver the baby vaginally rather than by cesarean section.

Possible risks. These procedures establish a greater need for a larger episiotomy. If forceps are used, there may be reddish-colored bruise marks on the baby's temples or cheeks for a few days; rarely temporary facial paralysis may result.

If vacuum extraction is used, it is common for the disc to leave a temporary bump on the baby's head where it was applied. Following vacuum extraction, there have been cases of fetal hemorrhage within the skull. Fortunately this is rare.

OBSTETRICAL MEDICATION: PREVENTION AND TREATMENT OF PAIN IN LABOR

Pain is not simply a sensory experience. It can become overwhelming, disrupting activity and leading to personality changes. Although the source of pain can be relatively the same from woman to woman, influences other than the actual stimulus modify pain perception. Reactions to a particular cause of pain not only vary among individuals, but reactions vary in the same individual at different times. An individual's reaction is based on past experiences, present attitude, mood, emotions, judgment, the significance assigned to the stimulus, and the attitudes conveyed by the attendants.

Many medications can alter the experience of pain during childbirth. No single drug is used routinely for all women. The methods used also vary from facility to facility. The use of medication during labor should be evaluated in terms of the mother's preference; the effects on the mother, baby, and labor process; the degree of pain relief desired; and the facility and skill of the person administering the medication.

Each medication has its own specific indication—and the limitations of each drug will vary under different conditions. Each has its own particular advantages and disadvantages. The medication used should cause the least degree of interference to the bodily functions of the mother and should not pose unusual risk to her baby.

Since each woman reacts to the pain of labor in her own unique way, the need for medication varies from woman to woman. You should consider the effects and limitations of the drugs so you can make a knowledgeable decision regarding their use when you are in labor.

Pain relief in labor is accomplished with the use of analgesia, which modifies the perception of pain, and anesthesia, which blocks sensation entirely. Analgesia may be psychological or chemical. Psychological modification of pain has been reviewed earlier. (See chapter 7.) Tranquilizers also are used in labor to relieve tension and anxiety.

Questions to ask your health-care provider and childbirth instructor about pain medications:

Comments by your health-care provider about pain medications:

Drugs Used: Benefits and Possible Risks

SEDATIVES

Drugs that ease excitement by producing a restful feeling.

Barbiturates: Phenobarbital (Luminal), amabarbital (Amytal), phentobarbital (Nembutal), butabarbital (Butisol), secobarbital (Seconal).

How they're administered: Orally or by IM (intramuscular) or IV (intravenous) injection.

Effect on mother: Reduce anxiety, possibly slow the heart rate, cause disorientation, lower blood pressure (B. P.). Administration of one of these drugs may allow mother to sleep.

Effect on labor: In excessive doses given at too early a phase, labor may be slowed.

Effect on fetus/newborn: These drugs can accumulate in the baby's tissue. They may lower Apgar scores, lessen sucking ability, slow respiration, decrease responsiveness, raise B. P., and/or cause poor muscle tone, especially in infants whose mothers received one of these drugs within twenty-five minutes of the baby's birth.

TRANQUILIZERS

Drugs capable of reducing anxiety and relieving tension. These drugs modify an individual's reaction to pain. They are frequently used along with narcotics.

Common ones are: hydroxyzine (Vistaril, Atarax), diazepam (Valium), promethazine (Phenergan), chlordiazepoxide (Librium), meprobamate (Equanil, Miltown), promazine (Sparine), prochlorperazine (Compazine), chlorpromazine (Thorazine).

How they're administered: Orally or by injection (IM or IV).

Effect on mother: Produce calm; may allow a mother to rest. Other effects may include dizziness, sleepiness, dry mouth, fluctuations in B. P., nausea, urine retention, disorientation.

Effect on labor: None known.

Effect on fetus/newborn: Effects may possibly include impaired ability to maintain temperature and impaired behavior in the newborn lasting for several days. Since these drugs are usually used in combination with others, their effects are difficult to determine on an individual basis.

ANALGESICS

Agents capable of reducing, abolishing, or altering pain perception. These drugs can benefit the fetus by stopping uncontrolled hyperventilation, which can be a mother's reaction to painful labor. They reduce the pain threshold so that an individual doesn't react to stimuli as being painful. When pain relief is inadequate, a mother may experience loss of confidence, fearfulness, anxiety and/or stress, which may affect her ability to cope with labor. Sensitivity to pain, rather than cervical dilation or the strength and frequency of contractions, is the cue for use of analgesics.

Narcotics: morphine, meperidine (Demerol, Mepergan), pentazocine (Talwin), alphaprodione (Nisentil).

How they're administered: By IV or IM injection. Nisentil may be given by subcutaneous injection.

Effect on mother: Produce a sense of separation between self and pain stimulus. Other effects may include depression, nausea, dry mouth, itchiness, dizziness, lowered breathing rate, raised B. P.

Effect on labor: Progress of labor may be slowed if given too early, or labor may go faster if drug is given during the later part of the first stage (7 or 8 cm.).

Effect on fetus/newborn: Disorientation, less interest in mother's voice, lower responsiveness, visual difficulties, bluish skin tone are all possible effects.

ANESTHETICS

Medications that completely block pain impulses by producing a loss of sensation. Can be given locally or regionally to numb a specific area, or if a general anesthesia is used, it can cause a loss of consciousness. Effects on the mother, her baby, and the progress of labor vary greatly with the drug, the dosage, and the route of administration.

Anesthesia: procaine (Novocain), tetracaine (Pontocaine), chloroprocaine (Nesacaine), piperocaine (Metycaine), lidocaine (Xylocaine, L-caine, Seracaine), dibucaine (Nupercaine), mepivicaine (Carbocaine).

How they're administered:

Types	*Areas*
Pudendal block	Rectal/genital area
Paracervical block	Cervix
Caudal blocks	Upper legs, lower pelvic area
Low spinal Spinal block	Legs, lower pelvic area, may extend up to mid-chest
Saddle block	Area that would touch a saddle
Epidural block	Upper legs and pelvic area

Effect on mother: Possible drowsiness, restlessness, dizziness, lowered B. P., lowered heart rate, or toxic reaction.

Effect on labor: Possible stopping or slowing of labor if given too early. The most extensive blocks can interfere with the mother's ability to aid in the expulsion of the baby.

Effect on fetus/newborn: If fetal distress exists when drug is given, fetal depression may become complicated.

Other Anesthesia: prilocaine (Citantest), bupivicaine (Marcaine).

How they're administered: Local infiltration, perineum, lower vagina.

Inhalation Anesthesia: cyclopropane or trimethylene, ether, halothane (Fluothane), methoxyflurane, nitrous oxide, trichloroethylene (TCE, Trilene, Trimar).

How they're administered: By inhalation through nose and mouth. Results in loss of consciousness.

Effect on mother: May cause lowered breathing rate, changes in heart rate, changes in B. P., and irregular heartbeat. Can impair the functioning of digestive tract, liver, and/or uterus. Can cause nausea, vomiting, depression, sleepiness, dizziness, disorientation, and postpartum hemorrhage

Effect on labor: Effect will vary with drug used. Contractions may be suppressed or may stop completely depending on the amount and the specific agent administered.

Effect on fetus/newborn: Baby must be delivered by cesarean section or forceps immediately following the administration of general anesthesia, thereby reducing the possibility of depression of the fetus and newborn.

OXYTOCICS

Agents that cause contraction of muscle fibers in mammary glands and uterine tissue. These drugs are used to stimulate or induce labor, to prevent postpartum hemorrhage, and to stimulate the letdown reflex when necessary for successful breastfeeding.

Some common ones are: synthetic oxytocin (Oxytocin, Pitocin, Syntocinon), ergonovine maleate (Ergotrate), methylergonovine (Methergine), sparteine sulfate (Spartocin, Tocosamine).

How they're administered: Through IV fluids, by IM injection, orally, or by nasal spray (for breastfeeding).

Effect on mother: Can elevate or lower B. P.; can cause strong contractions of longer duration, uterine rupture, nausea, headache, anxiety, swelling, vomiting, water intoxication.

Effect on labor: The quality of labor can change dramatically with the use of oxytocics, with contractions very quickly becoming stronger and longer. Oxytocics do not necessarily produce cervical dilation or progress of labor.

Effect on fetus/newborn: Can lead to lower oxygen in blood due to longer contractions and/or changes in heart rate.

APPENDIX D

SCRIPTURAL REFERENCES

All Things Work Together for Good

Ecclesiastes 3:1-14
Romans 8:28

Attentiveness

Hebrews 2:1

Being One

Philippians 2:1-2, 4

Blessings/Benediction

Hebrews 13:20-21
James 1:17
1 Peter 4:6-11
2 Peter 1:5-9

Breastfeeding

Isaiah 66:11

Childbirth

Genesis 3:16; 30:23, 24
Psalms 37:7a; 41:1-2; 71:6; 125:1
Ecclesiastes 3:2
Isaiah 65:23; 66:9
John 16:21
1 Timothy 2:15

Children

Psalms 103:17; 112:1-2; 115:13-15; 127:3-5
Proverbs 10:1; 13:1; 17:6
Isaiah 44:2-3
Matthew 19:14
Mark 9:36-37
Ephesians 6:1
2 Timothy 3:14-15

Children: Raising Them

Deuteronomy 6:6-7
Psalm 78:18
Proverbs 1:8-9; 2:1-5; 3:1-3, 11, 12; 4:1-9; 6:20-22; 13:1; 22:6; 23:22-25; 29:15, 17
Colossians 3:21
Hebrews 12:9-10

Comfort

Psalms 23:4; 119:76; 125:1; 145:18
Isaiah 61:2-3; 66:13
Jeremiah 31:13
Romans 15:4
2 Corinthians 1:4-5
2 Thessalonians 2:16-17

Confidence

Psalm 27:3
Proverbs 3:26
Ephesians 3:12
Hebrews 4:16; 10:35
1 John 2:28; 3:21-22; 5:14

Conscience-Cleansing

Hebrews 9:14

Creation

Psalms 8; 139:13-16
Isaiah 44:2

Discipleship: Its Cost

Matthew 13:44-46; 16:24-26

Encouragement

1 Thessalonians 4:18; 5:11
2 Thessalonians 2:16-17
Hebrews 3:13; 10:25

Facing Trials

James 1:2-8
1 Peter 1:6-7; 4:12-19

Faith

Matthew 17:20
Mark 11:22
Acts 3:16
1 Corinthians 16:13
2 Corinthians 5:7
2 Thessalonians 1:3-5

Hebrews 11:1

Family Relationships

Genesis 2:24
Psalm 128
Proverbs 5:18-19; 14:1; 18:22; 31
Ephesians 5:31-32; 6
I Timothy 3:1-11
Titus 2:35
1 Peter 3:1-8

Friendship

Psalm 133
Proverbs 17:17
John 15:13, 15
1 John 4:7-8

Gaining Aid

Psalms 5:1-3; 20:1-2; 54:4; 77:1-6
Isaiah 41:10
Philippians 1:19
Hebrews 6:10
James 5:13

Gaining Power

Zechariah 4:6
Ephesians 3:16-19; 6:10

Giving Thanks

Psalms 30:12; 75:1; 116:17; 118:21; 136:1-3, 26
1 Thessalonians 5:18

God's Greatness

Psalms 66; 71:14-24; 84; 92; 93; 95; 96; 97; 99; 100; 101; 107; 111; 113; 117; 118; 134; 135; 136; 144; 145; 147

God's Love

Psalms 136; 145:8-9
Jeremiah 31:3
Matthew 11:29-30

God's Protection (See Special Psalms)

Good Gifts

Psalm 85:12
Matthew 7:11
James 1:17

Guidance

Psalms 25:5; 48:14; 73:21-28; 119:105; 130; 143:110
Proverbs 3:6
Isaiah 45:3
John 16:13

Joy

Nehemiah 8:10
Psalms 5:11; 16:11; 20:5; 30:5, 11-12; 3:17; 40:16; 47:1, 6; 51:10-12; 52:9; 68:3; 70:4; 71:8, 14; 81:1; 86:4; 89:16; 90:14; 91:4; 100; 104:34; 118:24; 126:5; 145:5
Proverbs 12:20
Ecclesiastes 2:26
Isaiah 35:10; 55:12; 61:10
Matthew 25:21
John 15:11; 16:24
Romans 5:11; 14:17; 15:13
Galatians 5:22
1 Thessalonians 5:16
James 1:2
1 Peter 1:8; 4:13

Labor (Work)

Psalms 127:1; 128:1-2
Proverbs 10:16; 14:23
Isaiah 65:23
Matthew 11:28
1 Corinthians 3:8; 15:58
1 Thessalonians 1:3
Hebrews 6:10
Revelation 2:2

Making Plans

Proverbs 16:3, 9

Our Position in Christ

Romans 5:1-11
Hebrews 12:18-25

Peace

Psalms 4:8; 29:11; 34:14; 119:165
Proverbs 12:20
Isaiah 26:3; 54:10
John 14:27
Romans 5:1; 8:6; 14:17, 19
Galatians 5:22
Ephesians 2:14
Philippians 4:7
Colossians 3:15

Perseverance

Ephesians 6:11-18
1 Thessalonians 5:8
Hebrews 10:23-25; 12:1-12

Physical Training
1 Timothy 4:8

Prayer
Romans 12:12
Ephesians 6:18
Colossians 4:2
1 Thessalonians 5:17
James 5:16

Pregnancy
Psalms 51:5; 113:9; 138:8; 139:13-15
Ecclesiastes 11:5
Jeremiah 1:5

Protection
Deuteronomy 33:27
Psalms 91:9-15; 121:3, 5, 7; 145:20
Proverbs 12:21

Psalms to Highlight During Labor
Blessing—67:1
Covering—91
Creation—8
Deliverance—4; 142
Faithful love—117
God's Greatness—145
Help—63; 102:1-2
Protection—20; 121
Refuge—16; 23
Rest —62:1-4
Salvation—18:1-6, 30
Savior—27; 51:10-12; 61
Shelter—61; 62 (esp. vv. 5-8); 103:5

Purpose of Scripture
2 Timothy 3:16-17

Responsibility (Parental)
Proverbs 13:22
Luke 11:17
2 Corinthians 12:14
Ephesians 6:4

Rest
Psalms 4:8; 63:6; 116:7; 131
Isaiah 30:15
Matthew 11:28

Sharing Our Worries
1 Peter 5:7

Special Psalms
Homage—29
King of Glory—24
Music—33
Praise—34; 47; 48; 56:10; 57:9; 63:4; 64:10; 66:8; 67:3; 68:19, 26, 32; 69:30, 34; 71:32; 72:19; 79:13; 84:4; 92:1; 96:4; 103:20; 106:5; 109:1, 30; 119:108, 175; 145:3; 146:2; 147:1; 148; 150
Victory—21; 47; 48

Strength
Psalms 29:11; 31:24; 73:26; 84:5; 89:21
Isaiah 12:2; 30:15; 35:3; 40:30-31
Jeremiah 16:19
2 Corinthians 12:9
Ephesians 3:16
Colossians 1:11
2 Timothy 4:17

Submission (to God's Will)
Luke 1:38

Thought Patterns
Philippians 4:6-8
Colossians 3:15-17

Trust
Psalm 37:3-4

Two Together
Ecclesiastes 4:9-12
Song of Solomon 2:36; 8:7
Matthew 18:19-20

Words
Proverbs 16:24
James 3

Worldly Philosophies
1 John 4:1-6

GLOSSARY OF TERMS

Abdomen: The portion of the body containing the stomach, intestines, bowels, bladder, and uterus.

Abdominal wall: The muscles that form a corsetlike structure from the pubic bone to the ribs and breastbone, and from side to side across the abdomen.

Abruptio placentae: The premature separation of the placenta from the uterine wall.

Active labor: Regular uterine contractions associated with increasing dilation of the cervix and the descent of the baby.

Afterbirth: A term for the placenta, amniotic sac, and umbilical cord.

After pains: Cramplike postpartum contractions usually lasting up to forty-eight hours, resulting from the efforts of the uterus to expel the afterbirth and prevent bleeding from the placental site.

Albumin: A simple protein in all animal tissues that may be present in maternal urine during pregnancy.

Alveoli: The milk glands in the breast that secrete milk when stimulated by the hormone prolactin.

Amniocentesis: The removal of amniotic fluid with a syringe for diagnostic or therapeutic purposes.

Amnion: A thin, transparent, tough sac that holds the baby in amniotic fluid. (Synonymous with *amniotic sac, bag of waters.*)

Amniotic fluid: A clear to slightly cloudy fluid that protects the baby from injury in the uterus, helps to maintain an even temperature, and prevents the amniotic sac from adhering to the baby's skin.

Amniotomy: The artificial rupture of the amniotic sac performed by a physician.

Analgesia: The absence of normal sense of pain, produced by chemical, psychological, or other means.

Analgesic: A drug that relieves pain but does not induce a loss of consciousness.

Anemia: A condition in which there is a reduction in the proportion of red corpuscles in the blood, thereby reducing the capacity of the blood to carry oxygen to body tissues.

Anesthesia: The partial or total loss of sensation, with or without a loss of consciousness.

Anesthetic: A drug or gas that produces partial or complete insensitivity to pain.

Antepartum: The time before the baby is born. This term is also applied to the labor and delivery functions and staff of a hospital.

Anterior position: The crown of the baby's head is facing toward the mother's abdomen as it descends into her pelvis.

Anus: The opening of the rectum between the buttocks.

Apgar score: A means of evaluating a newborn baby's breathing, heart rate, muscle tone, reflexes, and color at one, five, and ten minutes after birth. Each of the five categories is assigned a value of 0, 1, or 2. A score of 7-10 is normal; 6 or less means that the baby requires medical assistance.

Areola: The pigmented ring of skin on the breast around the nipple.

Back labor: The condition during labor that results from the pressure of the baby's presenting part against the back of the mother's pelvis.

Bag of waters: See *Amnion.*

Ballotement: A term used to refer to the rebounding of the baby's head away from the examining finger of the nurse or physician. This indicates that the baby has not yet settled into the pelvis.

Bearing down reflex: The involuntary pushing effort of the uterus during the second stage of labor.

Bilirubin: A waste product of broken-down red blood cells, normally converted into a nontoxic substance by the liver before being excreted from the body. A high bilirubin level in the newborn results in jaundice.

Birth: The process by which the baby is expelled or removed from the mother's uterus and begins life outside the mother. This takes place about nine months or 266 days after conception, or 280 days after the date of the last menstrual period.

Birth canal: The term applied to the structure formed by the vagina and uterus when the cervix is completely dilated in the second stage of labor.

Blastocyst: The ovum during its second week of development when it is a hollow ball of cells.

Bradycardia: A slow heart rate. In the unborn baby and newborn, this refers to a rate of less than 120 beats per minute.

Braxton-Hicks contractions: Intermittent contractions of the uterus occurring throughout pregnancy that do not produce changes in the cervix and may not be noticeable until the last month.

Breast pump: A device used to draw milk from the breasts.

Breech presentation: The presentation of the child's buttocks instead of the head during childbirth.

Brow presentation: The presentation of the brow toward the cervix during labor, caused by the baby's chin being up rather than pressed toward the chest.

Caput: The baby's head.

Caput succedaneum: A temporary swelling on the baby's head.

Carpal tunnel syndrome: Loss of normal sensation and tingling in the fingers due to pressure on the inside of the wrist. During pregnancy, the condition is caused by fluid retention.

Catheter: A thin, plastic tube inserted into the bladder through the urethra to drain urine, or into the epidural space in order to inject an anesthetic.

Centimeters: The unit of measure used to measure cervical dilation.

Cephalic presentation: The presentation of the head during childbirth.

Cephalopelvic disproportion (C.P.D.): The condition in which the baby's head is larger than the space of the mother's pelvis.

Certified nurse-midwife: A registered nurse who is a graduate of an approved training program and who has passed a certification examination.

Cervix: The lower necklike segment of the uterus.

Cesarean birth/cesarean section: The birth of a baby through an incision in the abdominal and uterine walls.

Chorion: The outermost membrane surrounding the baby and the placenta.

Chromosomes: Small, rodlike bodies found in the nucleus of every human cell. These structures normally occur in pairs of twenty-three and contain the genetic material of the cell.

Circumcision: The surgical removal of the foreskin of the penis.

Coccyx: The tailbone.

Codeine: An addictive painkilling substance derived from opium.

Colostrum: The substance that precedes the production of breast milk, rich in proteins and high in antibodies.

Conception: The fertilization of the egg by a sperm that initiates the growth of a human being and triggers the onset of pregnancy.

Congenital: Present at birth.

Contraction: A unit of work performed by a muscle over a period of time. In labor, uterine muscles contract to dilate the cervix and press the baby out of the mother's body.

Crowning: The time during the second stage of labor when the largest part of the baby's head appears in the vagina and does not recede between contractions.

Cystitis: Inflammation of the bladder and urinary tract.

Demerol: An analgesic drug.

Diaphragm: A rubber cup that fits over the cervix as a barrier method of contraception. Also, the muscular membrane that separates the lungs from the abdomen.

Dilation: The stretching open of the cervix brought about by uterine contractions during labor.

Doppler: A form of ultrasound used to listen to and measure the baby's heart rate.

Eclampsia: A now rare condition of late pregnancy characterized by high blood pressure, severe headaches, visual interference, and convulsions.

Edema: The presence of an excessive amount of fluid in body tissues. Also referred to as fluid retention.

Effacement: The thinning and shortening of the cervix, measured in terms of a percentage.

Elective induction of labor: Induction of labor for convenience rather than due to medical indications.

Electrode: A small electrical conductor used to monitor the baby's heart rate directly during labor.

Electronic fetal monitoring (E.F M.): The continuous monitoring of the baby's heart rate through a transducer positioned on the mother's abdomen, by telemetry, or via an electrode inserted through the cervix and attached to the baby's scalp.

Embryo: The term used to describe the baby between the second and twelfth week of its development.

Endometrium: The lining of the inner surface of the uterus.

Enema: The injection of fluids into the rectum to empty the lower intestine.

Engagement: The entrance of the presenting part of the baby into the mid-pelvis.

Engorgement: Distention of the breasts with milk.

Epidural: Regional anesthesia produced by injected medication through a catheter into the epidural space of the lower spine.

Episiotomy: The incision of the perineum at the end of the second stage of labor.

Estriol: A form of estrogen found in the urine or blood during late pregnancy.

Estrogen: A hormone secreted by the ovary and placenta throughout the menstrual cycle and pregnancy.

Face presentation: The presentation of the baby's face toward the cervix during labor.

Fallopian tube: The duct that conveys the ovum from the ovary to the uterus.

False labor: Braxton-Hicks contractions that mimic labor in intensity.

Fertilization: See *Conception.*

Fetal distress: A term used to describe a shortage of oxygen to the baby resulting in a disrupted heart rate.

Fetus: The term applied to the baby after the twelfth week of pregnancy until birth.

Folic acid: A form of vitamin B vital to the production of blood cells and hemoglobin, especially during pregnancy.

Fontanels: The soft spots lying between the unjoined sections of the baby's skull.

Forceps: An instrument used to hold the presenting part of the baby and extract the baby from the vagina.

Foremilk: The milk that collects in the ducts behind the nipple between feedings and is lower in fat than the hindmilk.

Fundal massage: Massage of the uterus during the fourth stage of labor to assist the uterus in contracting and to control bleeding.

Fundal palpation: Checking the height of the uterus by feeling it through the abdominal wall.

Fundus: The rounded portion of the uterus from which the contractions originate.

Gene: The basic unit of heredity on a chromosome.

Gestation: The period between fertilization and birth.

Glucose: A sugar found in the blood that supplies energy to the baby.

Gravida: A pregnant woman.

Gynecologist: A physician who specializes in the problems of the female sexual and reproductive organs.

Hemoglobin: The iron-containing pigment of red blood cells where oxygen is stored.

Hemorrhage: Excessive bleeding.

Hemorrhoids: Swollen veins around the rectum.

Herpes genitalis: An infection caused by the herpes simplex virus, usually transmitted sexually, that causes painful blisters on the skin and mucous membranes of the male and female genitals.

Hormones: Chemical substances that stimulate various organs to act in specific ways.

Human chorionic gonadotropin (HCG): The hormone secreted by the chorion measured during a pregnancy test through the urine.

Hypertension: High blood pressure; in pregnancy a blood pressure above 140/90.

Hyperventilation: An imbalance between carbon dioxide and oxygen in the bloodstream created by overbreathing.

Implantation: Embedding of the developing baby into the lining of the uterus.

Induction of labor: The artificial production of labor.

Intravenous feeding (IV): The introduction of fluids, medication, or other substances into the body through a thin plastic tube inserted into a vein.

Intubation: Insertion of a tube into any hollow body organ as into the larynx or trachea.

Invasive techniques: Any medical procedure that invades the boundaries of the body.

Involution: The return of the uterus to its normal size after pregnancy.

Jaundice: A common condition of newborn infants in which the skin has a yellowish tint because of an accumulation of bilirubin in the bloodstream.

Labor: The series of stages during the process of childbirth through which the baby is born and the mother's uterus returns to a normal state.

Lactation: Breastfeeding a baby.

Lanugo: The fine, silky hair on the skin of a newborn baby.

Letdown reflex: The ejection of breast milk from the milk glands resulting in the flow of milk from the nipple.

Lie: The position of the baby in the uterus.

Lightening: The descent of the uterus in the abdominal cavity that accompanies the engagement of the baby in the pelvis.

Lithotomy position: The position for delivery in which the mother lies flat on her back with her legs placed wide apart in stirrups.

Lochia: The discharge of blood, mucus, and tissue from the uterus after the baby is born.

Meconium: The dark green or blackish substance that makes up the baby's first stool. If passed into the amniotic fluid before birth, it is often a sign of fetal distress.

Miscarriage: The loss of a baby before the twenty-eighth week of pregnancy.

Molding: The temporary shaping of the baby's skull to conform to the size of the birth canal during the second stage of labor.

Montgomery's glands: The small bumps around the nipple on the areola that secrete an oily substance that protects the nipples.

Multigravida: A woman who has been pregnant two or more times.

Multipara: A woman who has given birth to one or more babies.

Multiple pregnancy: The development of two or more babies during pregnancy.

Narcotic: A drug that produces stupor or sleep and is likely to be habit-forming.

Natal: Pertaining to birth.

Neonatal: The first four weeks of life.

Nicotine: A highly poisonous and addictive substance present in tobacco.

Nitrous oxide: A gas that can be used to produce general anesthesia.

Nonstress test: A test during pregnancy to measure the baby's heart rate.

Obstetrician: A physician who specializes in the management of pregnancy, labor, birth, and postpartum.

Ovary: The sexual gland in females that normally produces eggs and estrogen.

Oviduct: See *Fallopian tube.*

Ovulation: The periodic ripening and expulsion of the ovum from the ovary.

Oxytocin: The hormone, secreted by the posterior pituitary gland, that stimulates uterine contractions and the letdown reflex.

Palpated: Examined by touch.

Paracervical: A regional anesthetic injected into the cervix during labor.

Pelvic floor: The set of muscles attached to the pelvis that supports the contents of the pelvic cavity.

Pelvis: The bony ring that supports the spine and gives articulation to the lower limbs.

Pelvimetry: The series of X-rays that can be used to determine the exact measurements of the pelvis.

Perinatal: The period from the twenty-eighth week of pregnancy to one week after the baby's birth.

Perineum: The external area between the vagina and the rectum in the female.

Pitocin: The synthetic form of oxytocin used to induce or stimulate labor.

Pituitary gland: A small, rounded body attached to the base of the brain. It secretes a number of hormones that regulate bodily processes, including growth, reproduction, and lactation.

Placenta: The flat, oval structure attached to the uterus during pregnancy, which supplies nutrients to the baby, removes waste products, and secretes hormones.

Placenta previa: A condition in which the placenta lies over or near the cervix.

Posterior presentation: The crown of the baby's head is facing toward the mother's back as it descends into her pelvis.

Postnatal: After birth.

Postpartum: Following childbirth.

Preeclampsia: A condition in which a pregnant woman has high blood pressure, edema, albumin in the urine, and often an excessive weight gain.

Presentation: The position of the baby during pregnancy and labor.

Presenting part: The part of the baby lying closest to the cervix.

Preterm: A baby born before the thirty-seventh week of pregnancy and weighing less than five and a half pounds.

Primigravida: A woman during her first pregnancy.

Primipara: A woman who has had or is giving birth to her first baby.

Progesterone: A hormone produced by the corpus luteum and then by the placenta during pregnancy.

Prolactin: The hormone that causes glands in the breast to make milk.

Prostaglandins: Substances secreted by the body that stimulate uterine contractions.

Psychoprophylaxis: A method of childbirth popularized by Fernand Lamaze.

Pubis: The bones forming the front part of the pelvis.

Pubococcygeus muscle: The hammocklike supportive muscle of the pelvic floor that attaches to the pubis in the front and the coccyx in back.

Puerperium: The first four weeks after birth.

Quickening: The mother's first perception of the movements of her baby during pregnancy, usually between the fourth and sixth month.

Recti muscles: The bands of muscles running up the center of the abdomen from the pubic bones to the ribs.

Relaxin: A sex hormone that facilitates birth by causing relaxation of the pelvic ligaments.

Rooting: The baby's instinctive reflex of searching for the nipple.

Sacrum: The bone that forms the back of the pelvis at the base of the spine.

Show: The discharge of bloodstained mucus resulting from cervical dilation.

Sims'-lateral position: A semi-prone position with patient lying on left side, right knee and thigh drawn up, left arm along patient's back, and chest inclined forward so patient rests upon it.

Smooth muscle: Muscle that lacks cross striations (dark and light bands of stretched multinuclear fibers) that is found in structures such as the stomach and bladder.

Sperm: The male reproductive sex cell that fertilizes the ovum.

Sphincter muscle: Annular muscle surrounding and able to contract or close a bodily opening.

Spinal anesthetic: Regional anesthesia produced by injecting an anesthetic into the spinal fluid.

Station: The measurement of the presenting part in relation to bones in the pelvis.

Stillbirth: The delivery of a dead baby after twenty-eight weeks of pregnancy.

Stress: Any factor that requires response or change on the part of an organism or individual.

Stress test: A diagnostic test used during late pregnancy that measures that baby's heart rate under stress.

Stressor: Anything capable of causing wear and tear on the body's mental, physical, emotional, or spiritual resources.

Stretch marks: Light-colored lines appearing on skin that has been stretched during pregnancy.

Striae: See *Stretch marks.*

Subcutaneous injection: An injection given beneath the skin.

Suture: The surgical stitching of a wound.

Tachycardia: An abnormally fast heart rate in an unborn baby or a newborn, faster than 160 beats per minute.

Telemetry: A method of EFM that uses radio waves. See *Electronic fetal monitoring.*

Term: A pregnancy is said to be "at term" between thirty-eight and forty-two weeks of pregnancy.

Tocodynometer: A pressure gauge that records contractions. It is attached by a belt to the mother's abdomen.

Toxemia: See *Preeclampsia* and *Eclampsia.*

Tranquilizer: A drug that acts to reduce mental tension and anxiety without inducing unconsciousness.

Transducer: An instrument that is sensitive to the echoes of high-frequency sound waves that bounce off the baby's body and translate into an image on a recording device. See *Electronic fetal monitoring, Ultrasound.*

Transition: The third phase of the first stage of labor in which the cervix dilates from seven to ten centimeters.

Trimester: Period of three; one of the three phases of the nine months of pregnancy.

Twins, dyzygotic: Twins derived from two fertilized ova; fraternal twins.

Twins, monozygotic: Derived from one fertilized ovum that separated at the two-cell stage into two identical cells, each producing a separate individual; identical twins.

Ultrasound: Inaudible high-frequency sound waves used to outline the shape of the baby or other organs of the body.

Umbilical cord: The attachment connecting the baby to the placenta. It is surgically severed at birth.

Urethra: The canal that carries urine from the bladder.

Urinary estriol study: A diagnostic test used to measure the output of estriol from the placenta as a means of determining placental sufficiency. See *Estriol.*

Uterine inertia: Ineffective, weak uterine contractions during labor.

Uterus: The thick-walled, hollow, muscular organ of the female that serves to contain and nourish the unborn child.

Vacuum extractor: An instrument used as an alternative to forceps that adheres to the baby's scalp by suction and pulls the baby out of the vagina.

Vagina: The muscle/membrane tubelike structure that forms the passageway between the uterus and the entrance to the vagina between the external genitals. It receives the penis during sexual intercourse and is the canal through which the baby passes during birth.

Vernix: The creamy substance that coats the baby's skin while in the uterus to protect it from the amniotic fluid. It is not necessary to remove the vernix after the baby is born.

Vertex presentation: See *Cephalic presentation.*

Vulva: The external portion of the female reproductive organs, including the labia and the clitoris.

X-chromosome: The sex-determining chromosome carried by all eggs and one-half of the sperm. Its presence as a pair produces a female child.

Y-chromosome: The sex-determining chromosome carried by one-half of the sperm, never by an egg, that produces a male child.

Yeast infection: A fungal infection resulting in itching and inflammation of the vagina—characterized by a thick white discharge and caused by the growth of *Candida albicans.*

Yolk sac: The sac that carries and stores the nutrients for the developing fertilized egg.

Zygote: The developing egg between the time of fertilization and its implantation in the wall of the uterus.

Bibliography

Abouleish, E. *Pain Control in Obstetrics.* Philadelphia, PA: Lippincott, 1977.

Adams, J. *Understanding and Managing Stress.* San Francisco, CA: University Association, 1980.

Adels, J. H., ed. *The Wisdom of the Saints.* Oxford: Oxford University Press, 1987.

Ahlem, L. *Living with Stress.* Ventura, CA: Regal Books, 1978.

American College of Obstetricians and Gynecologists. *Planning for Pregnancy, Birth, and Beyond.* Washington, DC: ACOG, 1995.

Bean, C. A. *Methods of Childbirth.* New York: Dolphin, 1973.

Belsky, J. and Kelly, J. *The Transition to Parenthood.* New York: Delacorte, 1994.

Benson, H. *The Relaxation Response.* New York: Avon, 1975.

Billings, B. and Westmore, A. *The Billings Method: Controlling Fertility Without Drugs or Devices.* New York: Random House, 1980.

Blumenfeld, S. *The Retreat from Motherhood.* New Rochelle, NY: Arlington House, 1975.

Bonica, J. J. *Principles and Practices of Obstetrical Analgesia and Anesthesia,* Vols. 1, 2. Philadelphia, PA: Davis, 1967, 1969.

Bonica, J. J., et al. *Advances in Pain Research and Therapy,* Vol. 3. New York: Raven, 1979.

Bradley, R. *Husband-Coached Childbirth.* New York: Harper & Row, 1965.

Brazelton, T. B. *Families: Crisis and Caring.* Reading, MA: Addison-Wesley, 1989.

____. *On Becoming a Family: The Growth of Attachment.* New York: Delacorte Press/Seymour Lawrence, 1981.

____. *Touchpoints: Your Child's Emotional and Behavioral Development.* Reading, MA: Addison-Wesley, 1992.

Brenneman, H. G. *Meditations for the Expectant Mother.* Scottsdale, PA: Herald, 1968.

Brestin, S. and Brestin, D. *Building Your House on the Lord: Marriage and Parenthood.* Wheaton, IL: Harold Shaw, 1981.

Brewer, G. S. *The Brewer Medical Diet for Normal and High-Risk Pregnancy.* New York: Simon and Schuster, 1983.

Campbell, R. *How to Really Love Your Child.* Wheaton IL: Victor Books, 1977.

Carlson, K. J., Eisenstat, S. A., and Zipporyn, T. *The Harvard Guide to Women's Health.* Cambridge, MA: Harvard University Press, 1996.

Chambers, O. *My Utmost for His Highest.* New York: Dodd and Mead, 1935.

Chard, T. and Richards, M., eds. *Benefits and Hazards of the New Obstetrics.* Lavenham, England: Lavenham Press, Ltd., 1977.

Cooper, K. *The Aerobics Program for Total Well-Being.* New York: Evans, 1982.

Deutsch, R. M. *Realities of Nutrition.* Palo Alto, CA: Bull Publishing, 1976.

Dick-Read, G. *Childbirth Without Fear.* New York: Harper & Row, 1944.

Dix, C. *The New Mother Syndrome: Coping with Postpartum Stress and Depression.* Garden City, NY: Doubleday, 1985.

Donovan, B. *The Cesarean Birth Experience.* Boston, MA: Beacon, 1978.

Eheart, B. K. and Martel, S. K. *The Fourth Trimester.* New York: Ballantine, 1983.

Eiger, M. S. and Olds, S. W. *The Complete Book of Breastfeeding.* New York: Workman, 1987.

Eisenberg, A., Murkoff, H. E., and Hathaway, S. E. *What to Expect When You're Expecting.* New York: Workman, 1991.

Ells, A. H. *Family Love.* Nashville: Nelson, 1995.

Evans, Debra, ed. *Christian Parenting Answers.* Elgin, IL: Chariot, 1994.

____. *Heart & Home.* Wheaton, IL: Crossway, 1988.

____. *The Christian Woman's Guide to Personal Health Care.* Wheaton, IL: Crossway, 1998.

____. *The Christian Woman's Guide to Sexuality.* Wheaton, IL: Crossway, 1997.

____. *The Complete Book on Childbirth.* Wheaton, IL: Tyndale, 1986.

Everly, G. and Girdano, D. *Controlling Stress and Tension.* Englewood Cliffs, NJ: Prentice-Hall, 1979.

Fraiberg, S. *Every Child's Birthright: In Defense of Mothering.* New York: Bantam, 1977.

Goldfarb, J. and Tibbetts, F. *Breastfeeding Handbook: A Practical Reference for Physicians, Nurses and Other Health Professionals.* Hillside, NJ: Enslow, 1980.

Gots, R. E. and Gots, B. A. *Caring for Your Unborn Child.* New York: Bantam, 1979.

Gotsch, G. and Sears, W. *Breastfeeding: Pure & Simple.* Schaumburg, IL: La Leche League Int'l., 1994.

Gottschalk, W. "Problems and Risks of Obstetric Anesthesia," in *Risks in the Practice of Modern Obstetrics.* Aladjern S., ed., 2nd ed. St. Louis: Mosby, 1975.

Graham, H. *Eternal Eve—The History of Gynaecology and Obstetrics.* New York: Doubleday, 1951.

Greene, D. S. *79 Ways to Calm a Crying Baby.* New York: Pocket, 1988.

Haines, M. *The Child Within.* Wheaton, IL: Living Books, 1979.

Haire, D. *The Cultural Warping of Childbirth.* Milwaukee: ICEA, 1972.

Harrison, H. *The Premature Baby Book.* New York: St. Martins, 1983.

Hazell, L. D. *Common Sense Childbirth.* New York: Berkley Medallion Books, 1976.

Hotchner, T. *Pregnancy and Childbirth: The Complete Guide for a New Life.* New York: Avon Books, 1976.

Howard, J. G. *The Trauma of Transparency.* Portland, OR: Multnomah, 1979.

Huggett, J. *Two into One: Relating in Christian Marriage.* Downers Grove, IL: InterVarsity, 1981.

Huggins, K. *The Nursing Mother's Companion.* Cambridge, MA: Harvard Press, 1986.

Huggins, K. and Ziedrich, L. *The Nursing Mother's Guide to Weaning.* Boston: The Harvard Common Press, 1994.

Hunter, B. *What Every Mother Needs to Know.* Sisters, OR: Multnomah, 1993.

Jelliffe, D. and Jelliffe, E. F. P. *Human Milk in the Modern World.* New York: Oxford University Press, 1978.

Johnson, R. V., ed. *Mayo Clinic Complete Book of Pregnancy & Baby's First Year.* New York: William Morrow, 1994.

Jones, S. *Crying Baby, Sleepless Nights.* New York: Warner, 1983.

Jordan, B. *Birth in Four Cultures: A Cross-cultural Investigation of Childbirth in Yucatan, Holland, Sweden, and the United States.* Montreal: Eden, 1978.

Joy, D. M. *Bonding: Relationships in the Image of God.* Waco, TX: Word, 1983.

Kippley, S. *Breastfeeding and Natural Child Spacing.* New York: Penguin, 1975.

Kitzinger, S. *The Complete Book of Pregnancy and Childbirth.* New York: Knopf, 1996.

Kitzinger, S. and Davis, J. A., eds. *The Place of Birth.* New York: Oxford University Press, 1978.

Klaus, M. H. and Kennell, J. H. *Maternal-Infant Bonding.* St. Louis: Mosby, 1976.

La Leche League. *The Womanly Art of Breastfeeding,* 3rd ed. New York: Plenum, 1981.

Lamaze, F. *Painless Childbirth.* New York: Pocket Books, 1965.

Lamott, K. *Escape from Stress.* New York: Putnam, 1975.

Lawrence, R. *Breastfeeding—A Guide for the Medical Profession.* St. Louis: Mosby, 1980.

Leboyer, F. *Birth Without Violence.* New York: Knopf, 1975.

Leifer, M. *Psychological Effects of Motherhood—A Study of First Pregnancy.* New York: Praeger, 1980.

Lewis, C. S. *The Problem of Pain.* New York: Macmillan, 1962.

Macdonald, G. *At the Back of the North Wind.* Elgin, IL: David C. Cook, 1979.

McCaffrey, M. *Nursing Management of the Patient with Pain,* 2nd ed. Philadelphia, PA: Lippincott, 1979.

McNall, L. K. and Galeener, J. T., eds. *Current Practice in Obstetric and Gynecologic Nursing,* Vol. 2. St. Louis: Mosby, 1978.

Mead, F. S. *12,000 Religious Quotations.* Grand Rapids, MI: Baker, 1989.

Meichenbaum, D. *Cognitive Behavior Modification: An Integrative Approach.* New York: Plenum, 1977.

Melzack, R. *The Puzzle of Pain.* New York: Basic, 1973.

Meyer, L. D. *The Cesarean Revolution.* Edmonds, WA: Franklin, 1981.

Milburn, J. and Smith, L. *The Natural Childbirth Book.* Minneapolis, MN: Bethany, 1981.

Milinaire, C. *Birth.* New York: Crown, 1974.

Mills, N. "The Lay Midwife," in *Safe Alternatives in Childbirth,* D. Stewart and L. Stewart, eds. Chapel Hill, SC: NAPSAC, 1977.

Minirth, F., Meier, P., and Arterburn, S. *The Complete Life Encyclopedia.* Nashville: Nelson, 1995.

Myles, M. *Textbook for Midwifes,* 8th ed. New York: Churchill-Livingston, 1975.

Narramore, B. *An Ounce of Prevention.* Grand Rapids, MI: Zondervan, 1978.

____. *Help! I'm a Parent!* Grand Rapids, MI: Zondervan, 1972.

____. *Parenting with Love and Limits.* Grand Rapids, MI: Zondervan, 1978.

____. *You're Someone Special.* Grand Rapids, MI: Zondervan, 1978.

Navigator Studies. *God's Design for the Family.* Books 1-4. Colorado Springs, CO: NavPress, 1980.

Neifert, M. *Dr. Mom: A Guide to Baby and Child Care.* New York: Signet, 1986.

Newton, N. *Maternal Emotions: A Study of Women's Feelings About Menstruation, Pregnancy, Childbirth, Infant Care and Other Aspects of Their Femininity.* New York: Harper and Brothers (Paul B. Hoeber Medical Book Dept.), 1955.

____. *The Family Book of Child Care.* New York: Harper & Row, 1957.

Nilsson, L. *A Child Is Born.* New York: Delacorte/Lawrence, 1977.

Noble, E. *Having Twins.* Boston, MA: Houghton-Mifflin, 1980.

Oxorn, H. and Foote, W. *Human Labor and Birth.* New York: Appleton-Century-Crofts, 1977.

Page, E., Villee, C., and Villee, D. *Human Reproduction.* Philadelphia, PA: Saunders, 1976.

Parfitt, R. R. *The Birth Primer.* Philadelphia, PA: Running Press, 1977.

Paul, B. *Health, Culture, and Community.* New York: Sage, 1955.

Phillipp, E. *Childbirth—A Complete Guide to Every Problem.* Glasgow: Fontana/Collins, 1978.

Powell, J. *The Secret of Staying in Love.* Allen, TX: Argus, 1974.

____. *Why Am I Afraid to Love?* Allen, TX: Argus, 1972.

____. *Why Am I Afraid to Tell You Who I Am?* Allen, TX: Argus, 1969.

Pritchard, J. A. and MacDonald, P. C. *Williams Obstetrics,* 15th ed. New York: Appleton-Century-Crofts, 1976.

Rakowitz, E. and Rubin, G. S. *Living with Your New Baby.* New York: Berkley, 1980.

Reeder, S. J., Mastroianni, L., and Martin, L. L. *Maternity Nursing,* 14th ed. Philadelphia, PA: Lippincott, 1980.

Rekers, G. *Family Building: Six Qualities of a Strong Family.* Ventura, CA: Regal, 1985.

Ribble, M. *The Rights of Infants,* 2nd ed. New York: Columbia University, 1965.

Richardson, S. A. *Childbearing—Its Social and Psychological Aspects.* Baltimore, MD: Williams and Wilkins, 1976.

Riordan, J. *A Practical Guide to Breastfeeding.* St. Louis: Mosby, 1983.

Rokeach, M. *Beliefs, Attitudes, and Values—A Theory of Organization and Change.* San Francisco, CA: Tossey-Bass, 1970.

Romalis, S., ed. *Childbirth: Alternatives to Medical Control.* Austin, TX: University of Texas, 1981.

Rothman, B. K. *In Labor—Woman and Power in the Birthplace.* New York: Norton, 1982.

Sandberg, E. *Synopsis of Obstetrics,* 10th ed. St. Louis: Mosby, 1978.

Schaeffer, E. *A Way of Seeing.* Old Tappan, NJ: Revell, 1977.

____. *Affliction.* Old Tappan, NJ: Revell, 1978.

____. *Commonsense Christian Living.* Nashville: Nelson, 1983.

____. *Lifelines: The Ten Commandments for Today.* Wheaton, IL: Crossway Books, 1983.

____.*What Is a Family?* Old Tappan, NJ: Revell, 1975.

Schaeffer, F. and Koop, C. E. *Whatever Happened to the Human Race?* Old Tappan, NJ: Revell, 1979.

Schaeffer, F. *Genesis in Space and Time.* Glendale, CA: Regal, 1972.

Sears, M. and Sears, W. *The Birth Book.* Boston: Little, Brown, 1994.

____. *The Pregnancy Book.* Boston: Little, Brown, 1997.

____. *The Baby Book: Everything You Need to Know About Your Baby—from Birth to Age Two.* Boston: Little, Brown, 1993.

Sears, W. *Creative Parenting.* New York: Everest, 1982.

Selye, H. *Stress: General Adaptation Syndrome and the Disease of Adaptation.* Montreal: ACTA, 1950.

Seuss, Dr. *Happy Birthday to You!* New York: Random House, 1959.

Simkin, P., Whalley, J., and Keppler, A. *Pregnancy, Childbirth, and the Newborn.* New York: Meadowbrook, 1991.

Smedes, L. B. *Sex for Christians.* Grand Rapids, MI: Eerdmans, 1976.

____. *Forgive and Forget.* New York: Harper & Row, 1984.

____. *The Art of Forgiving: When You Need to Forgive and Don't Know How.* Nashville: Moorings, 1996.

Sternbach, R. A. *Pain: A Psychophysiological Analysis.* New York: Academic, 1968.

____. *The Psychology of Pain.* New York: Raven, 1978.

Sumner, P. E. and Phillips, C. R. *Birthing Rooms—Concept and Reality.* St. Louis: Mosby, 1981.

Trobisch, I. and Roetzer, E. *An Experience of Love—Understanding Natural Family Planning.* Old Tappan, NJ: Revell, 1981.

Trobisch, I. *The Joy of Being a Woman.* New York: Harper and Row, 1975.

Trobisch, W. *A Baby Just Now?* Downers Grove, IL: InterVarsity, 1978.

____. *I Loved a Girl.* London: Lutterworth, 1970.

____. *I Married You.* New York: Harper & Row, 1971.

____. *Love Yourself: Self-Acceptance and Depression.* Downers Grove, IL: InterVarsity, 1976.

Vellay, P. *Childbirth Without Pain.* New York: Dutton, 1960.

Wangerin, W. *As for Me and My House: Crafting Your Marriage to Last.* Nashville: Nelson, 1987.

Ward, T. *Values Begin at Home.* Wheaton, IL: Victor Books, 1979.

Welter, P. *How to Help a Friend.* Wheaton, IL: Tyndale, 1978.

____. *The Family: Stronger After Crisis.* Wheaton, IL: Tyndale, 1982.

Wertz, R. and Wertz, D. *Lying-In: A History of Childbirth in America.* New York: Free Press, 1977.

Wessel, H. *Natural Childbirth and the Christian Family*, rev. ed. New York: Harper & Row, 1983.

____. *Under the Apple Tree: Marrying-Birthing-Parenting.* Fresno, CA: Bookmates, 1981.

Wilson, C. W. and Hovey, W. R. *Cesarean Childbirth—A Handbook for Parents.* New York: Doubleday, 1977.

Woessner, C., Lauwers, J., and Bernard, B. *Breastfeeding Today: A Mother's Companion.* New York: Avery, 1996.

Wolfensberger, W. *Normalization.* National Institute of Mental Retardation. Toronto: York University, 1972.

Worthington, B., Vermeersch, J., and Williams, S. R. *Nutrition in Pregnancy and Lactation.* St. Louis: Mosby, 1977.

Wright, H. N. and Inmon, M. N. *Preparing for Parenthood.* Ventura, CA: Regal, 1980.

Wright, H. N. *Communication: The Key to Your Marriage.* Ventura, CA: Regal, 1974.

____. *The Pillars of Marriage.* Ventura, CA: Regal, 1979.

Yancey, P. *Where Is God When It Hurts?* Grand Rapids: Zondervan, 1977.

Young, D. *Bonding: How Parents Become Attached to Their Child.* Minneapolis: ICEA, 1978.

____. *Changing Childbirth.* Rochester, NY: Childbirth Graphics, 1982.

Young, D., ed. *Obstetrical Intervention and Technology in the 80s.* New York: Hawthorn, 1982.

Resources and Additional Reading

Birth Alternatives (birthing centers, home birth, midwives, labor assistants, doula services)

NAPSAC (National Association of Parents and Professionals for Safe Alternatives in Childbirth), Route 1, P. O. Box 646, Marble Hill, MO 63764 (573-238-2010). For a nominal fee, NAPSAC will send you a directory listing obstetricians, certified nurse-midwives, and childbirth educators.

National Association of Childbearing Centers, 3123 Gottschall Road, Perkiomenville, PA 18074 (215-234-8068).

American College of Home Obstetrics (ACHO), P. O. Box 508, Oak Park, IL 60303 (708-383-1461).

Association for Childbirth at Home International, P. O. Box 430, Glendale, CA 91209 (213-667-0839).

The American College of Nurse-Midwives (ACNM), 818 Connecticut Avenue NW, Suite 900, Washington, DC 20006 (202-728-9860).

California Association of Midwives (CAM), P. O. Box 417854, Sacramento, CA 95841 (800-829-5791). Publication: *Midwife Means "with Woman,"* an educational booklet about selecting and working with a midwife.

MANA (Midwives Alliance of North America), Box 175, Newton, KS 67114 (316-283-4543).

North American Registry of Midwives (NARM), 1044 Woodlawn, Iowa City, IA 52245 (319-354-5365).

National Association of Childbirth Assistants (NACA), 205 Copco Lane, San Jose, CA 95123 (408-225-9167).

Doulas of North America (DONA)/Pennypress Inc., 1100 Twenty-Third Avenue, Seattle, WA 98112 (206-324-5440).

Childbirth and Family Education, 415 Boxauxhall Road, Katy, TX 77450 (713-497-8894).

For Additional Reading

Mothering the New Mother: Your Postpartum Resource Companion by Sally Placksin (Newmarket, 1993).

Mothering the Mother: How a Doula Can Help You Have a Shorter, Easier and Healthier Birth by Marshall Klaus with Phyllis Klaus and John Kennell (Perseus, 1993).

Pregnancy and Childbirth Education

International Childbirth Education Association (ICEA/all methods), P. O. Box 20048, Minneapolis, MN 55420 (612-854-8660). Extensive book and publication list available upon request.

Apple Tree Family Ministries (ATFM/Dick-Read method from a Christian perspective), P. O. Box 2083, Artesia, CA 90702-2083. ATFM is an excellent source for natural family planning, birthing, and breastfeeding support from a Christian perspective. Founded by childbirth reform advocate Helen Wessel, ATFM is aiming to expand its educational and teacher-training ministry into the twenty-first century. Write for a copy of their newsletter and catalog.

American Society for Psychoprophylaxis in Obstetrics (ASPO/Lamaze method), 1200 Nineteenth Street NW, Washington, DC 20036 (800-368-4404).

American Academy of Husband-Coached Childbirth (AAHC/Bradley method), P. O. Box 5224, Sherman Oaks, CA 91413 (800-423-2397).

Childbirth Graphics, P. O. Box 21207, Waco, TX 76701 (800-299-3366, ext. 287). Informative, helpful publications and products for expectant parents, including excellent childbirth and breastfeeding booklets, educational videos, and a wide variety of useful, inexpensive pamphlets. Call or write for a free copy of their catalog.

Institute for Family Herbal Care, 85 Tunnel Road, Suite 12-A287, Asheville, NC 28805 (888-HERB-101). Offers 2 twice-a-year newsletters and various educational materials on herbs during pregnancy and after from a Christian perspective. Free membership available on request. Offers Naturally Healthy Pregnancy products as well as the book of the same title.

FOR ADDITIONAL READING

Beginning of Life: The Marvelous Journey from Conception to Birth by Geraldine Lux Flanagan (Dorling Kindersley, 1996).

A Child Is Born by Lennart Nilsson (Delacorte, 1990).

No More Morning Sickness: A Survival Guide for Pregnant Women by Miriam Erick (NAL-Dutton, 1993).

The Naturally Healthy Pregnancy, 2nd edition, by Shonda Parker (Naturally Healthy Publications, 1998).

The Pregnancy Book for Today's Woman: An Obstetrician Answers All Your Questions About Pregnancy and Childbirth and Some You May Not Have Considered by Howard Shapiro (HarperCollins, 1993).

The Pregnancy Book: Everything You Need to Know from America's Baby Experts by William and Martha Sears with Linda Hughey Holt (Little, Brown, 1997).

The Birth Book: Everything You Need to Know to Have a Safe and Satisfying Birth by William and Martha Sears (Little, Brown, 1994.)

The Good Housekeeping Illustrated Book of Pregnancy and Child Care (Hearst, 1990).

Unnecessary Cesareans: Ways to Avoid Them by Diony Young and Charles Mahan. Booklet available from ICEA.

The VBAC Companion: The Expectant Mother's Guide to Vaginal Birth After Cesarean by Diana Korte (Harvard Common Press, 1998).

The Birth Partner: Everything You Need to Know to Help a Woman Through Childbirth by Penny Simkin (Harvard Common Press, 1989).

Breastfeeding/Lactation Consultants

La Leche League International, 1400 Meacham Road, Schaumburg, IL 60168 (847-519-7730; 800-LA-LECHE). Extensive book and publication list available upon request from the world's largest mother-to-mother support organization.

International Lactation Consultant Association, 4101 Lake Boone Trail, Suite 201, Raleigh, NC 27607 (919-787-5181); www.ilca.com.

FOR ADDITIONAL READING

Breastfeeding: Pure & Simple by Gwen Gotsch and William Sears (La Leche League Intl., 1994).

Breastfeeding and Natural Child Spacing: How Ecological Breastfeeding Spaces Babies by Sheila Kippley (Couple to Couple League, 1989).

The Womanly Art of Breastfeeding, 6th rev. ed., by La Leche League International (La Leche League Intl., 1997).

Breastfeeding Today: A Mother's Companion by Candace Woessner, Judith Lauwers, and Barbara Bernard (Avery, 1996).

Dr. Mom: A Guide to Baby and Child Care by Marianne Neifert (Signet, 1986).

The Baby Book: Everything You Need to Know About Your Baby—from Birth to Age Two by William and Martha Sears (Little, Brown, 1993).

Unexpected Outcomes

C/SEC, Inc. (Cesarean/Support, Education and Concern), 22 Forest Road, Framingham, MA 01701 (617-877-8266).

Parents of Premature and High-Risk Infants International, University of Utah Health Sciences Center, 50 N. Medical Drive, Room 2A210, Salt Lake City, UT 84132 (801-581-5323).

National Organization of Mothers of Twins Clubs, P. O. Box 23188, Albuquerque, NM 87192 (800-234-2276 or 505-275-0955).

The Compassionate Friends, 900 Jorie Boulevard, Oakbrook, IL 60523 (630-990-0010).

Depression After Delivery, P. O. Box 1282, Morrisville, PA 10967 (215-295-3994).

Association for Retarded Citizens, P. O. Box 6109, Arlington, TX 76005 (817-640-0204).

United Cerebral Palsy Association, 66 E. 34th Street, New York, NY 10016 (212-481-6300).

FOR ADDITIONAL READING

This Isn't What I Expected: Recognizing and Recovering from Depression and Anxiety After Childbirth by Karen P. Kleima and Valerie D. Raskin (Bantam, 1994).

Having Twins by Elizabeth Noble (Houghton Mifflin, 1991).

Empty Arms: Coping After Miscarriage, Stillbirth, and Infant Death by Sherokee Ilse and Linda H. Burns (Wintergreen, 1985).

Sexually Transmitted Diseases

Office of Women's Health, Centers for Disease Control and Prevention, 1600 Clifton Road NE, MS: D-51, Atlanta, GA 30333 (404-639-7230); Web site: www.cdc.gov/od/owh/wh home.htm. One of eleven divisions of the CDC, the Office of Women's Health provides information on STDs, breast and cervical cancer, tobacco use, reproductive health, and violence.

National Institute of Allergy and Infectious Diseases, National Institutes of Health, Office of Communication, Building 31, Room 7A-50, 31 Center Drive, MSC2520, Bethesda, MD 20892-2520 (301-496-5717); Web site: www.niaid.nih.gov. Offers free consumer pamphlets and a publications list on STDs upon request.

FOR ADDITIONAL READING

Sexuality and Sexually Transmitted Diseases, by Joe S. McIlhaney (Baker, 1990).

Herpes Simplex: The Self-Help Guide to Managing the Herpes Virus by Philippa Harknett, (Thorson/HarperCollins, 1994).

Natural Family Planning Organizations

(For individual NFP groups, practitioners, and instructors in your area, send a self-addressed, stamped envelope with your request to the American Academy of Natural Family Planning, CCL, or the Pope Paul VI Institute.)

American Academy of Natural Family Planning, 615 S. New Ballas Road, St. Louis, MO (314-991-5766). Certification and membership directories available.

Couple to Couple League (CCL), P. O. Box 111184, Cincinnati, OH 45211-1184 (513-661-7612). Offers home study course in addition to an extensive network of individual NFP groups and instructors across the country. Write or call for their publication catalog and a reference to the group/instructor nearest you.

Pope Paul VI Institute for the Study of Human Reproduction, 6901 Mercy Road, Suite 200, Omaha, NE 68106 (402-390-6600). Catalog available.

Billings Ovulation Method Association, P. O. Box 30329, Bethesda, MD 20824-0239 (301-897-9323). Provides education and instruction in the Ovulation Method throughout the world.

FOR ADDITIONAL READING

The Christian Woman's Guide to Sexuality by Debra Evans (Crossway, 1998).

The Christian Woman's Guide to Personal Health Care by Debra Evans (Crossway, 1999).

The New No-Pill, No-Risk Birth Control by Nona Aguilar (Rawson, 1986).

Taking Charge of Your Fertility by Toni Weschler (HarperCollins, 1996).

INDEX